FLY RODDING THE COAST

FLY RODDING
THE COAST

ED MITCHELL

STACKPOLE
BOOKS

Published by
STACKPOLE BOOKS
5067 Ritter Road
Mechanicsburg, PA 17055

Printed in the United States of America

10 9 8 7 6 5 4 3 2

First edition

Portions of the section on silversides in chapter 8 appeared previously in *Scientific Angler's Flyfishing Quarterly,* summer 1992. Portions of the section on sand eels in chapter 8 appeared previously in *Fly Fisherman,* vol. 23, no. 1, December 1991.

Frontispiece by Glenn Wolff
Illustrations by Dave Hall
Color plates by Gary Mirando
Photographs by the author unless otherwise credited

Library of Congress Cataloging-in-Publication Data

Mitchell, Ed, 1946-
    Fly rodding the coast / Ed Mitchell. — 1st ed.
      p.   cm.
    Includes index.
    ISBN 0-8117-0628-1
    1. Saltwater fly fishing. I. Title.
SH456.2.M58   1994
799. 1'6—dc20   94-27249
                                                 CIP

To my wife, Sandy, who has endured and encouraged my fishing madness, and to my son, Eddie, who now shows signs of catching the bug.

And to my late brother-in-law, Andy Grella, I miss you buddy.

Contents

Preface ix

Acknowledgments xiii

Introduction 1

1. Tides: What the Fly Rodder Needs to Know 3

2. Reading Beaches 15

3. Reading Rips 61

4. Reading Points of Land 75

5. Reading Estuaries 87

6. Reading Man-made Structures 105

7. Reading the Weather 121

8. Matching the Marine: Baitfish and Beyond 131

9. Saltwater Flies: A Selection for New England 155

10. Saltwater Tackle 167

11. Knots 191

12. Striped Bass, Bluefish, Bonito, and Little Tunny   209

13. Fighting Your Quarry: From Start to Finish   243

14. Fishing at Night   261

15. Saltwater Fly Casting   275

16. New England Planner   293

17. Marine Conservation   305

     Bibliography   309

     Index   313

Preface

If fly fishing is a sport born of the beauty and complexity of the natural world, then ultimately every fly fisherman is, in his or her own way, a naturalist. Taking this a step further, one could argue that since the natural world is nowhere larger or more awe-inspiring than by the sea, coastal fly rodders fish in a very special place. Here, in the ocean's compelling vastness, they face the most powerful fish on earth while standing close to the origins of life and hearing the whispers of eternity.

I have fly-fished the coast of New England for more than fifteen years, and with each season my love for these salty waters grows. Home to striped bass, bluefish, and bonito, to name just a few, these are indeed enchanted waters. They offer the coastal fly fisherman a vital and challenging arena, a realm of many moods and faces. There are star-dusted nights, when each cast seems to reach out from the rim of the darkened world. There are stormy autumn days, when the surf pounds as stripers crack bait in the blue-green waves. And then there is the smell and feel of a dawn fog with its stillness, thick and unbroken except for the groaning call of a distant foghorn. Images such as these etch themselves deeply and afford saltwater anglers a sense of connection to a wider universe.

Who, for the most part, are these would-be saltwater fly rodders?

Primarily they are freshwater fly fishermen who have heard about the adventures of the coast and can no longer resist its lure. Some are seasoned trout veterans; others have only just begun. But they all have this in common: They must now convert their streamside knowledge to the foaming world of surf.

It is my plan to show freshwater fly rodders how to make the transition to the coast. I recognize that there are many light-tackle surf casters who, having seen the success of the fly rodder, would like to try too. These anglers are already acquainted with tides and coastal structure, but they need to further their knowledge of flies and fly-rod technique. I hope that what I have to say about reading the coast will help them too.

Even though saltwater fly fishing is over a hundred years old, the ocean is still a fly-rod frontier. And unlike the freshwater side of things, you cannot turn to lengthy shelves of angling books overflowing with the fruits of research. The first time a fly rodder leaves the safe haven of a trout stream and ventures forth, fly rod in hand, to stare out over these wide vistas, an uneasy feeling settles in. Is it really possible to fly-fish so large an expanse? Where are the pools, riffles, and runs that have so long defined the game? How do you begin when all of it looks so much the same?

I well remember those questions and the feelings that go with them. Looking up and down the beach, I had no idea where to begin. Everything looked so unfamiliar, so unlike the more encapsulated world of a trout stream. As much as I wanted desperately to catch my first striper on a fly, I could not but feel a bit helpless and more than a little out of place. It was as if nothing in my years of freshwater fly rodding had prepared me to face the coast.

At first, I made only sporadic visits to the coast, still preferring to do the bulk of my angling in fresh water. My trips to the salt were spur of the moment, without any prior planning. Naturally, this approach proved fruitless. And to make matters worse, the surf casters I occasionally shared the beach with looked more than a little perplexed to see someone with a fly rod in their midst, as if I must be lost, a trout fisherman who had somehow taken a wrong turn off the highway. A few of these anglers would come over and politely ask what I was hoping to catch. We could not possibly both be casting for the same fish, they must have thought. Surely I could not be thinking of trying to catch a striper or blue on such tackle.

All the while, however, there was a very seductive side to it. My fascination with saltwater fly fishing and the adventure it represented overcame any moments of doubt. And I continued to be drawn by the beauty of the coast—by the beaches, with their sense of solitude and majestic spaces, by the sea, with its rhythmic waves and seamless vistas. The chance to unite these things with my love of fly fishing became a magical notion. And I refused to let it slip from my grasp.

I began to realize that my poor results were largely the fault of my not having approached saltwater fly fishing more seriously. As I had once buckled down to face the challenges of freshwater angling, I now resolved to fish the coast as often as possible and to learn everything I could about how to fish the salt.

I made some important discoveries. I learned that although the waters looked featureless, there was in fact a lot of structure. And that it was imperative to work the right places at the optimal conditions of light and tide. At its core, saltwater fishing was the same as freshwater fishing: In order to succeed, one had to plan around the best opportunities and, above all, learn to read the water. So I began to piece together a strategy. And slowly things started to happen.

Success finally arrived on a cool June night. I had learned that to catch a striper, the hours before dawn held special promise. This particular morning, the tide would be ebbing strongly right through daybreak, making for perfect conditions in the mouth of a small tidal creek I planned to fish. The exiting current would pull baitfish out of their hiding spots along the banks and flush them downstream into the surf. And with luck, stripers would be there to dine.

I suited up, put on my stripping basket, and slowly walked down to the beach. Wading out onto a familiar sandbar in the mouth of the creek, I got myself and my gear organized. The surf was calm, and the ebbing currents swept each cast out to deeper waters. The first half hour of fishing was quiet. Thoughts flowed through my mind, and occasionally I just gazed at the stars. Suddenly the fly stopped cold. For a second it felt like it had snagged. Then suddenly the line began to throb, and it became apparent that this was the moment for which I had waited so long.

The fish pulled with a startling amount of determination—more than any trout I had ever hooked. The fly line in the stripping basket was yanked up and out through the guides as I fumbled to keep some tension on the line. The reel handle began turning wildly. With the fly rod bent deeply, I applied as much pressure as I dared, yet I was still losing ground. But the the initial run came to an end. The fish hung off in the darkness, resisting any efforts to move it. Slowly I gained the upper hand, working the fish toward me. Twice more the fish ran, but I was able to quickly bring it in check each time. The fish was finally tiring.

When it was nearly at my feet, I switched on my headlamp and looked down. The beam shone brightly over the light-colored sand, and the shallow waters appeared crystalline. Each pulse of the waves pushed ripples and foam across the bar, creating a mosaic of moving shadows along the bottom. In the middle of all that lay my fish, a striper, its side reflected up at me with mirrorlike brightness. Reaching down to grasp my prize, I felt strangely hypnotized by this fish and the backdrop of haunting shapes and patterns.

I unhooked the striper and held it upright in the foam. For a few moments I stared at this beautiful creature that I had for so long tried to catch. In my grasp, it seemed to represent all that was wild and primeval in the sea. Feeling the striper's growing strength, I slowly released my grip, and the fish shot off into the night. But that brief encounter created a lasting bond between angler and ocean. And it has left me to this day with a deep, abiding sense of wonder.

The coast and its wild game fish had turned out to be there for the taking. No matter how unsure a fly fisherman initially feels when confronted by the coast, no matter how difficult these endless stretches of water seem at first glance, the sea surrenders her secrets to those willing to persist.

There is really just one world of water. Success in fishing for one species always provides lessons that can be applied to fishing for another. And the knowledge learned in the sanctuary of a small trout stream is an essay in miniature for what anglers face in the brine. In every instance, from the beautiful brook trout high in its mountain hideaway to the muscle-packed bonito racing over an ocean reef, it is a game fish fully adapted to its surroundings, matching its strengths against the environment in order to survive. In every case, it is up to the fly rodder to discover how that strategy is put together, how the elements of structure, water temperature, current, and so on shape a fish's behavior.

Fishing the coast is easily as complex as fishing a stream, in my judgment even more so. Though my experiences come mainly from the New England coast, I believe they will prove helpful wherever the surf greets the shore. So let's head down to the sea, for I am eager to share with you what I have learned.

Acknowledgments

The pure joy of fishing has forever enriched my life. Yet writing a fishing book requires much more than a love of the sport; it takes time, perseverance, and above all, the help of friends. Please let me thank some of them here. To Angus Cameron, without whom I would still be pounding the keys. No would-be author could have a better friend, a better compass. No matter how many mistakes I made, you never became discouraged. Angus, thank you for the guidance. To Phil Farnsworth and Fred Hart for all the beaches we hiked down together, for all those nights we stood waist deep in the dark waves waiting for the next solid take. You are true friends and fine anglers.

To the fine folks over at River's End Tackle, Pat Abate for sharing his vast knowledge of the surf, and Sherwood Lincoln and Mark Lewchik for assisting me whenever possible, thank you all. To Kevin Pelletier and John Marona at S&M Fly Tackle, I truly appreciate the many times you helped me. To Barry Gibson and Whit Griswold at *Salt Water Sportsman,* who offered me my very first chance to write about this fascinating sport, thank you both for the opportunity; it meant a lot to me. To Brad Burns of Maine for his undying love of striped bass. You are an inspiration. To Terry Tessein for starting up the New England Coast Conservation Association. To Dave Foley for his knowledge of angling books and the chance to browse through his extensive collection. To George Terpenning, for his infectious love of angling. It is fun to watch you fish.

My biggest debt of all is to my late parents, both gone now, but not forgotten. To my mother, who encouraged me to pursue my ideas, though they often took a path others would have deemed impractical. Mom, you always allowed me to dream. To my strong and determined father, who as a young man left England and traveled the open ocean, several times around the world. Dad, you taught me self-reliance. Even when you were eighty years of age, landlocked for so many years, I could still see the seven seas dancing in your keen eyes.

Introduction

Coastal fly fishing is a game of complexities acted out across that vast stage where land and sea meet, where fresh and salt water mingle. It's the seasons. It's the tides. It's the sun, moon, wind, and waves woven into a rich and shimmering fabric of interconnections.

To fish these waters is to face an exquisite enigma, one that you can easily sense, yet not immediately solve. The trick is to simplify and organize your thinking, recognizing that the riddle's initial opaqueness is only the result of many transparent layers. Peel them apart and the coast comes to light.

If you could find a road that tightly hugged the coast so that as you drove, the shoreline would be forever in view, you would see mile after mile of seemingly unvarying water. But if you stopped occasionally and got out of the car, slowly scanning the shoreline, you would begin to see that like a stream, the coast is a variety of configurations and conditions. But instead of pools, riffles, and runs, the game now revolves around beaches, estuaries, and points of land.

Gradually, as you fish each of these varying coastal configurations, a strategy emerges. You start to recognize where fish hold and where the water is likely empty. The coast begins to look more and more familiar.

As weeks go by and the months with them, you witness the effects of temporal change. If configuration hints at where to fish, temporal change whispers when. Water temperature, light level, time of year, and especially tides all must be figured in.

The hatches we learned to love and follow streamside are also replaced. Instead of dreaming of mayflies and caddis floating down the currents toward the ring of a rise, the coastal fly fisherman sees flashing schools of sand eels and silversides gliding in the tide, racing to escape from powerful swirls. Anglers swap one excitement for another, yet the underlying theme remains the same. Flies are designed to match the aquatic life, and anglers learn how to present them naturally as they have always done.

1

Tides: What the Fly Rodder Needs to Know

It was half past two on a cool, starry October morning. High tide had crested at nine the previous evening, and for the next several hours the ebbing waters had pulled hard in their journey along the coast. Surf caster Fred Hart and I had just finished several hours of prime fishing at the tip of a point of land where hungry striped bass and bluefish hung in the swirling flow, taking full advantage of the strong currents that funneled food their way. But as the tide slowed and the water level receded, the fish had moved. And it was time for us to move along, too.

We were fishing a part of the coast that held excellent fly-rod potential but unfortunately was a ways from home. As a result, we did not get to work these particular shores as often as we would have liked, so each opportunity was savored and carefully planned. We had picked this night weeks before based on the time of the tides. There would be falling water late at night and an incoming tide that would start before dawn and push through the first light. It was a good combination for these pieces of coastal structure.

After securing our rods to the roof of the truck, we hopped in and moved off through the night. A short ride away, we parked at the end of a dirt road overlooking a long, crescent-shaped beach. I fumbled through our gear, found a thermos of coffee, and poured two cups. Except for the rhythm of the waves, the water was not moving, for it was dead low tide. It would be an hour before the incoming tide began to flood the beach in earnest.

Two short sandbars, both of which were partially exposed at low tide, lay close together, between them a narrow channel of deeper water. We could hear the waves as they lightly broke over the bars, forming a faint line of white foam just off the beach. At low tide, schools of a small baitfish called silversides sought protection in the quiet, shallow pockets of water left on the shore side of those sandbars. These pockets were a temporary haven from their constant enemy, the striped bass, which, because of the retreating water, had been forced to exit over the sandbars to deeper quarters. Soon the tide would reverse. And as it began to flood over the bars, those same stripers would use the rising waters as a highway back to their early morning meal.

We stepped from the truck, retrieved our rods from the roof, and walked down the long beach under a spray of icy stars. The rising water was just now beginning to cover the sandbars, and white foam formed as the breaking waves increasingly spread over them. Wading out, I trained my flashlight briefly near the water's edge to see if the bait was there. Sure enough, silversides nervously swam about, some leaping from the water and falling back like rain. Sunrise was still a couple of hours off, but already a weak glow rimmed the east. The stage was set.

Moving out from shore, each of us claimed one of the sandbars. Between us was the deeper channel; through that funnel-like opening, the bass would move on the flooding tide. The best place to fish was along the seaward edge of the bars, especially where they joined the channel leading to the beach. You could fish here only during a short window of time. Soon the incoming tide would send steep waves streaming across the bars toward shore. But for two precious hours, you could have schools of hungry bass ripping through the waves right at your feet while dawn spread across the eastern sky.

WHY TIDES ARE IMPORTANT

A river always runs. Around the rocks and through the cool forest, it winds downstream with a certainty of purpose. To fish it well, anglers learn to work the currents, probing the best pieces of moving waters skillfully with their flies. The coastal waters run too. With every tick of the clock, the ocean changes. The tides build and then recede with a rhythm older than life itself. This cycle is critical to the coast, for it stirs, enriches, and flushes the shorelines.

If you have ever fished a tailwater trout fishery—that is, one where the flow is regulated by a dam—you have already experienced a situation in some ways similar to how tides affect the fishing on the coast. In both situations, changes in water level and current greatly affect how, when, and where fish feed. When the river is low, the fish are grouped together in the remaining flow. Anglers wade out over the exposed or shallow bottom to reach the prime area, there to present their flies. When the dam releases water in a tailwater trout fishery, currents increase and the water level rises. The fish respond by taking up new feeding positions. Water temperature may drop and oxygen levels rise with this new water, further stimulating the fish. Frequently they spread out, moving to lies where the water previously was too shallow. Fly rodders are forced back toward shore by the deepening waters and must now find and fish new areas.

Tides are critical in the saltwater fisherman's hunt, because they play a central role in creating the feeding opportunities game fish seek. By controlling water level, tides control access. Rising waters allow larger game fish to visit the shallow areas where baitfish hide. Ebbing tides gradually take that access away again. Second, tides produce currents, and currents in the sea, like currents in a stream, aid game fish in their hunt. Finally, some types of marine life that game fish eat are available to them only on certain tides. Marine worms and crabs, for example, may remain buried at all but the higher stages of the tide.

A RISING TIDE

As the tide begins to flood in, the marine environment near the shore quickly transforms. Most obvious is the rise in water level, but there are many other less visible changes going on as well. This pulse of new water brings with it cooler temperatures, increased oxygen levels, changes in salinity, and frequently greater water clarity. This stirs the entire spectrum of marine life.

Game fish that were forced by lowering water to leave coastal shallows during the ebb tide are now able to reenter. So as the tide moves in, fish begin to move in, seeking places to dine. Often they approach the shallower parts of a beach by using deeper channels or bottom structures as passageways to shore. In the first few hours of rising water, the game fish are usually very concentrated, entering only areas of sufficient depth. Since they are concentrated, they are competitive and ready to charge a fly. As the water rises higher, the fish will spread out.

The flooding water also produces an increase in waves and tidal currents. Predators such as striped bass are powerful swimmers, able to steer through the most turbulent flow. Baitfish, on the other hand, are comparatively weak swimmers, and these conditions make it hard for them to navigate. They often become disoriented in the turbulence created by the waves, or are sucked into and drawn along by the stronger currents. Game fish gravitate to feeding stations wherever current and wave action are found, realizing that this will help them in the hunt. Once in place, they usually face into the tide.

Some baitfish hide, but they cannot afford to hide forever. The tide has brought fresh nutrients to the shore, and baitfish also need to eat. Marine worms and crabs must come up out of the bottom and move around as well, and like baitfish, they are forced to balance the need to eat with the increased threat from predators. Game fish sense the vulnerability of their quarry and search everywhere, even swimming up into coastal estuaries, trying to intercept schools of fish or other tasty tidbits.

A FALLING TIDE

As the tide begins to ebb again, game fish sense both the changing water level and the new current direction. In response, they move with the tide to new locations. Many game fish congregate around the mouths of coastal streams and rivers, where the downstream flow of the river is now matched in direction by the ebbing tide, creating very strong currents that pull baitfish out of hiding spots upstream. Fish feeding here will turn and face the tide.

Other game fish work the shoreline and grassy banks where baitfish have taken refuge, understanding that soon the receding water levels will force the bait to come out of hiding. As water levels continue to fall, game fish prowling shallow beaches first congregate in the remaining deeper areas, and eventually move away from shore entirely. Others that have been working areas of fast current also find themselves congregated together as the flow steadily diminishes in size and strength. Eventually they too must head out to deeper regions.

WHICH TIDE TO FISH

Every stage of the tide produces fishing opportunities somewhere along the coast. That's the good news. The bad news is that for most locations, good opportunities arise on only one tide, either the flood or the ebb. Furthermore, your very best chance at hooking a fish in a given spot often is restricted to a specific portion of tide. In some places, the window of angling opportunity may last just an hour or two.

As a result, the most critical decision a saltwater fly fisherman makes is which tide to fish. If you pick a stage of the tide when there are few game fish in your chosen location, even the best tackle is of little value. Many a newcomer to the salt has walked away frustrated for that very reason, not realizing that he or she simply picked the wrong tide. This mistake is a natural one when you consider that freshwater anglers are used to situations where the fish they seek are permanent residents of a given stretch of water.

Because saltwater game fish move from one location to another as the tide changes direction and strength, no one tide is correct for all locations. But every tide is the right tide for at least some locations. The trick is to be able to match a given fishing spot to the tide that will likely attract game fish to it. Saltwater anglers do this in a number of ways. They may seek advice from someone who fishes the place often. They may learn by trial and error. Or they may make deductions based on similar situations they have fished.

It is important to realize that the best tide means more than simply the presence of fish. It is the one that not only draws game fish to the particular shoreline you wish to fish, but also brings them into fly-rod range. The fish should be within casting distance and not lying in places too deep or too swift for fly presentation.

HOW TIDES WORK

The moon is the master of the tides. As it passes overhead, its gravitational attraction causes the earth to swell underneath it. That lifting occurs in both the land and the sea. It has been calculated that the ground rises as much as 20 inches. Yet because we are rising and falling with it, no change is perceptible. The sea, being less dense, rises and falls to a greater degree.

TIDAL RANGE

The most fundamental characteristic of the tides is the visible change in water level. Rocks and sand that are exposed at one stage of the tide may lie deeply submerged at another. This difference between the high and low levels of the tide is known as the tidal range. It is expressed in feet of water and can be found on some, but not all, tidal charts. This

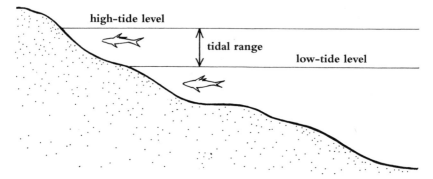

The vertical change in water level between low and high tides is called the *tidal range.*

tidal range is not a fixed number. It varies noticeably with the phases of the moon and is given as monthly average. Be aware, too, that the tidal range changes as you move from one section of the coast to the next. For example, the tide rises and falls a foot at Wasque Point on Martha's Vineyard; in Eastport, Maine, the tidal range is a full 18 feet.

It is important to know the tidal range of the places you want to fish. If you wade out through a deep hole to reach a sandbar at low tide, you must be careful how long you stay when the tide floods, or you might find yourself faced with a swim back to shore. Never assume when visiting a new part of the coast that the tidal range will be the same as that of your home waters.

THE TIME OF THE TIDE

Along most seacoasts, on average you can expect a high tide to be followed by a low tide every six hours and twelve minutes. So if high tide arrives at noon, anglers expect a low tide shortly after six in the evening. As a result, we have two high tides and two low tides in just over a twenty-four-hour period. This pattern is called *semidiurnal* and occurs along most of the Atlantic coast.

In some parts of the world, however, for complex reasons there is only one high and low tide per day (diurnal), or there is almost no tidal rise and fall at all. This is true in the Gulf of Mexico, parts of the Caribbean, Mediterranean, North Sea, Baltic Sea, Hudson Bay, and elsewhere.

When an incoming tide reaches its maximum water level, the tide is said to be *high* or to have *crested*. This moment is also called the *top of the tide*. After the tide has crested, there is a period of up to an hour where the tide is at rest, neither coming in nor going out. This period is appropriately called *slack tide* or *dead tide*. Once the ebbing tide has retreated to its farthest point, the tide is said to be *low* or we are said to be at the *bottom of the tide*. This is also followed by a period of slack water before the tide turns and begins to come back in.

The time of each tide's arrival can be followed on what is commonly called a tide table or chart. Tide charts also give the exact times that high tide crests and low tide reaches bottom.

Choosing and Reading a Tide Chart

Tide charts come in a wealth of shapes, sizes, and degrees of sophistication. They can be as simple as a daily newspaper listing of high and low tide for a popular beach or as detailed as an annually published paperback book that covers vast areas of the coast. Like a conventional calendar, all tide charts are good only for a particular year, so be careful not to use one that is outdated.

Most tidal charts contain limited information, giving the time of tide for only one or two specific locations. If the spots you wish to fish are not covered on the chart, you must determine the difference, if any, between your destination and the location on the chart. You can do this by keeping an eye on the rising water levels as you fish and making a mental note of the approximate time of highest water. Compare this time with the time published to determine how much your spot varies from the chart. This difference will always remain constant. Simple charts do not indicate tidal range, phases of the moon, or time of current. On the plus side, these charts are available for free or at a nominal charge and can be read at a glance.

The more complex charts, such as the *Eldridge Tide and Pilot Book* or the *East Coast of North and South America Tide Table*, published by the U.S. Department of Commerce, National Oceanic and Atmospheric Administration, are full of information and designed primarily for mariners. You will find the time of tide and the expected tidal range for hundreds of coastal locations. In addition, some contain tables on the times of sunrise and sunset, moonrise and moonset, as well as information on the tidal currents and even the weather. These tide charts are published annually and cost less than $10.

To use a tide chart, begin by finding the correct day and month. Remember that the time of tide given is for one particular location along the coast. The time of high or low tide for other locations may vary dramatically. Even a distance of only a few miles may make a significant difference in the time of expected tides. This is especially the case with inlets and the mouths of other estuaries. Here special care is needed to judge the time of tide accurately.

Other Types of Tide Devices

Other entries in the tidal information area are wristwatches, clocks, and computer software. The wristwatch idea is a good one, as long as the watch is waterproof and impervious to the salt. These watches, besides telling time in a conventional fashion, give the time of the tide and, in at least one case, the phase of the moon. Tide clocks come in tabletop and wall models. Naturally, a watch or clock is going to be set for the time of tide for only one location, so it will be limited in its use. Still, it can be helpful for fishing your favorite beach.

Tidal software is a very new thing. In effect, it turns your computer into a tidal information center capable of covering wide areas of the seaboard.

DAILY AND WEEKLY TIDAL PATTERNS

The tidal rhythm does not fit perfectly into our earth day, so the exact times of high and low tides advance daily. For semidiurnal tides, the rule is this: Expect the time of tide to advance about fifty minutes each day. If a particular beach on the coast has a high tide at 8 A.M. today, the tide will be high again tomorrow at the same spot at about 8:50 A.M. This may at first seem an insignificant amount of time, but over a period of a few days the tide moves several hours. If you do not take this into account, you may well miss the best hours of fishing.

This daily change also results in a weekly cycle. On the same beach at 8 A.M. seven days later, the tide will be nearly dead low. In one week's time, the tides reverse themselves. The time of day that once marked high tide now hosts low tide. In two weeks from the original date, the time of high again returns to about 8 A.M. As you can see, if you caught a good number of fish on a Saturday morning with the tide dropping, you cannot simply return the following Saturday and expect the same stage of the tidal. The tide will in fact be rising. It will be two weeks before conditions are the same.

MONTHLY TIDAL PATTERNS

Twice a month, on the new and full moon, the moon, sun, and earth align. When it happens, the sun's gravitational pull is added to the moon's, causing a greater than normal tidal range. Expect the highest high tides and the lowest lows, as well as the strongest tidal currents. These tides are known as *spring tides,* although anglers often call them *moon tides.* They occur each month around the new and full moons. Do not confuse "spring" in this context with its calendar meaning. The word as used here is derived from the Anglo-Saxon *springan,* meaning "to leap forth." At these times, the tidal range increases about 20 percent. If you normally see a tidal range of 5 feet, expect 7½ during a spring tide.

On the first and last quarters of the moon, the reverse situation occurs. Now the sun is working against the moon, resulting in weaker

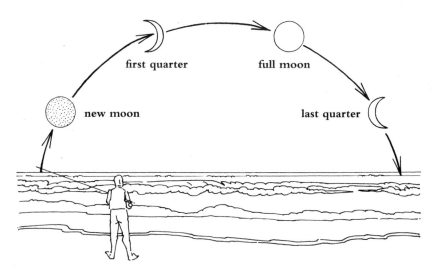

Moon phases. **Around the times of the new and the full moons, the tidal range is greater than normal. These are called** *spring tides.* **On the first and third quarter phases of the moon, tidal ranges are below normal. These are called** *neap tides.*

than normal tides. The high tide does not come in as far, nor does low tide recede as much, and currents are thereby reduced. These weakened tides are known as *neap tides*. Generally the tidal range is 20 percent below normal.

APOGEE AND PERIGEE

There is a wild card mixed into all of this. The moon's orbit around the earth is not round but elliptical, and therefore the moon's distance from the earth changes. At its closest point to the earth, the moon is said to be in *perigee*. At this time, the moon's gravitational pull is felt most strongly. High tides are higher than normal, and low tides lower. Conversely, when the moon's orbit takes it to its farthermost point from the earth, it is said to be in *apogee*. Now tides neither rise as high nor drop as low.

The strongest tides of the year happen when a spring tide occurs while the moon is in perigee. Then, rather than having a tidal range 20 percent above normal, you can expect a 40 percent increase. That is significantly more water moving in and out. A spring tide when the moon is in apogee is about a normal tide, because one cancels out the other.

TIME OF TIDE VERSUS TIME OF CURRENT

One reason tides are so important to anglers is because they create currents, which in turn attract feeding fish. So important are these currents to the quality of the fishing that some experts plan their trips around them. It seems logical that the time of tide would also be the time of current—that currents automatically start, stop, and change direction in locked step with the tide. This is not always the case, however.

For complex reasons, currents in some spots start, stop, and change direction out of synch with the tide, and thus the time of tide is not always the time of current. This is most commonly found where coastal rivers, salt ponds, and inlets greet the sea. Here you might be fishing an ebbing current while the tide is several hours into the flood.

The more involved you get in saltwater fishing, the more you come to realize how important this distinction between time of tide and time of current really is. Comprehensive tide charts such as the *Eldridge Tide and Pilot Book* have a separate table for the exact time each day when the current changes direction in specific locations. Learn to read these tables. You'll find it well worth the effort.

CURRENT SPEED

Game fish often prefer to dine when the current is at its maximum speed. This generally takes place around the second and third hours of the tide; the first, fourth, fifth, and last hour of tide usually have slower currents. The strength of the tide affects the maximum current speed. Spring tides have greater tidal ranges and therefore much stronger currents. Neap tides move less water and have weaker currents.

Most anglers prefer not to fish during slack tide or, for that matter, any time currents are weak or absent. This makes good sense. There is an exception, however. The best tide for an angler is the one that brings fish into fly-rod range. Swift currents may force feeding fish to stay deep, out of reach of even the fastest-sinking fly line. Furthermore, these fish will not move about freely or chase a fly far. As the tide weakens, current speeds abate, allowing these same fish to spread out and possibly come to the top. Now your chances of hooking one are much better. Remember this in locations where powerful currents are the rule.

2

Reading Beaches

Beaches are synonymous with the wide open world of the coast, the quintessential shoreline. Beaches can be defined by several common characteristics. A beach is a wide, flat stretch of shoreline level enough to freely walk around on, and unlike a deep cove or a jutting point of land, beaches tend to run along the water's edge in a fairly straight line.

Beaches exhibit a variety of personalities, however, regardless of their fairly simple and uniform appearance. Some are rocky, some sandy. Some have deep water nearby, others do not. Some lie in sheltered places, others are exposed and face the full force of the ocean. These differences are significant to fly fishermen, determining the best tackle and strategies to employ. Therefore, you can't treat all beaches as if they were the same. Beaches can be divided into two basic types: shallow and deep.

SHALLOW BEACHES

Shallow beaches are places where you can wade. Here the bottom slopes gradually out from shore, allowing anglers room to maneuver. The total amount of area you can wade depends on both the physical features of the location and the exact stage of the tide. Shallow beaches vary in size from a tiny stretch in the back of a small cove to vast, open sandy reaches. Some are covered with water even at the end of the ebb, while others, known as tidal flats, have large portions of their bottoms exposed at lower stages of the tide. But regardless of the differences, these places have much in common. And we can fish them with a single strategy in mind.

The composition of the bottom is usually sand or mud, with little in the way of rock. There are exceptions to this rule; for example, there are shallow beaches made up of cobble, especially in northern New England. The shape of the beach above the water line is usually simple and uniform, and there is little variation along the bottom under the waves. In fact, shallow beaches have the least amount of structure of any coastal configuration. Simply put, in these locations the land leading to the water varies little and the land under the water does the same.

Shallow beaches are fly-rod friendly. Over the years they have given me great pleasure. They rarely hold the trophy fish, but they often hold good numbers of fish. It's a fair trade-off, especially as any striper or bluefish hooked in these skinny waters puts up its most dramatic fight. Long runs are the rule, and bluefish are free to take to the air. If you do hook a large fish here, your chances of landing it are very good. There are few submerged snags where a bruiser could wrap or cut your line.

Because the water is shallow, sight fishing is more of a possibility here

Phil Farnsworth holds a big bluefish caught off a shallow sandy beach. It put up a spectacular fight.

than in deeper coastal locations. Actively feeding fish easily give away their positions with swirls and other surface disturbances. All of this adds a special dimension to angling. And that's not all shallow beaches have to offer: The freedom to wade, to get in the water and move about in search of your quarry, holds a strong appeal for fly fishermen. Certainly there is no greater thrill in all of light-tackle angling than hooking and fighting a fish while standing nearby.

For the most part, shallow beaches are sheltered beaches, shorelines not fully exposed to the open sea. There is less wind and wave, which makes casting and fishing easier. The fly rod has always been a more practical shallow-water tool than a deep-water workhorse. As a consequence, fly fishermen feel more at home on a shallow beach, and these beaches are especially appealing to newcomers to the sport. If you are a surf caster itching to try your hand at saltwater fly fishing, you will find shallow beaches a good spot to begin. In addition, if you are experienced with small swimming plugs and poppers on light line, you'll realize that small artificials are deadly in these types of locations.

These waters are the most difficult for anglers to read, however, because their uniformity makes it harder to determine where the fish are likely to be holding and therefore where to concentrate your fishing efforts.

Finding the Fish

Occasionally, feeding fish give their position away. The classic and most dramatic example is called a *blitz*. Here a large number of game fish herd the bait to the surface, slashing through it while accompanied by screeching gulls and terns overhead. Such feeding frenzies are thrilling and memorable events that saltwater anglers dream about in the same way trout fishermen dream about hatches. A blitz can be so massive and violent that it is visible for over a mile. Even the least-experienced angler can't help but notice the action.

Smaller feeding frenzies are much more common and lack the wild surface explosions of a full-blown blitz. A few tightly packed birds diving into the water is one sign to look for, although it may turn out that the birds are the only thing feeding. As a general rule, a pack of busy gulls is a better indicator of feeding game fish than a group of terns. Terns are content with just picking up tiny bait one at a time. Gulls are much more aggressive and need a real meal on the table before they get into the action.

A flock of busy birds often marks the location of a blitz, although there is never a guarantee. In this case, you can actually see the splash caused by game fish ripping through the bait.

Swirls are a surer sign. When you see them inside of casting range, you are in business. It is best to cast to either side of where you saw the swirl, not directly on top of it. The swirl marks a fish moving away, not a fish permanently holding in that spot. If you see quite a few swirls in a single area, cast to the center of them. More than one fish will see the fly, and they will compete to get it. A single swirl off in the distance is often hard to convert into a hookup. By the time you get over there, the fish is apt to be gone. But if the swirl repeats, make an attempt.

Another sign to watch for is what surf casters call a *slick*. As game fish tear into bait, fish oil is released into the water. This occurs more often with bluefish, which have sharp teeth, than with bass, which must swallow things whole. The fish oil floats to the top, creating a glassy smooth area of very calm water. It is lighter in color than the surrounding water, because its smooth surface better mirrors the available light. If you can reach the slick, or even the waters near it, with a fly, do so as soon as possible.

When I first started fishing, I heard stories about anglers who could literally smell the presence of fish. It sounded a little far-fetched. Now I know differently. Under certain conditions, you *can* smell fish. As the baitfish are torn up, they release an odor that is oddly sweet, similar to a melon held near your nose. In my experience, however, conditions have to be perfect in order to pick up the scent. There must be a lot of bait being consumed, and you need to be downwind of the event. Do not expect it to happen very often.

Unfortunately, things like blitzes, swirls, and slicks are infrequent events. Most saltwater fish you catch will be hooked sight unseen, and you need a more dependable way of finding the best spots to cover with a fly. Saltwater game fish, like freshwater ones, gravitate toward certain types of water, especially when feeding. The successful saltwater angler is one who can quickly identify those kinds of places—often called "good-looking" water—whether or not the fish are visible.

Along the coast, there are essentially three basic situations that strongly attract game fish. First, saltwater predators love current. And they especially like the intersection where slower, calmer water joins faster, more turbulent water. Trout anglers call this type of water a *seam*. Here, fish hold close to the current in order to feed from it, yet avoid sitting directly in the flow so as not to expend energy.

Second, saltwater predators want to be near forage fish or other food sources. Hence the old adage on the coast: Find the bait and you have found the fish. So any stretch of water rich in marine life is good-looking water.

The two calm patches of water are slicks created by fish oil released as blue-fish chopped up bait.

The third thing that attracts saltwater game fish is what anglers call *structure:* any place where the bottom undergoes a marked change in shape, depth, or composition. Game fish like structure for several reasons. Baitfish hang around these areas because their food sources are usually more abundant there. Structure also provides predators with a hiding place from which to ambush the bait. In addition, current and turbulence are often present here, both of which help game fish overpower their prey.

Pay special attention to the perimeter of any type of structure. Anglers call this an *edge,* and it is an excellent place to fish. For example, a sandbar might have a steep slope leading to deep water. A few fish may sit on the bar, but many more are apt to be along the edge of this dropoff. Even a simple shift in bottom composition from sand to stone creates an edge. Time and again you'll find saltwater game fish sitting or traveling along the edges of structure. Always keep this in mind.

Although the best water is characterized by the presence of bait, current, structure, or all three, finding such areas is not always easy. Often their presence is indicated only by subtle clues. Learning to detect these clues and where to look for them is a critical skill.

Reading a Shallow Beach

To learn how to read and fish a shallow beach, it is necessary to learn how to identify clues through firsthand observation. This knowledge also serves as a general introduction to reading all types of shorelines. Nautical charts can help in locating structure and possibly current, but day-to-day direct observation should be your primary tool.

Let me begin our investigation of shallow beaches by relating a personal experience. There are many shallow beaches in my home waters of Connecticut. One in particular is a densely settled beach. Its shores are packed with cottages, and a main road runs behind them. On a summer day, swimmers, boaters, and sunbathers swarm in all directions. At low tide, acres of sandy bottom lie exposed, and kids and families walk these flats collecting shells. It looks like many family vacation spots: easy to find, a little noisy, crowded, and not terribly fishy looking.

But at night it is a different world. Under the cover of darkness, stripers drift in and feed in the shallows. The bottom is fairly flat except for a series of shallow dips or depressions where the water is 12 to 18 inches deeper than the surrounding areas. A seemingly insignificant structure, these irregular areas in the bottom, ranging from roughly 30 to almost 100 feet in diameter, are nonetheless collection points for marine life. Wave and tidal currents are partly responsible, for they tend to deposit things there.

At high tide, the actual location of these holes cannot be seen from the beach. The only way anglers can find them is by accidentally wading into one, and if they did that, they would flush any fish holding there. At low tide, however, these depressions are easy to see. In fact, they often hold water even at dead low tide and appear as nothing more than large puddles in an otherwise vast exposed tidal flat. My friends and I learned their position long ago as well as their ability to hold the larger fish.

We also knew from past experience that one could not wade out to reach the best spots with a fly until at least two hours after high tide. So on a July evening with a high tide scheduled to crest at 10 P.M., we arrived at midnight. Rigging up, we walked down to the water. By counting cottages silhouetted against the streetlights, we lined ourselves up with the first of the dips in the bottom. On a falling tide, there is a modest current flowing from right to left down the beach. That meant that we needed to position ourselves to the right of the structure so each cast would be swept into the hole on the swing.

We had just begun covering the water when my fishing partner, Phil Farnsworth, said he heard a commotion to the right of us. Reeling in, we walked slowly along, stopping to listen every few feet. And it wasn't long before we came upon the source. A good number of stripers were rooting up sand eels in a series of depressions. The bass slapped their tails and rolled in the shallow water, which was only several feet deep. Quickly we got up current and cast to them. The swinging flies were instantly picked up, and the two hooked stripers blasted for deep water, pulling both of us into the backing. Surprisingly, the other fish did not panic and leave. They hung tight and continued to root up their dinner. So, after releasing our first fish, we got hooked up again in short order. This went on for hours, the fish slowly dropping offshore with the receding water, us wading forward and following along. Just at the hint of first light, the fish disappeared all at once as the tide went slack.

We hooked and released in the neighborhood of sixty fish between us with a few going 10, 12, or more pounds. It was fantastic fishing in any fly rod league. There had been moments when we felt like pinching ourselves to see if the whole experience had been real. And as we drove off, I could not help thinking about all the people sleeping in those cottages and how in a few hours these waters would be again a summer playground with not a sign of fishing anywhere.

Now the moral of this story isn't that shallow beaches are surefire fishing action. Far from it. They have their slumps like all fishing spots. The important thing is that they hold promise, especially for anglers who understand how to read these waters.

When you arrive on an unfamiliar beach, assume that the water in front of you has some spots that seldom produce fish, some spots that hold an occasional fish, and one or two places that usually have the most consistent action. Avoid the temptation to immediately start fishing, and instead spend a few minutes trying to identify the best water.

An observant angler learns a tremendous amount about an unfamiliar stretch of shore before ever setting foot in the water. Start by finding a vantage point from which you can see most of the beach. If you own a pair of binoculars, use them. The single largest visual element in front of you is the shape of the shoreline. Study it well, for shape is structure. Most shallow beaches run in a fairly straight line, and this uniformity makes them difficult to read. If you study the shoreline closely, however, you are apt to find places that are more irregular. These spots likely also have more bottom structure and thus should attract more fish. This correlation between the shape of the shoreline and the presence of bottom structure is true on a regional level as well: The most irregular stretches of an entire coastline have the greatest amount of bottom structure.

Next, look at the physical composition of the beach. In most cases, a shallow beach is composed primarily of one material, either sand or mud. There may be places, however, where the physical makeup changes. These shifts in composition signal accompanying shifts in bottom structure, water depth, resident marine life, and current, all of which affect the fishing. The boundary line between these different compositions qualifies as an edge. Pay particular attention to the part of the beach made up of the coarsest material. Usually this is a richer marine habitat. Rocks make a better environment for mussels, snails, and crabs than a sand bottom. This attracts baitfish, which in turn draws the fish you seek. So if you see an isolated patch of rocks running out into the water on a beach that is otherwise sand, investigate.

These are two good clues with which to approach an unfamiliar beach, but there are plenty more. A shallow beach is fairly flat, yet there is often a hint of incline as it nears the water. This incline or slope is a useful indicator of the relative water depth, as the slope of the shoreline is similar to the slope of the adjacent bottom.

When coastal game fish come near shore, they are sensitive to

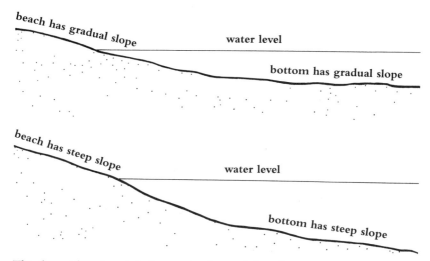

The slope of the beach indicates the slope of the adjacent bottom. Therefore, a steep-sloping beach has deeper water nearby than does a beach that slopes gradually.

changes in water depth. The shallower it becomes, the warier they become, and as a result, game fish often stay in the deeper water when visiting a beach. This is particularly true for the biggest fish. If you can quickly identify the deeper areas close to shore, you have a better chance of finding fish.

You can pick up information about water depths before you enter the water. Walk down to the water's edge a few hours after high tide, and study the beach both right and left as it runs off to the horizon. At a casual glance, there may seem little to see. Note whether the slope of the beach as it heads down to the water is equal everywhere or inclines down a bit more sharply in some areas. Hard to say? Try squatting down like a golfer lining up a difficult putt and look again.

Wherever the slope is greater, the water directly in front is correspondingly deeper. This change, although likely small on a shallow beach, could nevertheless be significant to the fishing. Fish close to shore make a habit of passing through and holding in the deeper areas. And although game fish will spread out over a shallow beach at high tide, as the water begins to ebb they increasingly congregate in the deeper places.

Here is another trick for finding pockets of greater depth. Some beaches are bordered by cottage after cottage. These residents own boats, and many moor them just offshore. These boaters understand the tides and bottom structure nearby. If you look along the shore, you may note that the boats are all a certain distance out. This may be in part a consideration to swimmers, but to some degree it marks the beginning of deeper water at low tide. This dropoff may be slight, but it holds angling potential. As the tide ebbs, you may be able to wade out to this dropoff line and work a fly along the edge. Also take special note of any substantially larger craft or sailboats. These guys draw more water, and their mooring location can mark a deep hole. If it is within casting range at low tide, it is a place to find a really good fish. A word of warning, however: If you hook a strong fish, it could wrap you up in those mooring lines, so apply full pressure immediately after the strike.

Studying the beach from a vantage point enabled you to identify the larger areas of irregular shape. Frequently, however, smaller variations go unnoticed from afar. These smaller areas may prove highly significant to the fishing, especially on beaches that lack any obvious structure. Head down to the water and sight along the line created by the water's edge. Is this line fairly straight as it runs toward the horizon, or does it meander? The water's edge on many beaches has a serpentine appearance, bulging seaward in some areas and cupping inland in others. It is important to look for these structures.

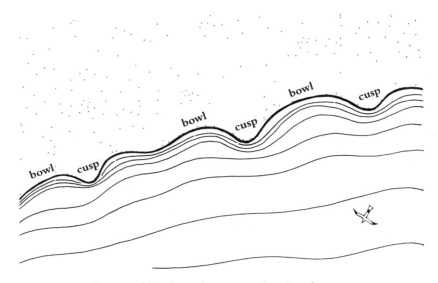

Cusps and bowls are important shoreline features.

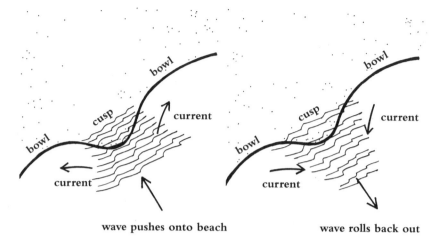

wave pushes onto beach   wave rolls back out

Waves produce subtle currents in both cusps and bowls.

The bulges are called *cusps*. A cusp might be a simple protrusion of sand only several yards across or a gentle arc hundreds of feet long. The cupped or indented parts of the beach are known as *bowls*. Both cusps and bowls are the result of the slope and shape of the bottom and signal the presence of bottom structure.

Most often a cusp is part of a slightly elevated area of the beach. This indicates that the water immediately in front of the cusp is apt to be shallower than surrounding areas of the beach. Bowls, on the other hand, are frequently connected to steeper sections of the beach and thus deeper water.

Waves can create current along the sides of a cusp, drawing fish to feed. This is particularly the case where the cusp protrudes a fair way. Each wave as it rides into shore hits the tip of the cusp long before reaching into the bowl. The portion of the wave that strikes the cusp is forced to slow down and break on the shore. Part of the wave's energy is thrust along the sides of the cusp, producing a current that shoots back into the adjacent bowls. Moments later, the portion of the wave that struck the cusp cascades back down the slope of the beach, draining seaward. This water draining off the tip of the cusp produces a second current, which pulls water out of the bowls. These currents follow one another with the steady rhythm of the waves.

Bowls may have less wave and current activity than the tip of a cusp, but they are very good places to fish. Here, nutrients suspended in

The shape of this shoreline reveals two bowls and a cusp. If you look closely, you can see that the cusp extends out underwater to the rock pile on the left side of the image.

the water tend to settle to the bottom. That food supply and the greater water depth attract baitfish to bowls to feed and hide from their enemies. Game fish lurk here too in hopes of corralling a meal for themselves. Thus, the most productive fishing spot is frequently right where the bowl joins the cusp.

Continuing your observation of the beach, turn your back to the water and face inland. Look at the terrain leading up to the beach. It might be dunes, flat ground, rolling hills, or some combination thereof. Although the beach may be flat from years of coastal erosion, it probably once looked much like the ground immediately inland. Thus, wherever the land leading to the beach undergoes a change in elevation, the beach most likely once had a similar shape, and the water directly in front may well still have some type of corresponding bottom structure. Generally, where the ground inland is steep, there is deeper water close to shore; where the land is low, there is a shallow bottom. On more than one occasion, this has helped me find a prime fishing spot I would otherwise have missed.

Just as changes in the shoreline speak of changes in bottom structure, so do changes in the appearance of the water. These include variations in color, wave patterns, and the water's surface. In some cases, the look of the water is your primary clue to the location of an important piece of structure or current.

Water color is affected by many things. Storms can cloud it, silt-laden estuaries turn it muddy, and so on. Water depth also changes water color. Where the water is clear and the bottom sandy, a shift in depth can produce a dramatic color change. Here, the deeper the water, the darker and bluer it looks; the shallower the water, the lighter its color, often leaning toward pale green. Where you see a sudden color shift from pale green to deep blue, there is an equally sudden dropoff on the bottom. A fly moving along this edge between shallow and deep is an inviting target for game fish.

In shallow, clear water, the color you observe may be a result of bottom composition. Sandy bottoms reflect the light penetrating the water column, making the water look yellow or pale green, especially on calm, sunny days. Rocky bottoms reflect little light, and the water over them appears dark brown. Thus on shallow beaches, water coloration may identify edges where the bottom changes from sand to rock. Remember, a large school of baitfish can darken the water, too. This doesn't happen often, but the angler should consider the possibility.

Wave action is another excellent indicator of water depth. As a

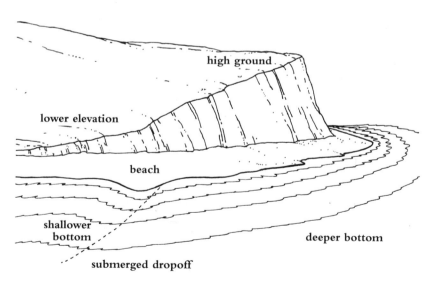

The elevation of the land can be a clue to the bottom structure on an adjoining beach.

wave moves over an area of shallow water, the friction of the bottom causes the wave to slow down and get much steeper. Eventually the wave gets so steep that it starts to break, tumbling forward and spilling in a cascade of white foam. This happens most often right at the water's edge. Yet in certain situations, waves may break a good distance out from the beach. On a tidal flat, the waves may begin breaking several hundred feet from the water's edge and continue to break all the way to shore. This is particularly true at lower stages of the tide, when the water is less deep. If you study the area of breaking waves, it will help you learn the shape of the shallower portions of the beach.

Note where the waves first begin to break offshore. This is the edge at which the shallow beach joins deeper water. It is an excellent place to fish at low stages of the tide. There will likely be a change in water color here as well.

Occasionally you see a group of breaking waves totally surrounded by calmer water. This type of wave pattern marks an isolated shallow reef or bar. On many beaches, these structures, like the surrounding bottom, are composed of sand, hence the common name *sandbar*. They can

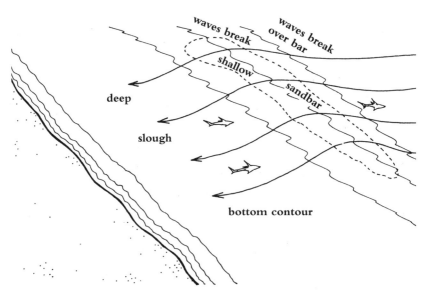

Wave action is a good indicator of the position and size of sandbars and sloughs.

produce a fairly narrow band of breaking waves that on some beaches
might extend for a considerable distance, often running roughly parallel
to the beach itself. The waves first break along the seaward or outside
edge of the structure. Where they stop breaking marks the inside edge.
Both edges are prime places to wet a fly.

The exact stage of the tide determines how easy it is to find the
position of a sandbar. At high tide, the bar is harder to locate because it
is deeper underwater. Still, an experienced eye might pick out the bar
simply by noticing a change in water color. The farther the tide drops,
the more the waves actively break across the bar on their journey
toward shore. This makes finding the bar quite easy. So heavy are these
breaking waves on some sandbars that you can determine the bars' location by sound as well as sight. At low tide, the sandbar may be totally
exposed, giving you a more complete picture of its shape and size.

Often there is a pocket of deeper water between the shoreline and
the sandbar, known by anglers as a *slough* (pronounced "slew"). Here
again the waves are a clue. In such locations, the waves break over the
sandbar but quiet down again as they continue on toward the shore. You
can also find a slough by wading at low tide. A slough forms a lane of
deeper water along which game fish travel the beach in their quest for
food, and it is probably the only place you will find them at the lowest
stages of the tide.

The last clues to look for are signs of current, as fish are greatly
attracted to moving water. Breaking waves cascading down the slope of
the beach produce a type of current called the *backwash*. Anyone who
has ever stood in the foam at the water's edge has felt this. Your feet sink
in the sand as the current pulls around your ankles. Sometimes game
fish feed near the water's edge to take advantage as the backwash stirs up
things hiding on the bottom, such as crabs and amphipods. Baitfish are
drawn here to feed as well.

Tides are the largest producer of currents on the coast. Though we
tend to think of tides as water moving straight in to the beach on the
flood and then straight back out on the drop, tides more often move at
an angle to the shore. This forces tremendous amounts of water to brush
along the coast, creating wide areas of moving water. In general, because
of their uniform shape, beaches have less current than more irregular
places, such as points of land or inlets. Nevertheless, the current you do
find is significant to the fishing.

You can locate current in several ways. I often keep an eye on my fly line during the retrieve. If it swings to the right or left, it indicates the presence of a flow. Even a weak current can be spotted this way. Stronger currents can be felt tugging at your waders. Also, the more current there is, the more turbulent the water surface becomes. Watch too for lines of floating debris or foam. This tactic can help you locate currents even from a considerable distance.

Inside of a large area of current, look for places where the current is markedly faster than the surrounding waters. These areas of increased current are called *rips*. Like riffles in a stream, rips are caused by water traveling over or around structure. Rips may be the most consistently productive type of water you can fish. Because of their great importance, chapter 3 is devoted to them.

Making a Wading Tour

Since a shallow beach affords the opportunity to wade, you can discover a great deal about the bottom structure firsthand. Do this as a preliminary to your initial fishing trip. Start by checking your tide book for a daytime low tide, particularly one on or around a new or full moon, when the tide will be especially low. A perigean spring low tide is better still. Water levels will be extremely low, affording you an excellent view of the bottom structure.

Walk down toward the water, but stop well short of it. First, get an idea of where the high-tide line is. It will help you form a mental picture of the beach at high water. At the moment, the high-tide mark is apt to be considerably above the present water line. Look for the wrack line, a dark line of debris on the dry sand running roughly parallel to the present water line. In general, it will be 1½ to 2 feet wide, consisting of seaweed and bits of wood and contrasting well with the light-colored sand.

There may be a second, less-distinct line that lies even farther inland from the water. This line often contains larger pieces of wood. This is the spring high-tide line, which the water reaches on the new and full moons.

Piers, pilings, and other man-made objects supply another way to gauge the high-water mark. At low tide, there is likely a dark collar on these objects that extends from the present water level up to the height of the full tide. This stain results from the material being wet during higher stages of the tide.

Walk the exposed area between the high-tide line and the water.

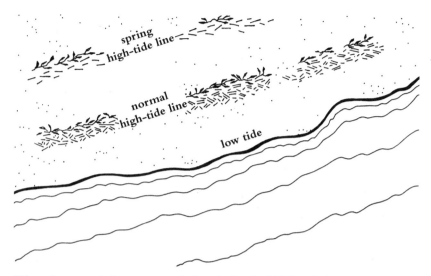

spring high-tide line

normal high-tide line

low tide

When the water is low, you can judge the level of high tide by looking for the wrack line, a band of weeds and other marine debris on the beach. A less discernible line farther inland marks the spring high-tide level.

Do you see a trough or groove in the beach? Perhaps there is one just below the high-tide mark running parallel with the water line. This is a result of the digging action of the waves during high tide. Where water depth is sufficient, stripers and bluefish herd baitfish into this area during the flood tide, especially in low light.

Now wade into the water, zigzagging back and forth to cover as much area as possible. Look for signs of bait, current, or structure. Note any significant-looking alterations in the bottom, including holes, depressions, changes in bottom composition, sandbars, and dropoffs. Remember that these are covered at higher stages of the tide, so you need to get a firm idea of exactly where the best structures are located. To do this, you can make rough sketches, pick some landmarks on the shore, or even pace off a structure from a visible marker above the high-tide line.

As you wade, be alert for current or signs of life. At this stage of the tide, both are usually at a minimum, but you may still find evidence. The presence of baitfish, crabs, or skates is a good sign. Note if they tend to congregate in certain areas. Much of the resident marine life found on sand and mud beaches is of the burrowing type, such as blue crabs, clams, and marine worms. They are able to dig into and hide in the bot-

On a new- or full-moon low tide, a shallow tidal flat may lie fully exposed. Note the subtle bottom structure, including pockets of deeper water and sandbars. Six hours from now, all of this is hidden under 3 feet of water. *Photograph by Phil Farnsworth.*

tom. During the daytime, the place usually appears to be little more than a water-covered desert, but if you wade the beach at night with a flashlight, you'll see a great deal more activity, because most resident marine life is nocturnal.

Small baitfish such as silversides and sand eels call these shallow beaches home. These forage fish are transitory during the day, moving in and out with the tide. Because of the minimal bottom structure, they move freely up and down the beach a good deal as well. If the schools are large, they are easy to see. Other signs can give away the position of even a few tiny fish. As you wade, you may catch a glimpse of them as they jump out of the water in an attempt to get away from you. Also pay attention to the surface of the water. These fish often dimple as they feed. If you want to get a close look at the local forage fish, use a minnow net.

Keep an eye out for areas of the bottom containing submerged plants. These spots are much more attractive to marine life than bare sand. Perhaps the most common of these underwater grasses is *Zostera marina,* better know as eelgrass. It is well adapted to protected beaches where tidal current and wave action are light. Its leaves are dark green,

Always look for signs of baitfish. Here sand eels are feeding on the surface over a sand bottom.

flat, and ribbonlike. Look for it starting just below the low-tide mark and extending out a considerable way to deeper water.

If you can, return to the beach during a daytime high tide, and observe how things have changed. See if you can pick up the subtle clues from the shape of the beach or the surface of the water that identify the bottom structures now covered by water. Use the landmarks you picked out earlier to help you.

Once you have fully examined a beach, you might think your work is over. But the coast is a living entity. Everything here is subject to change. Sand bottoms are soft and particularly prone to the forces of ocean storms. Many a spring I have visited a place I knew well, only to find that winter reshaped it. Holes grow and then fill in, points of land erode, and sandbars wax, wane, and move, all courtesy of the forceful sea. It's all part of the adventure of fishing the coast.

Tide Selection for a Shallow Beach

Generally the first hours of an incoming tide hold promise, particularly on days when that stage of tide occurs at dusk, dawn, or even night. Why pick low light? Game fish to a fair degree avoid shallow water in strong light, probably because they feel vulnerable. Also, baitfish are more susceptible to ambush in lower-light conditions, and game fish take advantage of this. Furthermore, many beaches are busy with swimmers and boaters during the heat of the day. Not only does that make fishing more difficult, but the noise drives fish away.

The second, third, and fourth hours of the ebb are also productive, again in low or changing light. Not only does the ebbing water create beach currents, but the fish seem to feed harder when they sense the tidal door closing. Striper and bluefish do gradually drop back offshore, but the decreasing water levels may allow you to follow them out for some distance.

During the hours near the crest of the tide, game fish use the greater depth to spread out along the beach. Then the fish are the least concentrated, and you need to cover as much water as possible. These moments of maximum water, however, are the times when the largest fish are apt to enter a shallow beach.

At the bottom of the tide, or dead low, when the water is at its shallowest, the fish have moved out to deeper water. Be aware, however, that though this is frequently the poorest time to fish, on some shallow beaches it holds a unique angling situation. If there is a deep hole, dropoff, or other edge that you can wade out to and reach with a fly at low tide, do it! Many times game fish group there waiting for the tide to return. A very big fish could be in that hole. When fish are clumped together, they are also very competitive, which means that they will attack the fly to prevent their comrades from getting it first.

Fishing a Shallow Beach

Your first trip in the salt should be arranged with an emphasis on safety and comfort. Night fishing, though very productive, is definitely out until you are more familiar with both saltwater fishing and the place you have in mind. Instead, plan a dawn trip on a day when the tide is appropriate. Pack your gear ahead of time, and double-check that you have all the things you want along. A list of basic equipment is given at the end of chapter 10.

The weather on the coast is a real factor in your fishing. Chapter 7 gives a more detailed look at this part of the sport, but here are some basics you should know for your first trip. The night before your outing, listen to the weather report. Note the direction and the speed of the forecasted wind. If the wind is going to come off the land, it shouldn't be much of a problem. If it will be off the water, however, that changes things considerably. An onshore wind of 15 knots or less is fine. You should be able to cast well enough to fish. If the wind will be over 15 knots, consider waiting a day for better conditions. When you have more experience casting in the salt, winds over 15 knots are less of a problem. Heavy rains or thunderstorms are also good reasons to postpone your trip.

Sometimes the weather the day before your fishing trip is a consideration. Shallow sand beaches are greatly affected by prolonged periods of high wind. When the wind first begins, the turbulence they create may attract feeding fish, but the longer the high winds persist, the more likely you should fish elsewhere, especially if the wind lasts for more than a day. In areas of shallow water, strong wind creates waves that break quickly as they approach the shore, stirring up the soft bottom and sending clouds of sand into suspension. Game fish tend to avoid such waters, perhaps because it is difficult to see their prey in the clouded water or because the sand gets in their gills. Choose another time or place to fish.

Arrive at the beach about an hour before sunrise. Even though the sun has yet to show, you should have a fair amount of light. Do not be tempted to wade wet, even in the summer months. Though the dangers are not great, there is plenty out there to ruin your day. Bare feet and legs are exposed to crabs, sharp shells, broken glass, and the tail ends of skates. Jellyfish are also a problem. The big, reddish-brown lion's mane jelly *(Cyanea),* so common along the Northeast coast in the warmer months, is responsible for most problems. Fortunately, it is not extremely powerful. Storms can drive its supercharged offshore cousin the Portuguese man-o-war *(Physalia)* into shallow water, however. You don't want to tangle with this guy, so waders are in order.

Head down to the water and look for signs of feeding fish: a blitz, a swirl, concentrated bird activity, or a slick. If you see any of these, move to that location and begin fishing immediately. More likely than not, however, you will not find any visible signs of feeding fish. At this point, begin studying the beach for structure and current. If you have already done so before this visit, use your notes or landmarks to get your bearings.

If you plan to wade out a long way from shore on an expansive tidal flat, take a compass reading before you enter the water. If thick fog rolls in while you're out there, it may be difficult to remember the way back.

This is especially important in areas of the coast where fog is persistent and the tidal range is great. True, such situations happen rarely, but play it safe.

Begin to cover the best holding water, starting with those areas closest to the water's edge. Remember that the more water you cover, the greater the chance of finding fish. You and your fishing companions should spread out to maximize the area you cover. Each angler should cast in a fanlike pattern to increase the amount of water the fly travels through.

Start the retrieve as soon as the fly lands on the water. Fish are extremely sensitive to something new entering their environment, and as a result, most strikes come within the first 20 feet of the retrieve. Therefore, it is critical that you get in immediate contact with the fly. This is especially true in shallow water, but it is a good general rule wherever you fish. One exception is those times when you need to give the fly a chance to sink deep.

Work each place for five to ten minutes, or until it is clear that you have covered the water well. Then move along to your next location. If the entire beach is less than 200 yards long, I might cast a dozen or so times over a likely holding spot, and then slowly move down the beach or wade out to the next one. Repeat the process down the length of the beach. The lower the water becomes, the farther back the fish are apt to drop offshore, so wade out as the opportunity arises, and be sure to cover the various bottom structures you discovered when you scouted earlier.

Should you or your partner hook a fish, get a strike, or simply see a fish make a pass at the fly, cover the surrounding area intently. Saltwater game fish often feed in groups, so where you found one fish there are likely to be others. If fish continue to follow the fly without taking, change retrieve speed. Try faster first. If that fails, give them something different: Change fly size and color. Regardless of the outcome, remember this spot. At the same stage of the tide on another day, it will likely hold fish again.

Working with the Waves

Where moderate to large waves are coming into shore at a noticeable angle, it is best to work with them rather than against them. Casting straight out from shore forces your fly line to ride up and over each incoming wave. This creates slack in your line and lessens your contact

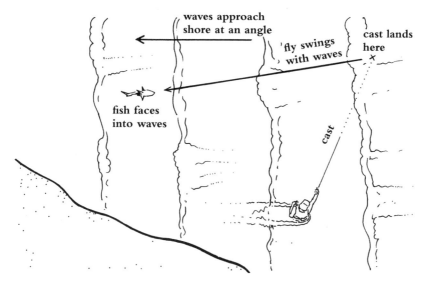

Whenever possible, work with the angle of the waves. It helps you better control your fly.

with the fly. Casting in a direction parallel to the face of the waves has two advantages. First, you can work the fly in the space between two waves, called a *trough of the wave*. This greatly reduces or even eliminates the slack in your line, allowing you better feel and control of the fly. Also, game fish will likely be facing into the waves. Casting with the waves allows you to swing the fly in a more natural manner.

Sometimes, given the circumstances, you cannot help but cast directly over the incoming waves. When that happens, you should take steps to help maximize your control of and feel for the fly. If you are using a floating line, switch to an intermediate or possibly even a sinking line if conditions allow. That will reduce some of the slack. Next, pick your fly carefully. Unweighted patterns are the worst things to use in these situations. Because they are so light, the waves really lift them. A heavy fly sinks down into the water far better, eliminating some of the slack. And if it has a wide head, the fly will create increased resistance coming through the water as you retrieve it. That resistance translates into better control and sensitivity for the angler.

Waves approach a beach at a steady pace and with a fairly constant distance between them. If you are forced to cast over the waves, you can help yourself stay in touch with the fly by adjusting the retrieve speed. If the waves are coming close together, one right after the other, momentarily speed up the retrieve as soon as you sense yourself losing touch with the fly. This removes some slack from the line. Once you are in control, return the retrieve speed to normal until you sense trouble again. If the waves are widely spread apart, adjust your retrieve speed to match the forward speed of the waves. The fly is least in control when it lifts up the back of a wave or falls down the wave's face. If you retrieve faster than the rate at which the waves are advancing, your fly is constantly riding up and over the waves. Instead, let the fly ride in the trough between two waves, then use a retrieve speed that allows it to advance forward without overtaking the wave in front of it. These techniques are critical when fishing beaches exposed to strong surf.

DEEP BEACHES

The basic concepts and rules given for fishing on a shallow beach carry over to deeper waters, with a few adjustments in the details to match various deep-water situations.

Along many beaches, the bottom drops away quickly from the shore and is often 4 or more feet deep at the water's edge. Wading is not possible or at best extremely limited, permitting anglers to move out only a few feet even at the lowest stages of the tide. The only exception is found where a shallow structure, such as a sandbar, swings to touch the shore. These deep beaches also, in general, have increased exposure to strong wind and waves.

Deep beaches can be a challenge, requiring anglers to make adjustments. In some locations, these adjustments are simply a matter of a few changes in tackle and technique. In others, where the surf roars and the winds race, meeting the challenge can be a major task. These are the great beaches whose majestic grace was so eloquently described by writers such as Beston and Thoreau. But for all their beauty, they are going to test you and your equipment to the fullest. So why do it then? For the sheer exhilaration of facing a challenge, for the unmatched solitude and beauty of these wild places, and for the trophy-size fish that call these waters home.

Many years ago, an experience on outer Cape Cod taught me a fundamental lesson about fly fishing in heavy water that has helped me fish in strong surf ever since. We were working hard, but 25-knot winds were making casting extremely difficult, and large waves boomed on the shore. Still, we saw surf casters hitting middle-weight bass and blues at very close range. That was encouragement enough to continue. But after more than two hours of struggling, we had not had a single strike. Then I learned why. I saw my fly riding down the face of a wave, and a big blue latched on to it. It was a real eye opener. I saw the strike, but I never felt it. And equally important, as quickly as I could react, I still could not set the hook fast enough. The waves were lifting my fly line so much that large amounts of slack were created between me and the fly. Only now did I realize just how much. This fish was probably one of many that had struck my fly, all of them totally unknown to me.

On an exposed beach, with its big waves, you cannot wade in to adjust your angle. So what did we do? For one thing, our intermediate fly lines were not giving us enough control of the fly. A high-density fast-sinking line would cut down into the waves and thereby reduce some of the slack. Heavily weighted flies were needed, too. And finally, picking a slightly more protected beach could ease the whole process. So we rerigged and studied our charts that night as the wind rattled the motel windows.

The following dawn found us farther down the coast, where the mountainous dunes behind us gave some shelter from the wind. The heavily weighted flies we had tied last night were knotted to the line. I dotted my leader with twisted-on lead as well. This was still big surf country, and waves thundered at our feet. And casting this rig was no picnic. It was more of a backhanded lop than anything else. Yet within minutes, my rod bowed deeply as I struck a fair-size striper, the first fish of the trip. The thrill of fighting and trying to land this warrior in the pounding surf was intense. I had two other fish in short order as the light of day broke over the North Atlantic. It was something I will never forget.

Overall, learning to fish deep beaches involves the same strategies used to investigate shallow beaches. There is an important distinction to be made, however. There are two distinctly different types of deep beaches: those composed mainly of sand and those of rock. While similar in many respects, each has its own special character and fishing requirements.

Deep Beaches of Sand

Like shallow beaches, deep beaches of sand come in a wide range of sizes. Some are small, covering less than 100 yards of shoreline; others are better measured in miles. The amount of surf also varies. At one end

of the spectrum there are the deep beaches along the ocean side of
Cape Cod, especially from Eastham northward. Here the waves thun-
der, pound the beach with raw power. With their mountain-high dunes
and endless horizons, they are the most asethetically compelling of
beaches. And likely at the same moment the most difficult to fly-rod. At
the other end of the spectrum, there are deep beaches of a somewhat
gentler nature. Here the surf is less severe, and both the land leading to
the beach and the bottom itself are a bit more gradual in slope. The
southwest coast of Rhode Island holds many such places.

Feeding fish are no more likely to be visible along a deep beach
than along a shallow shore. Given the greater depth, fish are, if anything,
harder to spot. So again anglers must rely on their ability to read the
water. The good news is that deep beaches in general have considerably
more bottom structure than shallow beaches. Therefore, you can expect
sandbars, holes, edges, cusps, and bowls to be both more numerous and
more dramatic in scale.

As with a shallow beach, start your investigation by finding a vantage point, and observe the shoreline. Identify where the land nearest
the water has the greatest irregularity of shape. Next, look for places
where the composition of the beach changes.

Cusps and bowls are bigger and easier to spot on the deep beach.
On some deep sand beaches, cusps reach gigantic proportions. It is

**Look for changes in shoreline composition. Where this sand beach turns to
rock is likely a good spot to fish.**

entirely possible for them to be 100 feet or more across. They jut out into the sea like large, stubby fingers. The oceanside beach on outer Cape Cod is a fine example of this type of coastline. Where found, these giant cusps are a major feature of the beach and, as you might expect, a critical part of learning how to fish these waters. The distance from one bowl to the next might be upward of 100 yards. These beach features are produced by complex and conflicting currents, some moving seaward, formed as the pounding waves crash then retreat back down the steep incline, others moving shoreward, produced by tidal flow and general wave direction, still others moving parallel to the water's edge.

The currents you find along the sides and tip of the cusp are the same as on a shallow beach. Because of the heavier surf associated with deep beaches, however, these currents are all much stronger. In fact, they frequently are powerful enough to be called rips. Rips, as I mentioned earlier, are extremely productive places to fish and are covered in detail in the next chapter. Couple increased current strength with increased water depth, and you see why even the largest stripers and bluefish feed around the cusps on a deep beach. Furthermore, the current coming off the cusp's tip often is focused enough to create a break, or cut, through any sandbar paralleling the shore.

Of course, even without cusps, surf coming into shore results in the formation of current. Where waves strike the beach obliquely, surf pushes water along the shoreline. These are called *longshore* currents.

In my experience, one of the best spots to find the bait, and therefore the fish you seek, is where the bowl turns seaward at the base of a cusp. You can further refine your strategy by looking at the angle at which waves are approaching the shore. If, for instance, you are standing onshore in the middle of a bowl and the waves are moving ashore in a left-to-right direction, the right side of the bowl will have more current and collect more bait-attracting food. It is therefore the place to start fishing.

Now turn your attention from the beach to the water. Look for signs of submerged structure. Remember, a line of breaking waves out from shore might signify a sandbar. These bars are likely to run roughly parallel to the shoreline, but in some cases they may be angled in toward the beach or have some other type of irregular shape. At lower stages of the tide, some sandbars are fully exposed and very easy to identify. If you find a sandbar, note as best you can where it likely begins and ends. It is good to sketch or photograph the area for future reference.

If you see a long line of waves breaking offshore, broken by a calm

This angler is fishing a cusp on a deep beach. Note the wave action around the cusp and the slope of the beach.

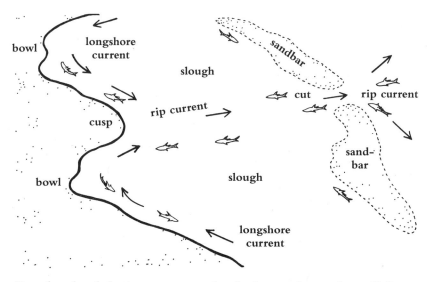

On a deep beach, bottom structure—sloughs, bars, and cuts—is usually larger and more dramatic than that found on a shallow beach.

area of dark water in the middle, you have found a sandbar with a channel cutting through it. This break, or cut, is an extremely important entrance and exit point for game fish moving to and from the beach. If it is within casting range, it deserves your fishing attention.

After a breaking wave crosses the sandbar, it may not break again until it reaches the shore. Just as it did on a shallow beach, this indicates the presence of a slough between the shore and the sandbar. These pockets of water, much bigger and deeper than the ones found off a shallow beach, hold both baitfish and game fish and can be very productive places to fish. Because of their depth, they often hold fish even at the lowest stages of the tide.

There are also apt to be smaller pockets of greater water depth. These depressions, or holes, are no less important here than the ones associated with shallow beaches. Observing water color and wave activity can help you locate them. These spots are a lot easier to see from the high vantage point than they will be down on the beach. So try to line these spots up with some kind of landmark to help you locate them again later.

As on shallow beaches, waves often cut a small trench parallel to the water line, called a *trough*. On deep beaches, the backwash is much more powerful, and therefore the trough is usually far more pronounced.

Changes in water color often reveal changes in the bottom. The dark water just above center on the right side marks a shift from sand to rock. Fish travel along this edge. In the bottom quarter of the image, you can see a change in water color running across the entire photograph. This is the dropoff at the edge of the trough. Many fish feed here, especially at night. In this case, it is only a rod's length out from the water line.

Expect fish to feed right here, practically at your feet. Game fish can trap bait in the trough, and the constant action of the waves uncovers small marine life such as amphipods. Striped bass often dine in the trough for just these reasons.

Occasionally you find a deep sandy beach where the bottom closest to the water line is a wide, flat shelf. This shelf starts at the high-tide mark and runs out under the surface of the water for 20 feet or more before it suddenly drops off to deeper water. Some surf casters call this structure the "first bar." If you ever fish the shoreline of southwestern Rhode Island, you are bound to run into this type of structure. Think of it as a large plateau tight to the shore. Game fish love to feed along the edge of this dropoff. Furthermore, they tend to travel along this lip when they want to move up and down the length of the beach to chase bait. I have seen this done by stripers, bluefish, bonito, and little tunny.

Since you cannot wade these beaches, for the most part, the existence of this shelf and its accompanying dropoff may go unnoticed. The shelf is easiest to locate during the last hours of the outgoing tide or the first few hours of the flood. Waves riding into the beach will start breaking as they cross the dropoff, and they will continue to break as they ride up over the shelf and head to shore. Reaching the dropoff with a fly is considerably easier now, because the lower water levels not only identify the exact location of the dropoff, but also allow you to work your way closer to it. On days when the surf is very calm, you may be able to wade out on the shelf at low tide. Still, given the breaking waves and the fact that the water is rarely lower than waist-deep, you will probably get wet.

Waves pile water up onto these shelves, and somehow that water must drain back off. As the water drains seaward, it produces a current along the bottom headed from shore toward the dropoff. That current is part of what makes the dropoff such an attractive feeding spot in the first place. Since the shape, slope, and depth of any shelf are not perfectly uniform everywhere along the entire beach, in a few spots the current around the dropoff may be much greater. These spots are called *runouts.*

A runout is a place where the water pressure built up on the shelf can drain seaward. This exit point actually pulls water from neighboring areas of the beach. Here is how it happens. As water is forced up on the shelf by the surf, it hits the shore and runs back down. Sometimes this water heads straight back out along the bottom. Where there is a runout nearby, however, this water moves parallel to the water's edge toward the channel, where it exits out to sea.

Runouts are a type of rip. Look for patches of dark, nervous-looking

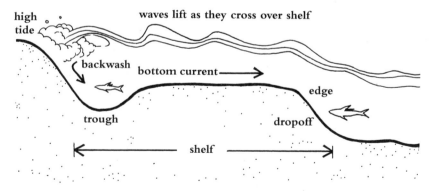

Deep beaches may have a shelf, or first bar, extending out from the water line. Expect many fish to feed and travel where the shelf drops off to deeper water.

Chip Bates has hooked a striper right where a shelf on the bottom drops off to deeper water. Note how the wave on the right side of the image lifts as it crosses the leading edge of that structure. *Photograph by Phil Farnsworth.*

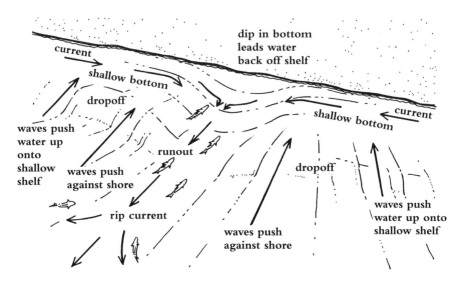

On beaches with a long, wide shelf, look for runouts. These are spots where the water forced up onto the shelf by waves drains back off, forming a current or rip line.

water. Another way to spot a runout is to watch the foam created by the breaking surf. Where the runout is located, you commonly see a fairly distinct line of foam pushing out to sea. These runouts are super places to fish, and I find more and larger fish here than at any other part of the dropoff.

Once you have learned as much as you can from your vantage point overlooking the beach, head down toward the water. The beach grass of the dunes will end somewhat abruptly and give way to all sand. Near this transitional area, you will find a noticeable dark, narrow, broken strip of dried seaweed and other floatable objects. This line marks the extent to which the spring high tide climbs the beach. The distance between this line and the normal high-tide mark may be considerable, because the tidal range is great on a deep beach.

Continuing on toward the water, you will often travel across fairly level ground. Surf casters call this area the *backshore* part of the beach. Eventually you will come to a spot where the beach suddenly takes a 90-degree drop. This drop may be less than a foot or as much as several feet. At the base of this drop, the beach begins a more gradual incline that leads down toward the water. At the bottom of this incline is the low-tide water line. The incline itself is called the *foreshore* and marks the separation between the normal high- and low-tide marks. The area at the top of the incline is known as the *berm* or *berm crest*. The peak of this

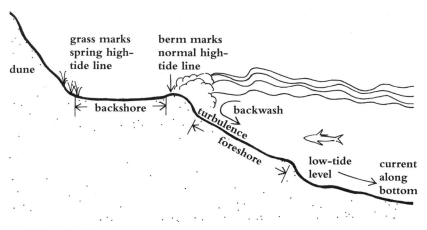

Backshore, backwash, berm, and foreshore are some beach terms you will hear.

crest marks the normal high-tide line, and in six hours, the waves will be breaking over your footprints.

Now sight along the beach toward the horizon, studying the slope of the beach as it extends down to the water. As with the shallow beach, you are looking for the deepest pockets of water next to shore. Any point at which the beach drops more abruptly to the water likely leads to an area of greater water depth that has fishing potential. In many cases, though not always, these areas of deeper water are parts of the bowls you identified from your earlier vantage point.

Best Tides for a Deep Sandy Beach

Saltwater fly rodders can fish a deep sandy beach on any tide. Even at the lowest stages of the tide, there is enough water for game fish to move about. But you are likely to find the biggest fish at the highest stages, when currents and waves are strongest, and smaller fish at lower stages of the tide. Despite this general rule, however, there are times when low tide and even dead low tide are very productive. The reduced water levels, coupled with the reduction in waves that lower water brings, allow you to move out from shore a bit and cover important pieces of bottom structure that would be out of reach at high tide. As always, tides at night or in low-light levels are generally the most productive.

Fishing a Deep Sandy Beach

For your first fishing trip to a deep beach, I recommend that you plan a dawn trip. Not only is dawn a productive time to fish, but with the rising light safety and comfort are enhanced. The exact stage of the tide is somewhat less important on these steep beaches, so you can visit the beach at any stage you wish. Naturally, as you gain experience, you will refine your understanding of the best tide for a specific beach and will want to try other times of day and night as well.

It can be very difficult to keep in touch with the fly when fishing in the surf. Therefore, besides your intermediate fly line, it is important to have a sink-tip or full-sinking line and weighted flies. You will also need a foul-weather jacket, regardless of the weather, to wear along with your waders for protection from spray and surf.

As always when fishing the coast, upon arrival look for signs of feeding fish, such as a swirl, diving birds, fish breaking the surface, or a slick. If no signs are found, begin working the areas of structure and

**The author caught this striper along the edge of a mussel bed that forms a
bar extending out from the beach.** *Photograph by Phil Farnsworth.*

current you located earlier. Move to those spots on the beach where the
slope indicates a pocket of deeper water. Cover the holes near shore,
indicated by darker-colored water. If the beach has both cusps and
bowls, work these areas, covering different pieces of water with each
cast. If no strikes are forthcoming after half an hour, consider moving to
another cusp. Generally the action on steep beaches will be concentrated in small areas. The trick is to find which spot presently holds the
fish. As you did on a shallow beach, you and your fishing partner can
spread out to better locate the action.

Regardless of the presence or absence of offshore sandbars or the
bowls and cusps found on many exposed locations, remember that some
fish are right in the trough practically next to you. On a deep beach, the
trough takes on increased importance for two reasons. First, since you
cannot wade out, this is one area of turbulence and current that you can
always cover with a fly. Second, because of the heavy waves and deep
water, on a steep beach even the largest fish is apt to dine right here.

It is imperative that you are ready to fish this water well. Poppers
can be effective, but they are difficult flies to work well in a heavy surf.
Furthermore, even in calm conditions, poppers are not the easiest flies
to drive home when a fish latches on. Subsurface flies are a better bet,
unless there is a lot of seaweed suspended in the water. In that case, the

subsurface fly will get rapidly fouled with the weed, whereas a surface fly might ride right over it.

If the water is not loaded with seaweed and you are using a sub-surface fly, the problem is to get the fly and fly line down through this heavy surf. You must gain both line and fly control. Working against you is the fact that the wave closest to the caster tends to carry the fly line high on its back in an arc. This produces slack between the angler and fly and pulls the fly upward away from the fish as they charge after it.

This is exactly why you should be carrying a sinking line and a weighted fly. The key here is to be able to feel the fly's weight during the retrieve. If you cannot, you have too much slack in the setup, and a heavier fly or faster-sinking line is in order. In the strongest surf, a lead-core shooting head may be the only effective answer. Use at least one or two line weights greater than the rod is rated for. Remember, you do not have to throw 80 feet of line in this situation. The fish could all be very close to your position, so use a relatively short throw. As conditions become more moderate or in locations where the surf is never extreme, go back to a slower-sinking line or sink tip.

On some deep beaches, there is a fairly dependable current moving parallel to shore, known as a longshore current. This current is a feeding lane for game fish. Most run for great distances, often well within fly-rod range. A piece of driftwood or flotsam moving down the beach is one indication. Study too how your fly line swings during the retrieve. Don't look for anything dramatic, as these currents are often weak. You fish it much in the way you would fish a stream, by casting down and across the flow.

Longshore currents are mainly created by the direction of the waves as they approach the shore. Since wave direction is a factor of the pre-vailing wind, these currents tend to always run in the same direction regardless of tide. On a very straight beach, one without strong cusps and bowls, this current could run unbroken for miles. Pay special atten-tion to where the current crosses any change in the bottom, such as a hole or a sandbar. That is a hot spot.

Once in a while you will come across an extremely swift tidal cur-rent running directly along the shoreline in the manner that a longshore current does. This happens most often on beaches near the mouth of an inlet where the tide range is 10 feet or more. Here the tide is pushing so fast and hard to fill a salt pond or bay that a tremendous amount of water races along, perhaps reaching or exceeding 8 knots. Wading is dangerous, but even working from shore is no picnic. Even though you are casting directly out, after the fly line lands it is immediately swept 90 degrees to one side, often right back to the beach. Anglers call this phenomenon tidal sweep. By using a sinking line and fly in conjunction with a well-placed uptide cast, you may be able to stay in business. I have seen some beaches, however, where on a full or new moon tide, the sweep is more than you can really handle.

Another type of current found on deep sandy beaches is created by channels cut through sandbars. These cuts attract many fish. Unfortunately, some are out of fly-rod range, but many are fishable and deserve attention. During the first of the incoming tide, the path of least resistance for water flooding in to the beach is through these channels. Striped bass and bluefish will use the channel in two manners at this point. Some will travel through on their way to the pockets inside the sandbar where baitfish have been hiding at low tide. Others take up position in the cut itself and feed on things sucked into the channel by the current or uncovered on the bottom by the increased turbulence.

A fly cast here is very likely to draw a strike. And because the water level is relatively low at this stage of the tide, you have your best opportunity to reach it. Since a good percentage of these cuts line up with a corresponding cusp on the beach, an angler standing on that cusp is in the very best position to reach the cut with a cast. If a surface popper or slide fails to draw action, do not hesitate to switch to a sinking or sink-tip line and a streamer. These are commonly very effective here.

Eventually, as water levels continue to rise, the tide is increasingly able to move directly over the sandbar rather than funneling through the channel. As this happens, the currents in the cut slow. But gradually the dynamics are changing, and in ways you might not expect. As the flooding tide steadily pushes water over the bar, the water level between the bar and shore can actually rise slightly higher than the water level outside the bar. This produces pressure, which in turn produces current. Now the channel takes on a seaward current as it becomes an exit for water on the shore side of the bar to return seaward. Striped bass and bluefish are now in the cut facing toward you and feeding in the flow.

At the crest of high tide there is little current in the cut. As the ebb gets under way, however, slowly the water inshore of the bar is pulled out to sea again. The lower the tide gets, the more the sandbars become walls or dams restricting the ability of the water to move back out to sea. The cut therefore becomes the easiest and fastest place for water to exit the beach. The current picks up in the channel, and so does the fishing. And the lower water stages once again allow fly rodders to get out from shore and possibly reach this fertile piece of bottom structure.

Just as with shallow beaches, waves and tidal currents tend to move at an angle to the beach. You should always try to position yourself, if possible, so that the fly will swing with any flow. This is the most natural presentation and also tends to keep the fly line tighter, giving you more control over the fly. For example, over many steep beaches, the first thing to look at is the direction of the waves as they come ashore. If they are moving from left to right, get to the left of the best-looking water and cast quartering to the right so that the fly is swept back with the waves.

Some steep sand beaches have sandbars that curve in toward land and join the beach at the foreshore. Usually such a sandbar is very easy to locate because of the breaking waves it generates. You may have spotted the bar while viewing the beach from your high vantage point. Another type of bar that sometimes comes all the way into the shoreline is a mussel bar. Here the sand bottom gives way to a bar made of cobble-size rock. This bar gets its name from the blue mussels that

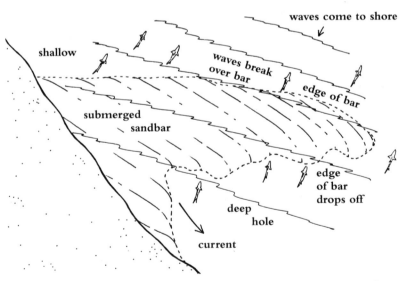

Some sandbars are attached to the beach, providing anglers an opportunity to wade out. Expect most fish to be along the edges of the bar.

thickly colonize such locations by adhering to the stones. A mussel bar is biologically a far richer and more productive spot than a bar composed solely of sand. It draws baitfish and crabs to it, which attract the striped bass and bluefish. If you locate a mussel bar, particularly one surrounded by the more barren sand bottom, be sure to fish it!

Wading out on either of these bars attached to the beach is going to give you access to some deeper pockets and a good many fish that you otherwise could not reach. But caution is advised. First of all, there may be strong, unexpected waves, one of which could knock you down. Pay attention to the incoming water, with an eye to large waves crossing the bar. A foul-weather jacket and a wader belt are in order. Use the belt supporting your stripping basket to also hold the bottom of your foul-weather jacket tight to your waders, reducing the chance of a wave riding up under the jacket and soaking you. Also, because these bars are adjacent to deeper water, take care not to inadvertently wade off the bar. The sand bottom will be easy wading, but the rock bottom of a mussel bar will likely be slippery, so felt soles or cleats are needed. It is best to investigate such bars slowly and only when the seas are calm and the tide is dead low. In some cases, the remaining ebbing flow or the first push of the incoming tide will produce a fair current as well, further attracting game fish.

Right where the bar joins the beach, you may find a deep hole to either side. This is an excellent place to wet a fly and can be covered with a cast even at high tide. As you move out onto the bar, look for other places where the bar drops off to deeper water; these edges attract fish. Cover both sides of the bar and especially the tip. The bar may deepen in places, only to rise back up again a short distance farther out. If you wade through these dips and continue on, be sure to take that increased depth into account when judging how long you can fish into the rising tide. For example, after a few hours of incoming water, you may still be in only knee-deep water at the far offshore end of the bar, but that dip between you and shore that was so easy to cross a few hours ago might now be chest-deep water.

If you feel a distinct current crossing the bar, use it to present the fly. By that I mean cast directly across the current and let it swing your fly off the bar toward deeper water. Game fish are highly tuned in to these currents and will patrol the edges of the bar, searching for food swept over it by the moving water. The current will take your fly right to the fish. The actual direction of this current changes with the tide.

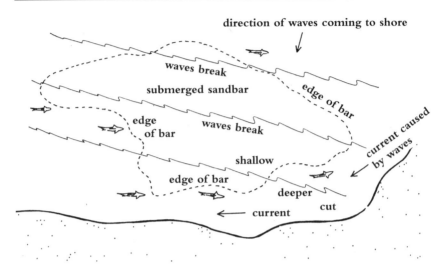

Some sandbars are separated from the beach by a short channel called a *cut*.

In some locations, a large, irregular sandbar comes close to shore but is separated from the water's edge by a deep cut. This cut can be a highly productive place to fish when waves or the tide creates a current through it. And given its proximity to shore, it is easy to reach with a fly. In a few rare cases, it may be possible to wade through the cut at dead low tide and reach the sandbar itself. At that point, you can fish all around the perimeter of the bar. Pay special attention to dropoffs, where the bar joins deeper water. On overcast days or at night, some fish could be on the bar itself, so cast ahead as you move around. Do all this with the greatest care, and first make several daytime visits to familiarize yourself with the area. Note how quickly the tide rises to cover the bar. Be sure to take note of the depth of water in the cut itself. If you are fishing the incoming tide, this area will deepen with the passage of time; take care that you do not become stranded on the bar.

Just like shallow sand beaches, these steep sandy locations are always in flux. And what you find in terms of structure this season is likely to be gone or greatly changed the next. Even from summer to fall, the shape and position of sand structures can change radically. A single large storm can rearrange the beach. The forces of wind and tide are that great here. Winter brings heavy seas and a series of strong coastal storms. So these are very much living places, and you will have to be ready to relearn them from time to time.

Another possible clue to finding fish on steep sand beaches is to look for high bluffs or dunes that line the shore. Where the cliffs are the highest, the water in front is often the deepest, and where the cliffs are much lower, the bottom is often shallower. If you can find a place where a line of high cliffs suddenly drops down low, try fishing right in front of that point. Likely the bottom here is an edge between deep and shallow, and it can be an excellent place to find plenty of fish.

Deep Rocky Beaches

Rocky beaches are very fertile fishing areas with a character all their own. The predominant size of the rock of which the beach is composed can range from stones you can hold in your palm to rocks the size of a watermelon. There may also be single or small groups of rocks along the shoreline that tower far above the rest. Furthermore, just offshore, some submerged rocks may be large enough to break the surface, showing at certain or all stages of the tide.

Moving around on these rocky shores can be a real problem. Rather than simply walking, you are often climbing. It means moving slowly and demands at least felt-soled boots or a full set of metal cleats. In some spots, however, even cleats do not supply the total answer, especially in

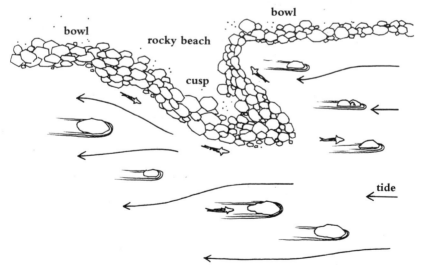

Rocky beaches have bowls and cusps too.

the intertidal zone where rocks may be draped with a thick coat of rockweed, sometimes called wrack *(Ascophyllum* or *Fucus)*. Metal cleats may not be long enough to totally penetrate this growth and supply solid footing. So take care.

Pay a low-tide visit, and start off if possible by getting an overview of the area you wish to fish. Like a deep sandy beach, these rocky stretches are rarely straight runs, and there is a lot of structure.

There are apt to be bowls and cusps. Also note any large rocks that are showing through the surface just offshore. Like rocks that break the current in a trout stream, these create protected pockets in the flow and are excellent lies for feeding game fish. Some of the rocks on the beach that are now completely exposed at low tide will be covered later as the tide rises. Therefore, these rocks, especially the larger ones, will provide similar lies at higher tides.

As you walk down toward the water, study the color of the rocks to get an idea of how much of the beach is covered by high tide. A band of noticeably darker rocks, called the *black zone,* runs parallel to the water's edge and marks the upper regions of the daily high tides. Be very careful! The dark color is produced by a blue-green algae, and these rocks are extremely slippery. A fall here could be dangerous to you and your tackle. Metal cleats, felt soles, or some combination thereof are required, and a staff can be helpful. The inland edge of the black zone is

Anglers work a rock-lined bowl.

A flat rock can provide an excellent casting platform. But be careful—some rocks are very slippery.

not a hard and fast line, given the difference between neap and spring high tides.

As you continue toward the water, the black of the rocks becomes studded with light-colored barnacles. This is the line covered by even the weakest monthly high tides, the neap tides. A look up and down the beach from this point should give you an idea of how things will look six hours from now.

Note any large, flat-topped rocks located in the black zone or the upper barnacle zone. These can make excellent platforms from which to fish as the tide crests. By standing on one, you can get an idea of the area your cast will cover and what bottom structure it will reach. Note where the fly or fly line might snag up as well; you can easily get hung up on a rocky shoreline. As you move closer to the present water line, note other rocks that look like good casting platforms for other stages of the tide.

On a rocky shore, it is easy to find reference points, such as large rocks or a series of larger rocks, to mentally mark the structures you have found. Use these aids to help you fish during both the day and especially the night. By carefully noting how the tide covers the various larger rocks, you can also tell at a glance the relative stage of the tide.

These beaches, with their hard rocks, are resistant to change. Unlike sandy beaches, these rocky shores are relatively permanent, and little in the way of structure changes from season to season. Each visit will find the same rocks to use as reference points or casting platforms.

Best Tides for a Deep Rocky Beach

The best time to wet a line on these rocky beaches, especially for large fish, is generally the two hours on either side of high tide, for the same reason as with the other types of beaches: Fuller water allows big fish an opportunity to cruise close to shore. Also, high water produces the most wave action, which disorients small baitfish and tips the scale in favor of large predators.

As good as the flood is, often at high water the best edge or piece of structure is out of fly-rod range. Lower stages of the tide could possibly allow you to work your way out far enough to cover this potential gold mine. This may mean wading out through fairly deep water to reach a key rock from which to cast. It is tricky business. Learn to use the rocks around you to gauge the tide's progress. By studying which ones are exposed and which are still submerged, you will know when to make your move.

Unfortunately, rocky beaches have the most seaweed associated with them. In many locations it is not a problem, but in others it can be a major obstacle. Avoid beaches where the surface is a permanent weed-bed extending way out from shore. In some weedy areas, however, one tide will be far easier to fish. You can find this out through trial and error.

Fishing a Deep Rocky Beach

Floating lines and poppers have their place on these deep rocky beaches, as they did on the sandy variety. They are good tools for covering a lot of water, and they can keep your fly up out of any seaweed. If no strikes are forthcoming, however, switch over to an intermediate or sinking line and a sinking fly. Use a "countdown" system to work the fly at various depths. For example, you could begin by starting the retrieve immediately after the cast lands on the water. On the next cast, count to ten before beginning the retrieve. On the next, count to twenty, and so on. This allows you to work the fly at various depths. Be aware that there are a lot of things here on which the fly could become snagged, including the rocks themselves and seaweed. Therefore you might want to use a bend-back or Clouser to avoid this problem.

If you elect to climb up on a rock, take care. Before you climb aboard, watch how the waves are breaking over the rock you wish to fish from. If large waves are striking the rock hard and with a good deal of spray, you risk getting knocked down. Pick another spot or wait for the tide to drop. Once you find a safe spot, be sure to position your feet firmly. Take extra care if waves will be hitting your legs.

Caution is also required when getting down off a rock. It is all too easy to fall. If you must turn your back on the waves in order to climb down, watch the rhythm of the advancing waves and choose your moment accordingly. If the waves are separated by long intervals, it should be easy to time your movements. If they are close together, it is harder to do so. When you are heading ashore, turn to look behind you every few seconds so that a large wave does not surprise you from behind.

One more problem you will face on these beaches is that the barnacles and mussel shells are very sharp. They can quickly rip your waders and easily slice through a leader or badly nick a fly line. To cut down on wader wear and tear, avoid sitting, leaning back on, or rubbing against the rocks, except perhaps in the black zone. Carry spares for both your leader and fly line. At the very least, have complete leaders ready to go.

As you fish, periodically stop and check the hook. Occasionally you will hit a rock on the backcast and dull or break the point. Run your hand down the leader to check for frays, especially after fighting a fish. Very often in the course of a battle the leader will, unknown to you, get dragged over sharp submerged objects. Run your hand along the leader in its entirety, not just the tippet. If you feel nicks, replace it. Even with this precaution, some fish still will cut you off, frequently higher up on the leader than you might expect. At the end of the trip, check your fly line and backing. They also may be ready for some maintenance.

Many rocky beaches have a special kind of edge that is often patrolled by game fish. It can be difficult to find and even to fly-fish, but you should be aware of it. Underwater someplace offshore, the rock bottom may end and an all-sand bottom begin, marking the transition between open deep waters and the more confining sloped bottom of the beach.

Surf casters, with their stronger rigs, can reach this edge from their perches on the beach, but in many cases fly rodders cannot. Still, there are some beaches where this edge is within fly-casting range or where you can work your way out to it at low tide. Beaches of small cobble-stones may be gradual enough in slope to allow you to wade out to fish this area around the hours of dead low tide. A man-made structure such as a jetty can sometimes enable you to reach this zone.

3

Reading Rips

Restless and ever changing, the ocean pulses with life. It has a way of speaking to us, quietly alerting all who listen to the wealth within its depths. Never is this voice more electrifying than when it whispers that fish are near. And nowhere do anglers hear that message more clearly than in those swift waters called a *rip*.

A rip is a confined area of water where the current is markedly faster than its surroundings. Rips come in sizes from a few yards of tightly focused current to wide expanses covering acres of ocean. They exist everywhere along the coast, from shallow beaches to deep ones, from points of land to inlets and estuaries. Some are known only to the anglers who regularly ply a particular stretch of shoreline; others are clearly marked on navigation charts and are common knowledge.

A rip's increased current speed is caused by the presence of structure. The structure may be a naturally occurring object like a sandbar or man-made, such as a jetty. Either way the result is the same: When the current flows over, around, or through this structure, it increases in speed. The size and shape of the structure help to determine the size and shape of the rip.

Every rip has current, but not every current is a rip. It is the nature of a rip's current relative to its neighboring waters that makes it distinctive. Typically a rip is a focused lane of stronger current located inside a much broader area of weaker current. The water along an entire stretch of beach may be slowly moving in one direction with the tide, but where that current travels over changes in the bottom, the current becomes defined and strengthened into a rip. And this is where fish are most likely to feed.

The very same type of thing happens on a trout stream. In nearly every part of a pool, there is a downstream flow; still, the pool's currents are not everywhere equal in terms of speed or the feeding opportunity they present. Parts of the currents are slow and ill defined and therefore less attractive to trout. Elsewhere the pool's current is focused by its passage over or around various kinds of structure. For instance, at the head of the pool, there are usually spots where the flow funnels between rocks, forming strong tongues of faster current. These currents are attractive spots for trout to feed and are similar to rips.

SOURCES OF RIPS

All rips require a source of energy to get things rolling. The usual sources are tidal currents, coastal river flows, and wave action. Less typical sources include power plant and dam releases. Most of the rips anglers encounter are tidal in nature. These rips are usually created when flooding or ebbing currents move over an uneven bottom, such as a shallow reef. Here the change in depth between the reef and the neighboring bottom causes an increase in water speed. The greater the differential between the two depths, the faster the rip runs. Another common tidal rip forms wherever tides move around a point of land. Again, the current increases as the water pushes hard to reach its destination.

Waves produce rips, although in general these are weaker than tidal rips. Since wave height and direction are tied to wind and weather, ultimately the rips they create are less predictable. Still, they are important, especially in places where tidal rips are scarce. Waves climbing over a cusp create small but nonetheless significant rips, and runouts are rips produced by wave action. Also, as waves break and then cascade back down the slope of a beach, they form seaward currents right at the water's edge. Standing in the surf, you can feel the water pull around you. This too might be thought of as a rip. And many a good fish is hooked right here, practically under an angler's feet.

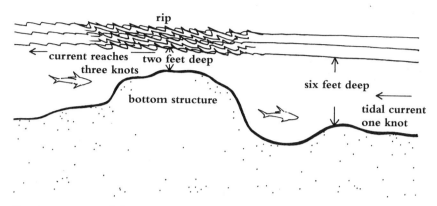

Bottom structure defines and accelerates a rip. The greater the change in bottom depth, the faster the rip runs.

At times, the character of a rip is the result of two or more forces. When the wind and wave are pushing hard in the same direction as a tidal rip, the rip builds. When the wind opposes the rip, it forces waves against the current, slowing the speed of the rip but making its surface more turbulent. When the force of a river's exiting flow joins the pull of an ebbing tide, rips gain strength. When the tide reverses, new rips form but they are often weaker.

Coastal river dams with release gates or spillways produce rips. Since these dams may unfortunately stop the migration of anadromous fish, these rips are often loaded with fish seeking to head farther upstream.

Power plants are found on both the shores of tidal rivers and the coast itself. Often they have one or more discharge tubes that emit water in a powerful focused flow. The resulting rips look simple enough, but they may well have their own special character. In some cases, the water discharged by a power plant is 10 degrees or more warmer than the river or the surrounding sea. This heated water stimulates the local ecosystem, attracting the entire food chain from bottom to top. As a result, the power plant's release site may hold fantastic fishing, especially during parts of the year when the remaining coastal waters are far too cold to produce any action. These artificially created habitats also attract species of game fish not normally found along that part of the coast. Some migratory game fish, notably striped bass, winter over in these areas, creating a year-round fishery where normally one would not exist.

TIPS FOR SPOTTING A RIP

Saltwater fly fishermen absolutely must be able to spot a rip. It is crucial. Fortunately, during the day, many rips are clearly visible, even to the relatively inexperienced angler. Still, a trained eye not only sees more of them, but also locates the smaller ones, finding them even in low light.

Begin by scanning the surface of the water. Rips appear as lines or patches of water that contrast with their surroundings. Frequently the first thing that catches your eye is the increased speed of the surface. In addition, rips also have increased turbulence and wave action associated with them. This too makes them stand out.

Not every surface disturbance turns out to be a rip, however. Sometimes it is nothing more than a patch of water stirred up by an isolated gust of wind and has no current associated with it. Anglers call this phenomenon *wind lines*. But make it a rule to investigate all promising-looking areas and find out for yourself whether they have current.

Occasionally rips contain lines of foam or floating debris, or show changes in water color or clarity. These things all make a rip more dis-

The dark water in the center of the image is a rip. This angler is wading along the upcurrent edge of the rip, called the *rip line*. You can see a second rip farther out.

tinct. Another valuable clue has to do with the limited ability of a rip's surface to reflect ambient light. When water is calm, it acts like a mirror, bouncing back much of the available light. Conversely, a rip's turbulent surface tends to break up the light, reflecting back little. Therefore, rips appear much darker than the surrounding water. Often this contrast in brightness makes a rip visible for a considerable distance, especially on a calm, sunny day.

There are still other ways to identify a rip. When you cast across any current, it causes your fly line to bow in a downcurrent direction. By casting across different parts of the current, you can even pinpoint where the swiftest areas lie. And if you wade into a rip, you feel the pull of the water around your waders. Experienced fishermen become so highly tuned to all these methods that they can find a rip even at night. This type of ability is a surefire ticket to angling success.

As you look for rips, always keep in mind that they are temporal. Some exist for the entire duration of a tide; others come and go in far less time. Small rips along an open beach may form and disappear in the span of fifteen minutes, a subtle reflection of changing water levels. Therefore, no one visit to any given stretch of shore will turn up all the rips in that location.

FISHING A RIP

Every season, rips produce more fish for me than any other type of water. I think of them as my bread and butter, and you should too. Still, as productive as these places are, you must learn how to properly tap their potential.

One of the first tidal rips I ever fished is on the Lyme, Connecticut, shore. Years ago, I would approach it with no real strategy. I went with little regard to tide stage, and cast wherever I felt like casting. Sometimes I caught fish; many times I did not. Over the course of several seasons, I got to know the place well—its bottom, the bars, and where the rip held its fish. I saw it in many moods: various winds, tidal stages, and phases of the moon. Now I fish it differently.

This rip lies just off the shore of a shallow beach. The bottom here is a mixture of sand and small rocks. Wading out during low tide, you discover that the bottom grades slowly, and eventually a mussel bed and sandbar join in. About 200 feet out from the high-tide line, the water deepens rapidly, and it appears you can go no farther. Still, if you search slowly, you find a long, narrow underwater ridge that heads straight out.

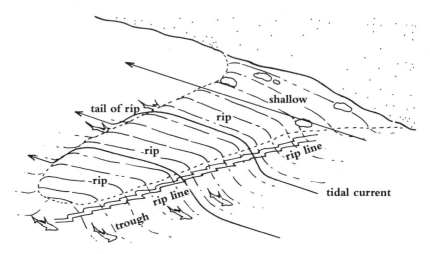

Fish often sit either just ahead of or just below the rip line.

During full or new moon low tides, it is possible to get onto this ridge and wade out a good deal farther from shore. To the left of the ridge, the bottom drops off only slightly before it shelves off again to form a wide submerged plateau. To the right of the ridge, it is a different story. Here the bottom drops off 2 or 3 feet, forming a long trough that runs the entire edge of the structure.

During an ebbing tide, the current travels roughly parallel to the beach. When the dropping water nears the submerged reef, it moves up and over it. This produces a strong surface disturbance called a *rip line,* which marks the beginning of the rip as well as the entire leading edge of the structure. (Be aware that anglers often use the term to refer to the entire surface of a rip, especially when the rip is long and narrow. I will use it only for the rip's starting point and leading edge.) The rip line is very visible as you walk the beach or cruise by in a boat. It starts to form about an hour after high tide and continues until dead low.

If you arrive at the start of the drop, you cannot wade out far enough to reach the better water. In short, it is not a productive time to be there. But if you show up two and a half hours after high tide, you can get out to the rip and cover it well. When that stage of the tide coincides with dusk or dawn, your chances of hooking a fish are even better. Yet regardless of the light level, it makes a good deal of difference where you cast the fly.

Fish in this rip hold slightly upcurrent of the rip line. In many other

The author caught this little tunny from the beach where a strong rip comes tight to the shore. *Photograph by Gary Mirando.*

rips, they may hold downcurrent of the line; it depends entirely on the shape of the bottom structure. Here they are directly in front of the ridge on the deeper side, and like all fish in a rip, they face forward into the flow. If you fish mainly the turbulent water downtide of the rip line, you rarely do well. Instead, position yourself so that the fly lands in the smooth glide above the rip line. Then the current can sweep the fly back to the waiting fish sitting along the edge.

Because of the way fish congregate in a limited area, it is entirely possible for two anglers standing only several yards apart and using the same equipment to have completely different rates of success. One can constantly hook fish, the other go without a single strike. I have seen this happen on many occasions, not only here, but in other rips all along the coast as well.

Accuracy and Timing

The keys to fishing a rip well, therefore, are accuracy and timing. Accuracy is important because game fish—particularly the better fish—elect to hold only in certain parts of a rip, while other parts of the rip might be barren. Timing is critical because rips are temporary and you must be there when the rip runs. And even when a rip runs, its ability to attract and hold game fish is not constant. It waxes and wanes with changing conditions, including such things as stage of the tide and light level.

Rips, like all coastal structures, have some spots that hold fish regularly and others that rarely do. The experienced angler reads a rip with that in mind, seeking to identify those areas where fish are likely to be holding. The first important prerequisite of any good holding place is protection from the full force of the flow. Like trout in a riffle, saltwater game fish cannot afford to be constantly fighting the current. Dips or holes in the bottom, midcurrent obstructions such as rocks, and the edges of the rip where it joins slower water all offer shelter. Here fish can slipstream the main forces of the rip, yet remain close enough to dart out and grab a meal when it comes by. Where this type of shelter is not available, the rip is apt to be barren.

Though you rarely know every facet of bottom structure in a rip, certain areas are easy to see and deserve your fishing attention. Very often the best place to fish is right at the rip line.

Usually there are protective pockets for fish to hold in immediately above or below the rip line. I will call this general area the head of the rip. From the fish's standpoint, these places are frequently the most desirable lies, because fish sitting here get first crack at the food entering the rip.

The rip line identifies one good area, but there are other clues to look for as well. Any obstruction that deflects the rip's flow produces a potential feeding spot. Some obstructions break the surface and are easy to locate. Perhaps the most common example is a protruding rock or series of rocks. Under the waves, these create pockets in the current that are ideal for fish to sit in.

Not all obstructions stick up through the surface. Many more are submerged and therefore difficult to see. An observant angler can find them by studying the surface of the rip. Where the current travels over or around a large submerged object, the surface of the water abruptly changes. It may hump up, literally lifting, or it might boil into a swirling back eddy. Also scan the surface of the rip for breaks in the current that seem to fan out into a wakelike pattern.

Fish in a rip, like fish everywhere on the coast, are sensitive to water depth. The bigger fish seek the rip's deeper holes. If you can locate those holes by noting changes in water color or other direct observations, you increase your odds of hooking the best fish. Sometimes these deeper spots are near the head, but they may just as likely be elsewhere. I have fished plenty of rips where the only deep holding water was considerably downcurrent of the rip line. Here the head can be very shallow and hold primarily small fish, while the real brutes are closer to what might be called the tail of the rip. The only time these tackle busters cruise up to the front is under the cover of total darkness.

Inside a large rip, there will be one or more places where the current runs faster than others. These faster lanes of water funnel more food, and therefore game fish gravitate here, especially when a nice holding spot lies near this flow.

Once you have a solid handle on where fish sit in a rip, you need to think about when to expect them to be there. Some rips are so short-lived that you simply fish them when they are in motion without making any other distinctions. Tidal rips, however, are another story. Many of them run for four or more hours. During that time, the rip's size, current speed, and depth change. And as you might expect, all of these factors influence the fishing.

Each tidal rip has its own character, and you can only fully discover its personality by fishing it many times. Some generalizations can be made, however. In a shallow rip where the water is never deeper than

4 or 5 feet, the stage of the tide may have a direct bearing on the size of the fish you encounter. The larger fish are most likely to feed during the hours of greatest depth, the smaller ones when water levels are reduced.

In many other tidal rips, water depth is less of a factor, and the quality of the fishing hinges more on current speed. Here the rule is this: When the current is greatest, the fishing is best. Usually a tidal rip reaches its maximum speed about two or three hours after the water starts moving. Note that this is not necessarily the same thing as two or three hours after the time of tide. Also, because the strength of any tide varies with the phase of the moon, expect stronger tidal rips on the new and full moons and weaker rips on the first and third quarters.

Here is a seeming contradiction: In a very deep, powerful tidal rip, the best time to fly-fish might be when the current is weakest. Why? During the period of maximum flow, the fish could be sitting right on the bottom. Thus it would be extremely difficult to get a fly down to them through the swift current. As the rip slows, these fish move up off the bottom, and you are better able to deliver a fly to them. Moreover, in some deep rips, the only time the fish feed on the surface is when the current stops at slack water.

Periods of low or changing light levels are always important and productive times to fish on the coast, and rips are no exception. So expect to find peak action in any rip when that rip runs through dusk, dawn, or into the night. With a tidal rip, you can consult your tidal chart. Even if you have a specific part of a tide you want to fish, you can pinpoint the exact day and hour to be on the water. When you get to this level of strategy making, you are really becoming a veteran of the salt.

Presenting a Fly in a Rip

The most popular way to present a fly in a rip is to cast at a 90-degree angle across the current. The fly is then allowed to travel down and across the rip on a fairly tight line. Sound familiar? It should. This is exactly how wet flies are often used for trout. In fact, it is fair to say that all your experience in working a fly through the currents of a stream will prove highly useful in a rip.

A second or two after the cast lands on the water, I usually begin a slow retrieve. This helps me keep in contact with the fly. You can, however, delay the start of the retrieve until the fly is much farther downrip. With a weighted fly or a sinking line, this delay allows things an opportunity to sink. And it gives you a slow, more natural drift. All of these techniques are most effective with streamer- or slider-type flies and least useful with poppers. (See chapter 9 for more details on flies and methods to retrieve them.)

Before you make the cast, station yourself upcurrent of the water you wish to cover. First read the rip to identify the best holding spots, and then work your way into position above them. Remember that the fish sitting below you will be facing forward into the current. The idea is to make a cast long enough that the fly swings right in front of their noses.

Anglers used to spinning tackle are going to be surprised by how quickly the fly line picks up speed after hitting the water. This happens because the relative thickness of the fly line offers the water plenty of surface area to push against, far more than monofilament. When the fastest part of the current lies between you and the fly, the fly line may even quickly outpace the fly, creating a belly in the line. Note that the greater the belly becomes, the less control and feel you have for the fly.

Most strikes come at the end of the swing as the fly line starts to straighten below you. If no strikes come, you have several options. You can continue retrieving the fly back until you are ready to pick up and make another cast. You can permit the fly to hang in the current for a while, occasionally jigging it in hopes of drawing interest. Or you can even peel additional line off the reel and allow the fly to fall farther downrip, thereby covering new water. All of these approaches are standard wet-fly techniques.

Fish that strike at the end of the swing usually hit hard. Still, strikes at other points in the retrieve may be much more subtle. Therefore, it is imperative that you stay in touch with the fly at all times. As soon as the fly lands, lower the rod tip to the water and point it at the fly. As the fly progresses down the rip, follow it with the rod tip. This is especially important if you are fishing from an elevated perch, such as a large rock, or from a boat that has a fair amount of freeboard. Besides, a high rod tip can make it difficult to properly work a fly.

This procedure does two critical things. First, it reduces the amount of slack and thereby improves your ability to set the hook when the time comes. Fish in fast water are apt to slam the fly suddenly, and it is easy to be caught off guard. So pay strict attention. Second, by following the fly with the rod tip, you tend to slow the speed of the fly. And slowing down the fly can make it more attractive to fish that must fight the current to catch it. You can also control the fly's speed by varying your retrieve speed. But this business of fly speed is a tricky matter. Some fish may not even try to strike a fly that is traveling too fast. On the other hand, if a fly is traveling very slowly, this might allow some fish to observe it closely, leading to refusals. You need to experiment to find the most effective speed for the conditions.

Another way to work a fly in a rip is to retrieve it directly across the current, which shows the fly broadside to the fish. This works with all types of flies, including poppers. First, get directly opposite the water you want to fish. Then cast across the current or just slightly upcurrent, and begin retrieving immediately. One place this method works well is right down the face of a rip line. Where you can do it, this presentation may show the fly to several fish in a single cast. Unfortunately, retrieving directly across a current is difficult to do, especially where the flow is swift. For one thing, you must avoid letting the line belly in the current. Casting slightly upcurrent is a help, but the freshwater technique of mending line is useful too. If you are unfamiliar with it, ask an experienced fly fisherman to demonstrate.

Finally, there is the most difficult, and some argue the most natural, presentation. Fish sitting in a rip are expecting bait to come more or less straight at them. To present a fly in this manner, you can do one of two things. If possible, position yourself directly downcurrent of where the fish are holding. Then cast straight up the rip beyond the holding area and retrieve toward the fish. Frequently this is not feasible, since it means wading into the rip. As an alternative, you can get below and to one side of the fish, and then cast up and across the flow.

As natural as this presentation is, it is also very hard to control. If you have used this method in a trout stream, you already know why. The fly is being pushed toward you by the current, and it is easy to lose touch with it. Once you lose touch, you can miss strikes and find it difficult to set the hook even on the ones you do feel.

Using a popper is one possible solution. It allows you to see the strike in the way a dry fly does. Another helpful option is to use a sinking fly line with a heavily weighted fly. By going deep, your offering travels slower and is less buffeted by the current. You gain back some control. Adjust the retrieve speed constantly to maintain that control, and keep the rod tip very low or even underwater. Overall you'll get better results.

In a few situations, the rip's depth, speed, or location makes it impossible to get in position to fish across or down and across the current. Here I use an upcurrent presentation, not because it is realistic, but because there is no alternative. It is a problem, but on the bright side, these places receive less fishing pressure for that reason.

A Few Final Thoughts

The most spectacular time you can work a rip is when predators herd a large school of bait into the current. Now you have a blitz and the water boils with action. If you are within range, you are sure to get a strike. Still, a few tips are in order. The game fish responsible for the attack may be there in a wide range of sizes. Some parts of the rip could hold school-size fish, other areas jumbos. Watch for trends during the battle, and move accordingly.

With all this surface activity, few anglers ever think about using a sinking fly. If the rip is deep, however, getting the fly down may well prove deadly. You are likely not only to catch more fish, but to get the bigger ones. Occasionally you'll even find different species working at different depths. In the fall I have seen blitzes with bluefish right on top, bass under them, and bonito mixed in deep, especially along the edge of the fastest part of the current. So by counting down the fly as it sinks, you may be able to effectively target specific game fish.

Though rips do not always hold fish, they do hold fish for longer periods than most other types of water. Saltwater game fish generally roam in search of food and are therefore rarely still for long. But rips have so much to offer in the way of bait, current, and structure that fish sit here for a considerable time. As a result, unlike fishing an open beach, where dropping a fly on the nose of a game fish is a bit like hitting a moving target, anglers working a rip can repeatedly present the fly to fish that are more or less stationary. Therefore, you have a chance to change fly size, color, and retrieve speed in hopes of provoking a strike with less concern that the fish will move away. Take advantage of this and experiment while fishing a rip. I have had fish repeatedly swirl on a fly, only to be hooked on subsequent casts after a small change in presentation.

When a fly comes within range, fish in a rip are generally far less selective than fish in places of slow or nonexistent current. This is for the same reason that trout in a current are less selective than trout in still water. In both cases, predators have to make snap judgments in order to catch food quickly going by them. Counterbalancing that somewhat, fish in a rip are less apt to chase a fly for a great distance. Doing so would waste precious energy. So a fish sitting deep in a rip is reluctant to climb through the current for a fly traveling overhead, and if your fly is far to the left or right of a fish's position, it may refuse to fight the current to get it. A fly that either comes reasonably close or swings in front of a fish's nose, however, stands an excellent chance of getting taken.

When a fish takes the fly in a rip, the weight of the fish and the force of the current go a long way toward setting the hook. But these forces also mean that you should not react with a great deal of force, as the combination of events might pop the tippet. Do not try to horse the fish up through the flow, either. You'll probably break it off.

SAFELY WORKING A RIP

Wading in a rip can be dangerous in the same way that wading a swift river can be. So caution is required, particularly with a rip that is both strong and close to deep water. If you can feel the current pulling sand or gravel from under your feet, consider moving to a slower area. Never wade more than knee-deep unless you are very familiar with the location and feel certain you are not at risk. Always use a wading belt to cinch your wader tops. Wear felt soles; consider metal cleats wherever rocks compose a large part of the bottom. A wading staff can be a help, too.

4

Reading Points of Land

Tonight there are no stars. Even the moon is dark, and the air hangs with a stillness that only a summer's night can bring. Pat Abate, Phil Farnsworth, and I walk slowly over the rough terrain, carefully moving forward in our flashlight's beam. Our destination is a coastal point of land reached only by a long hike, made even more arduous by our waders. Yet the effort needed to get there assures us that few other anglers will attempt this trip, and we can nearly always have the place to ourselves.

As we near the extreme end of the point, the ground behind us rises up in a bluff at our backs; out front, the tip juts far into the ocean night. This is a rocky place. The largest rocks line the shore like eerie sentinels, jet black masses whose looming silhouettes can be seen even in the weakest light. Over the course of many visits here, they have become our friends. Some are important landmarks, helping us establish our exact position on the point; others are favorite casting platforms overlooking prime waters. And now we are nearing a group of rocks that is our outpost of sorts, a spot to store some gear for the evening, a thermos of coffee, and a spare rod.

In front of us lies a long, jagged, needle-shaped pile of rocks jutting into the night. Some are totally exposed, some partially submerged, some hidden from view; together they form a reef. After checking our gear, we move out onto it. Experience has proven that the first few hours of the flooding tide are best here, and we have planned this visit accordingly. As the tide floods, it will stream over this narrow ridge of rocks, traveling from one side of the reef to the other. Much of the bottom lies exposed now, revealing thousands of densely packed blue mussels, but as we proceed farther out, we come to where the tide is already starting to reclaim the reef.

Moving first through ankle-deep water and then knee-deep, we finally reach a place where we can wade no farther. Here the tide swirls wildly over the uneven bottom and boils noisily between the boulders in a dark maelstrom. It is a rip, a classic piece of water with fish written all over it. Later, when the tide deepens and spreads out over the point, the rip will change, losing its special character, but for now many good fish are concentrated here in the pockets of this narrow, streaming flow. The striped bass usually take spots close to the boulders, sitting behind and alongside or in front of them. Some of the bluefish do that too, but overall they seem to prefer hanging farther upcurrent, along the edge where the rocky bottom turns to sand.

A sinking fly runs the chance of hanging up in the many rocks, so we tie on black sliders, which will ride the top. Cast across the current, the fly swings downtide in a wide, sweeping arch, creating a wake across the surface. Any fish that sees this disturbance overhead rockets up to intercept it. The takes are violent, and the crashes can be heard by anyone nearby. Even a 5-pound fish is a worthy adversary, using the current to its immediate advantage, testing both angler and tackle.

A fish in the teens is going to rock you into your socks. Feeling the sting of the hook, it catapults down and across the rip, crashing between the boulders at breakneck speed in an all-out attempt to reach deeper water. With your rod bent to the corks, you must lean back all you dare in hopes of turning the fish. First the fly line disappears, then you are quickly into the backing, and with each passing moment the possibility of getting cut off climbs. You feel the fish's raw power through the rod tip as it sulks somewhere off in the darkness, angrily shaking its head. There is nothing like it in the world.

Points of land are places of conflict. Jutting out against the sea, they set a host of forces in motion. Rips run around them, currents converge, waves pound, and the wind seems to howl a little harder. And in this eternal flux, game fish love to feed. Not surprisingly, when saltwater anglers talk about their favorite spots, points of land often come up. Some of these points are nothing more than a small bump in the shoreline. Others are large, prominent headlands, some of which are angling legends, nothing short of hallowed ground: Race Point, Gay Head, Napatree, and Montauk, for example. Large or small, points of land are places to be remembered, places where fish come to a fly.

INVESTIGATING A POINT OF LAND

Before fishing an unfamiliar point of land, again plan a daytime scouting trip. It is best to arrive during the last hours of the ebb, because the low water exposes a lot of structure, and since the tide is still in motion, you might find a tidal rip, too.

For the sake of this investigation, the point can be divided into three main parts: the area around the tip, and the shorelines leading to it on either side. These separations are only imaginary boundaries and blurry at best. Nevertheless, they provide a useful framework.

The tip is often of greatest interest to anglers, as it commonly hosts the finest fishing. This area is constantly under attack by wind and waves, and it frequently has the strongest currents and the best bottom structure. Still, the fish aren't going to jump into your boots; it is up to you to find them. Nevertheless, armed with what you already know about reading beaches and rips, it is not going to be that hard.

Study the tip following the same techniques used to examine a beach. Run your eye along the contour of the shoreline in front of you, looking for the most irregular parts, as this is where you'll often find the best bottom structure. At times the most irregular thing about the tip is that there seems to be more than one of them. Generally, one tip is clearly the most prominent in the sense that it is largest or juts out the farthest. There may also, however, be several smaller protrusions, or "false points," along the shoreline. Expect the most prominent tip to have the best fishing, but do not overlook the false points. Many times they turn out to be an essential part of fishing a point of land, accounting for a good portion of the catch.

Some tips have a major piece of underwater structure called a *reef.* This reef is a shallow, submerged ridge usually extending outward from the tip of a point of land. Tips that come to a sharp, narrow point seem most likely to have this type of structure. Blunt, gently rounded tips, on the other hand, less commonly have reefs, but exceptions do exist.

Near low tide, the reef may even be fully exposed. If it is not, water color or wave action may give away the reef's exact position. Also, reefs often have rips and therefore may be associated with rip lines. Underwater, these reefs create a sharp edge that really concentrates game fish. If the reef is exposed, you may want to move out onto it, but proceed with the utmost care. Reefs are notoriously tricky to walk or wade. If the reef is still partially covered with water, the situation is tougher, especially where current is present. Use caution.

Next, examine the shoreline around the tip closely for any areas where it switches composition. A change in physical makeup marks another underwater edge. Note changes in water color that might confirm the presence of underwater fluctuations in depth and bottom composition. Take special interest in any rock formations that show through the surface of the water. Not only could they have fish associated with them, they might prove a valuable landmark for you on return trips.

Even if you have already found one rip in conjunction with the reef, be on high alert for the presence of others, given their fish-attracting abilities. Look everywhere for signs of a rip line or turbulence. Try to determine where the currents are located in relation to the point and how they cross the tip itself. Do they seem to come straight over the tip

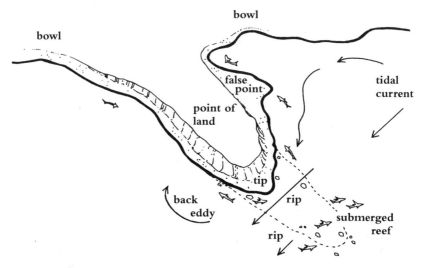

Points of land and their various connected structures and currents hold excellent fishing.

A line of white waves marks an underwater reef extending out from this point. Dark water on the left is a rip cause by tidal currents crossing that structure.

or to travel up the side of the adjoining beach and then swing over the tip at an angle?

Some points have no rips; others may have tidal rips on both the flood and ebb. The shape of a rip and the angle at which it crosses the point are apt to vary dramatically from one tide to the next. One tide generally offers better fly-fishing opportunities than the other, because the resulting rip is easier to reach with a fly or simply holds bigger fish. Experience will tell.

Now turn your attention to the beaches on either side of the tip. These shorelines are particularly productive because, in a sense, they are the edges of the entire point. Expect fish to travel along them and hold to feed in the better spots. Note if one side of the point is deeper than the other or receives stronger surf. This side might hold the better fish. Investigate both sides for rips, current, and bottom structure.

Next, check out the bowls formed where the point joins the mainland. These two bowls are usually very different in size, shape, and depth. The bowl facing more directly into the prevailing wind should be the shallower of the two, especially if the bottom composition is sand, and should hold more baitfish. The bowl on the lee side of the point could be much deeper and an excellent hiding spot for a large fish. Spend some time getting to know these areas.

BEST TIDES FOR FISHING POINTS OF LAND

If the point has a tidal rip, that alone could determine the best hours to fish. Where none exists, the following generalities hold true whether the point is composed of sand or rock. High water will bring the largest fish closest to you, so the last hour of incoming tide through the first hours of the drop are prime if you are looking for the biggest fish from the shore. These hours also have the most wave action, however, and frequently are the hardest to fly-rod. So there is a price to pay. On some points, the surf may be so rough at the top of the tide that fly rodding is totally impractical.

The best tide is the one that both attracts game fish and brings them into fly-rod range. Many points of land have fish working the area at nearly all stages of the tide. But unfortunately, they may lie in places you cannot reach with a fly or be so scattered that it is difficult to locate them. If there is a shallow reef connected to a point of land, you have your best chance to wade out and fish it at times of low water, either during the first part of the incoming tide or the last part of the outgoing. The hours around dead low tide will allow you to move out the farthest on the reef, but the fish may have left the area entirely by this stage of the tide.

FISHING A POINT OF LAND

To fish a point of land, use the information you acquired on your scouting trip to cover the better water. Once you are in place, do not be quick to give up that location, even if the action is slow. Some times it takes a while for fish to move in. Once you feel certain the water in front of you is unproductive, move to a new location where your fly will probe a different part of the structure or current. Be sure to cover any false points in the area.

Some fish are likely sitting right at your feet in the deeper pockets very close to shore, allowing the turbulence of the waves to stir up a meal or two. To search for these fish, try positioning yourself, if possible, so that you can cast more or less parallel to the shoreline. This presentation gives these fish a good broadside view of the fly.

As always, be alert for signs that you have moved a fish. Repeat the same cast immediately if you felt a tap or saw a swirl or the wake of a fish following the fly. If that does not work, change the retrieve speed, the action you give the fly, or both. If that fails to get any interest, rest the fish briefly and cast elsewhere for a couple of minutes. Then cast a fly of a different color and size back to the original spot. Sometimes that provokes a solid strike.

Working a Reef

Where you can wade out from shore on a shallow or exposed reef, do so if the situation looks reasonably safe. Fish holding along a reef, like all fish around structure, repeatedly gravitate to the same spots. Therefore, every fish caught helps you locate other fish on return trips. Over time you should be able to pinpoint specific places where smaller fish hold and other places where bigger fish hang out.

Portions of a reef covered with only knee-deep water might still hold good numbers of fish, even a few large ones. Nevertheless, it is safe to assume that the biggest fish will be sitting on either side of the reef where it joins deeper water. If there is a tidal rip traveling over the reef from right to left, some of the biggest fish are apt to be upcurrent on the right edge of the reef, where they get first shot at bait being drawn

This rocky reef lies exposed at low water. The white line of barnacles indicates the high-water mark. As the tide floods over the reef, smaller fish take up station between the rocks. The bigger fish hold along the edges of the reef where it drops to deep water.

along by the current. Casting a fly upcurrent to these fish has its share of problems, however, as discussed earlier. A weighted fly in this circumstance is a big help. By sinking, it offers more resistance to the current's attempt to push it along, allowing you better feel and control of the fly. Try to work a fly right along the upcurrent edge of the reef. I guarantee that fish will be sitting here.

Next, use any existing current to swing a fly across the edge and onto the reef itself. Do not forget that there likely are fish on the downcurrent side of the reef as well. Use the current to swing a fly to them, too. If the tide is rising, expect more fish to move onto the reef itself. If the tide is dropping, expect any fish on the reef to drop off and move farther out from shore.

Free Lining a Fly

When working the rip off of the tip of a point of land, one problem you are apt to encounter is finding the fish out of fly-rod range. In some cases, you can hear and see fish erupting offshore and are in the frustrating position of watching them blast bait while you stand by helplessly. Here is a trick that might save the day.

Make your cast across the rip current, then begin to strip line off the reel and allow it to feed through the guides as the fly swings downstream. Shaking the rod tip back and forth is a help in getting the free line to exit the tip-top. If the flow is strong, you can use it to pull out all

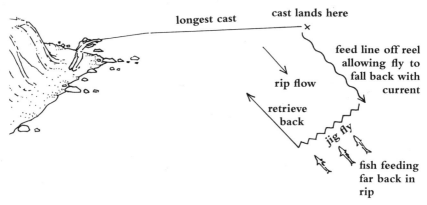

Free lining is a technique that allows you to reach fish out of casting range.

of the fly line and as much of the backing as you dare. Using this technique, which I call "free lining," you can present the fly up to 400 feet away. You can use a floating or intermediate fly line. In a very swift current, a full-sinking line might perhaps be the best.

This technique does present some very real problems in fighting and landing any fish that strikes, since you have a very limited amount of line left on the reel and you must bring that fish a long way upcurrent. But these problems are more than made up for by the fact that this is the only way to reach those fish. I have seen the same technique being used by surf casters in a rip. They cast across the current, and then open the bail on the spinning reel. This allows a shallow running or floating lure to be pulled out into the rip as the angler freespools line. Here, the technique is known as freespooling, and it works well.

Once the fly has reached the full extension of the line, you can let the fly simply hang in the rip, retrieve back slowly, or jig the fly. Jigging is often the best method. Here is how it is done.

With the fly hanging directly downcurrent on a tight line, and the rod tip low to the water and pointed at the fly, make a single strip of about 8 inches. Then release the line you have just gained slowly through your fingers. As soon as the fly is tight again, repeat the procedure. Picture for a moment what is happening to the fly. First it darts ahead 8 inches, then it falls back with the current to its original position, only to dart ahead again. It is simple, and it draws fish like crazy.

Working the Calmer Water
The calmer water associated with points of land can hold real promise as well. There commonly are places just off the flow where back eddies are formed. These eddies are tight to the shoreline, well within fly-rod range, and are usually found immediately to one side of the tip. You can pick out these locations by studying the surface of the water. A back eddy will have a smoother surface and perhaps a distinguishable slowly revolving current. Floating debris is frequently trapped there as well; this is very easy to see.

Here the current slows, sometimes to a near standstill. These pockets of slow-moving water become collecting spots for a fair amount of the suspended food that settles out. Every trout fisherman has seen a smaller version of this phenomenon in a stream, where a back eddy off the main current forms a rich feeding ground. And as on a trout stream, the angler has a right to hope for a big fish here.

Large fish, especially large stripers, lazily feed in these back eddies, particularly at night. With very little effort, they can cruise slowly and dine on an extended menu of seafood. There are likely several different locations from which you can present a fly through this water. One of the best ways to begin covering this area is to cast the fly so that it crosses from the faster main current into the slower eddy. In this way you show the fly to any fish that may be sitting at the very edge of the fast water. After covering this water, concentrate on casting directly into the back eddy. Once you have the fly in the backwater, do not be in a hurry to get it out. Retrieve slowly, especially at night, and even try letting the fly hang for long periods of time in the weak current. You will find that this idea works.

Turn next to the beaches adjoining the tip on either side. These beaches deserve consideration for several reasons. First, there might be a back eddy close to where the sides join the tip. Next, if you find strong current at the tip, you often also find strong current on the beaches leading to it, which means that there are attractive feeding areas here. Also, the baitfish do not spend all their time at the tip and could very well be feeding or hiding along these beaches.

Cover these shores using the techniques discussed in chapter 2. If the beach forms a large bowl at the base of the point of land, do not overlook its potential. These spots are frequently good producers. Stop and cover this water as a matter of course, both on your way out to the tip and on your way back in. In this way, you can maximize your coverage of the point.

BARRIER BEACHES

Barrier beaches are very special points of land. Rather than jutting outward, these long, slender strips of land lie parallel to the coast, frequently running in a north-south direction. These coastal configurations extend out and stretch across the mouth of a bay or estuary, creating a physical barrier between the mainland and the sea.

Barrier beaches are formed by natural forces that transport grains of sand along the coast and deposit them in an ever-growing projection of land. At the outer end of the barrier beach, the currents create a fist-shaped tip, which characteristically curves back around toward the mainland. This curved tip is referred to as a *sand spit*, although you sometimes hear the entire barrier beach called by this name. If you look at a map, you will see that outer Cape Cod is in essence a giant barrier beach, with

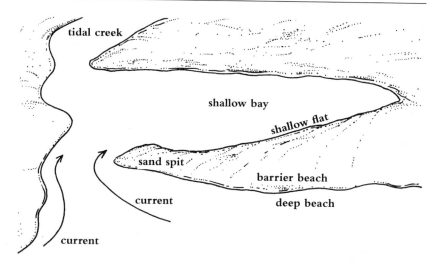

Barrier beaches offer a variety of fishing options from shallow to deep.

Cape Cod Bay being the protected waters on the mainland side, and Provincetown located on the sand spit.

One of the interesting things about fishing a barrier beach is that it gives you a choice of fishing three different types of water. On the mainland side, you find shallow, sheltered waters often lined with salt marshes and sources of fresh water. These places teem with resident baitfish and, like other shallow coastal locations, are easy to fly-fish. A short distance away, on the seaward side, you have exposed beach with a heavier dose of surf and wind, as well as the promise of larger fish. And where the water enters and exits the bay, you are apt to have very strong rips to cover with a fly.

Some Fishing Differences

In my home state of Connecticut, Griswold Point at the mouth of the Connecticut River is a barrier beach. Having fished it for some time now, certain characteristics of barrier beaches seem evident. Ironically, their great length both provides a lot of area to fly-fish and restricts the number of fishermen who take advantage of them. For example, Griswold and some other barrier beaches do not allow four-wheel-drive vehicles, so you must walk out. And a mile hike or more in waders, especially on a warm day, is no picnic, but it does separate those who really want to fish from those with less desire. On Cape Cod, however, with the necessary permits, you can use four-wheel-drive vehicles to visit places like Nauset and Sandy Neck.

Unlike most other points of land, barrier beaches often have some of their best fishing at spots other than the very tip itself. This is probably because the outside beaches leading to the tip have a good deal of current and structure. If you get a chance to visit these special kinds of points, be alert for signs of good-looking water all the way out to the tip itself. Keep an eye out for sandbars, holes, and rips when working a barrier beach.

5

Reading Estuaries

Ultimately fresh and salt water meet, for every stream, river, and creek on earth sets out for the sea. The places where the two finally mix are known as estuaries. Yet beyond their role as a meeting place for different waters, the world's estuaries supply a fundamental link in the survival of many forms of marine life. Marine experts believe that on the Atlantic coast, 80 percent of the fish caught by recreational and commercial anglers spend at least some part of their life in an estuary. This shows the critical role estuaries play in our marine fisheries. Game fish such as striped bass, shad, salmon, sea trout, and weakfish either reproduce here or move through these waterways to spawning beds farther upstream. Estuaries are also essential areas for the survival of baitfish. Bay anchovies, herring, mummichogs, silversides, and sand eels use these waters to spawn in, as a nursery area for their young of the year, or simply as places to feed.

Bodies of water as large as the Chesapeake Bay and Long Island Sound qualify to be called estuaries. Yet for our purposes, it is the smaller estuaries—the tidal creeks, salt ponds, and coastal rivers—that require special attention. These smaller estuaries, with their biological richness and their role in hosting seasonal runs of spawning fish, are ideal spots for saltwater fly fishermen. Small estuaries also are easier to fish than the open coast. The surrounding land affords shelter from the wind, and the force of the ocean surf is eliminated or greatly reduced. And because these areas look more like inland waters, they have a sense of familiarity that aids freshwater anglers in making the transition to the salt.

FISHING COASTAL RIVERS

Coastal rivers supply some of the best fishing on the seaboard, offering opportunities for both shore-based fly rodders and those who prefer to fish from a boat. The lower ends of these estuaries and especially the waters around the mouth often account for the bulk of the angling action, although in the spring, when striped bass chase herring, the fishing could extend for miles upstream.

Rivers often have a defined channel of deeper water. This channel, while an important route for boaters navigating the river, is also an important piece of fishing structure. It serves as a pathway for fish moving up and down the river, particularly during spawning runs of striped bass and baitfish such as alewives. A detailed navigation chart of the river is a great help in locating the exact position and width of the channel.

Game fish also use the channel as a kind of base of operations. When the tide is rising inside the river, game fish come up out of the channel and spread out into shallow areas of the river to feed. This is similar to the pattern on shallow beaches, where fish move into shorelines on rising water. As the tide ebbs, these feeding fish are forced by the reduced water levels to fall back to the safety of the deeper channel. Thus working a fly near the edges of the channel is productive, and the first hours of rising water and the last hours of the drop offer excellent opportunities to intercept fish.

The very largest stripers and bluefish in the river may rarely leave the channel at all. Instead of joining their smaller cousins in chasing tiny baitfish in the shallows, they hunt bigger prey closer to deep water. The dropoffs at the edges of the channel are good places to look for these resident monsters. Sinking flies and perhaps sinking fly lines are needed to reach these fish, so be prepared.

If you prefer to fly-fish from shore, as I do, the channel is often out of casting range. A careful study of your navigation chart, however, should reveal locations where the channel swings in tight to the riverbanks. Wherever the river bends, the channel often favors one bank or the other. Islands in the river present another chance to get close to the main flow while fishing from shore. The channel may hug an entire side of an island, or it may just come close to one end of the island, usually the downstream tip.

The type of shoreline you find along a river determines your fishing strategy in much the same way as it has done for other parts of the coast. Some riverbanks are steep, hosting deep water. Some are rocky. Others are shallow and soft, with bottoms of mud or sand. Use the techniques discussed earlier to work here too. For example, many coastal rivers have shallow beaches and tidal flats that extend out from shore. In essence, you work these like similarly shaped ocean beaches. If the bottom is not too soft, you can wade out and fish. At low tide, you may even be able to get far enough out to reach the channel or pockets of deeper water. And you should expect game fish to come onto the flat with the flooding tide and retreat back to the channel as it gets late in the drop.

One thing that is different about the shorelines inside a coastal river, however, is the amount of current you find. There is apt to be a great deal more than on the exposed coast. And this is especially true wherever the shoreline of the river forms a point. Rivers are also home to a great number of rips. Work them hard and carefully, for as on the open coast, rips here supply the best opportunities of all.

The mouth of a tributary is another hot spot. Here, the exiting flow of a smaller river or creek joins the main flow, making an ideal location for baitfish and game fish alike. Be on the lookout for the possible presence of a bar just outside the mouth of the tributary. The dropoff on the main river side of such a structure is a great place to work a fly. Usually a dropping tide produces the best action and the strongest rips.

Small coves along the river are also important holding areas for baitfish. These are similar to the bowls on a beach and deserve your angling attention. Once again, strong dropping currents are usually best. The ebb sucks small fish out of the calmer backwaters and draws them toward the center of the river itself. I especially like to fish any tidal rip located at the mouth of a cove.

Because of the industrialized nature of most rivers, there are also many man-made structures that alter both the flow and character of a river. Bridges, jetties, breakwaters, and marinas create, change, and shape

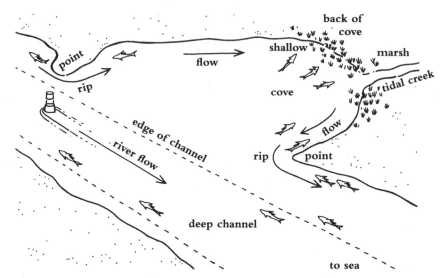

Inside a coastal river, coves, points, rips, and the edges of the channel are worth investigating.

currents while providing feeding and hiding places for both baitfish and game fish. There are some fine fishing opportunities in and around these places. The next chapter looks at them in detail.

MIGRATION RUNS

Several species of baitfish and game fish make spawning migration runs along the coastal estuaries. These include two herrings, the alewife and the blueback. The alewife is found from Nova Scotia to North Carolina; the blueback ranges from southern New England to Florida. Their runs are generally springtime events, although there are exceptions, based largely on geographic location. When these spawning runs coincide with times of the year when game fish are active, there are great fly-fishing opportunities. To find out where these runs take place, ask local anglers or the state department of marine resources.

A third type, the Atlantic herring, spawns near shore and uses the lower ends of estuaries as nurseries for its young-of-the-year. Its importance is most clearly felt in the coastal rivers of the Gulf of Maine. This baitfish draws striped bass, although in some locations the run may precede the spring arrival of bass migrating northward.

Striped bass also spawn in coastal rivers in the spring. Not surprisingly, their spawning run is often matched fairly closely to the appearance of herring in the river. This gives the bass a rich source of food during a strenuous time. Though you should not fish for stripers in the exact areas of a river where spawning takes place, it is inevitable that anglers will fish for them during the upstream migration and their return to sea. As long as this is largely a hook-and-release situation, there is no inherent wrong in doing so, except where the water is very low in salinity and warm. Here hook-and-release mortality is probably unacceptably high.

Another important springtime migratory run is that of the American shad, which by the way are herring too. Shad are found along nearly the entire Atlantic coast, often in great number. One of the best runs in the country takes place in the Connecticut River. This run starts as early as April, and the fish travel the river northward through parts of Massachusetts. Salmon and sea-run trout are also anadromous game fish. Unfortunately, their runs are not anywhere near their historical levels either in size or range. Therefore, fishing is extremely limited and found only in a few locales.

TIME OF TIDE AND TIME OF CURRENT

In an estuary, both the time of tide and the time of current can be confusing. Here is what is going on. As tide tries to enter a coastal river, it must push against the existing downstream flow. This slows the tide's progress. For example, although high tide may have crested along beaches just outside the river mouth, the tide inside the river may not be high for two hours or more.

The time of tide gets later and later as you travel farther upstream. Therefore, the time of high tide at the mouth is often considerably different than just a couple of miles upriver. The same thing happens on the ebb. The ebb begins at the mouth while the tide is still cresting at locations upstream. This is similar to the situation a trout angler faces in a tailwater stream where the flow is regulated by a dam that periodically releases water. And just as in that tailwater trout stream, fly rodders generally can move upstream or downstream to meet various stages of the flow. So, for example, you could fish the first of the falling tide near the mouth of the river, and then travel upstream to another location to catch the first of the ebb there, simply following the tide's progress from one spot to another.

The time of current in an estuary can appear to be even more out

of synch with neighboring shorelines than the time of tide. Understanding this phenomenon is a critical part of fishing an estuary, because
the fish are many times more likely to be feeding while the current is in
motion. Here is part of the key. Salt water is heavier than fresh water.
Therefore, an incoming tide can actually enter an estuary and move
upstream along the bottom while the lighter fresh water is still ebbing
downstream along the surface. This incoming ocean water is call a *salt
wedge*.

During the first hours of the incoming tide, this produces the illusion that the tide is still falling. The fresh water on top is dropping
toward the river mouth, and a fly cast across the surface current swings
toward the sea. But if at this moment you were to drive a stick into the
shore right at water's edge, you would shortly find that the river is actually rising. This is why good tide books include tables for both time of
tide and time of current.

In terms of a hypothetical fishing trip, suppose you hear that there is
great fishing in the mouth of a particular estuary when the current is
ebbing. You look in your tide chart and find that the time of high tide at
the river mouth is noon. So you add one hour for slack tide and arrive
around one o'clock, expecting to see an ebbing current. Much to your
surprise, the current is still incoming, and you are told by a local angler
that the ebbing flow will not begin until two o'clock or three o'clock.
Sound impossible? It happens. This is why I recommend that you use a
comprehensive tide chart such as the *Eldridge Tide Book*. It gives you
more accurate information with which to fish.

THE SALT WEDGE

Some saltwater species entering an estuary ride the salt wedge upstream
so as to not expose themselves to low levels of salinity. This is particularly true of species like bluefish and bonito, which have less tolerance
for fresh water than other fish, such as striped bass. The actual extent
upstream to which these less tolerant species can move is largely determined by how far the saltwater wedge travels. The volume of freshwater
discharge is a factor too. Knowing how far saltwater game fish travel
upriver will help you determine where to focus your efforts.

A useful indicator is the shape of the river mouth. Generally there
are two extremes: wide, shallow mouths and deeper fjord types. The
composition of the banks is a help in identifying each. Shallow rivers
generally have sandy or soft soil banks; the deep, fjord-style mouths are

Angler Steve Cicoria works the edges of an estuary where it leads to the open coast.

more likely rocky. In shallow, sandy rivers, the salt wedge does not push upstream more than a few miles; in deeper, rocky rivers, it can travel much farther.

In Connecticut, there are two classic examples only a few miles apart. The Connecticut River has a wide, shallow mouth with a channel averaging 20 feet or less in depth and fairly strong freshwater discharge. The banks are soft with sand and mud predominating. As a consequence, the wedge does not push upstream very far, and you would not expect to catch bluefish more than a few miles from the mouth.

The Thames River, to the east, has a much deeper mouth, with few tidal flats and a channel that reaches 40 feet deep and more. The ground is hard and rocky. Here there is a large wedge that travels some 15 miles upstream. A bluefish blitz can take place right into the downtown areas of Norwich next to the river. Many of the rivers in Maine also have this deep fjord type of structure.

FISHING TIDAL CREEKS AND STREAMS

Fishing the smallest coastal estuaries such as tidal creeks and streams is not as complex as fishing large coastal rivers, but they still hold fine angling opportunities. For one thing, there is a lot of bait to be found in these places. Herring runs are possible even in freshwater flows so small that you can jump over them. It is estimated that a single acre of salt marsh produces 10 tons of organic material each year. That in turn sustains a great deal of marine life.

In many areas, these seemingly insignificant estuaries are closely guarded secrets shared by seasoned coastal anglers. Barely much more than a trickle, they may still be home to large schools of silversides, mummichogs, and other baitfish. As a result, predators prowl the waters adjacent to the mouth, especially on a dropping tide, and may enter if water depths allow. These small estuaries are great locations to fish, particularly at night or at dawn.

Where a tidal creek joins the salt, it may form a small, shallow delta extending out from the mouth. In some cases, at low tide the delta is exposed and large enough that you can wade out onto it. Regardless of the size, try to establish where the delta ends and suddenly drops off to deeper water. The best fish will be working along the edge of this dropoff on an exiting current. If water depths allow game fish to enter a small estuary, you will find good fishing up inside too. Walk the banks and cast your fly to cover the best-looking areas.

Along the banks of many tidal estuaries, you'll find aquatic plants.

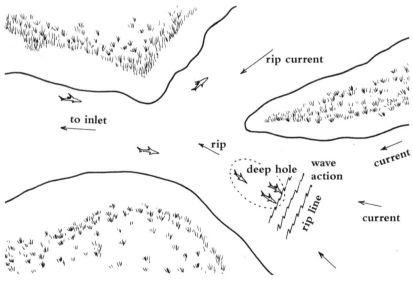

Inside an estuary, rips, holes, and places where currents converge are important fishing areas.

Some of them prefer fairly dry soil, but a few grow right down into the intertidal zone. The most common one is cordgrass *(Spartina alterniflora)*, a straight, smooth-leaved plant that stands about 2 feet tall. At high tide, small baitfish hide among this flooded grass. Striped bass and bluefish know it and patrol the outside perimeter of the grassy area. Try casting your fly along the edge of the grass. It is a deadly technique during the last hour of the flood and the first hours of the ebb.

While you are working inside the creek, study the surface of the water for the presence of a rip line or back eddy. Be sure to work your fly through any you find. Also watch the surface of the stream for turbulence that marks where current is moving over changes in the bottom structure. Deep holes in the streambed are favorite hiding spots for game fish. Pay special attention to bends in the stream. Here you are apt to find bottom structure along with deeper water and increased current.

Look over a topographic map of your coastal area and identify all the small estuaries nearby. Study them closely. Those with the largest drainage area or most extensive salt marshes are apt to produce the best fishing.

Some words of caution: First, the banks of some creeks and even the shorelines of some larger rivers have holes in them, so move slowly and be careful where you step. And ticks can be a problem along the marshes and bordering fields of the coastline, and in the wooded and grassy areas along inland streams. With Lyme disease on the rise, care is in order.

FISHING SALT PONDS

Salt ponds are shallow lagoons of salty water frequently separated from the open ocean only by a thin strip of barrier beach. They are found all along the coast, although some areas have more than others. Like most types of estuaries, they offer good fishing in a location protected from the winds of the open coast.

The tide usually enters these ponds through a narrow opening or inlet, refreshing the pond daily with water from the sea. Many times there is some source of fresh water, usually at a spot far inland to the rear of the pond, although the overall salinity is close to that of the open coast. This fresh water, however, may be enough to support a herring run in the pond. If it does, the herring will draw good numbers of both striped bass and bluefish into the pond.

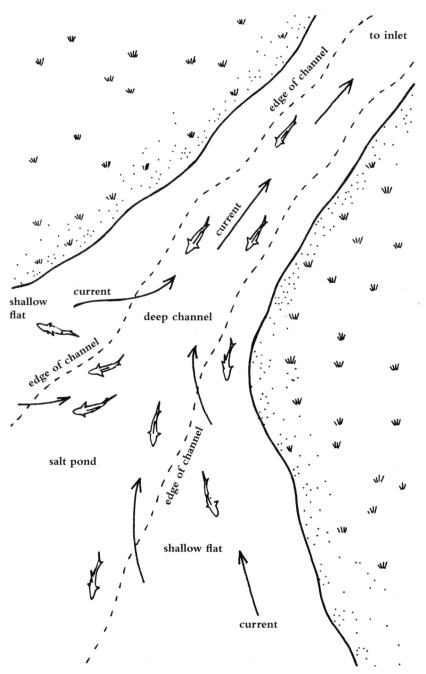

Inside a salt pond, the bigger fish are usually sitting either along the edges of the channel or on the channel bottom.

The fishing in and around inlets can be some of the best on the entire coast, and they deserve plenty of attention. Inlets tend to shoal over with sand and eventually seal off the ponds from the sea. In order to keep them open to navigation, many have been reinforced by man-made structures such as breachways or jetties.

Like a river, a salt pond often has a main channel that extends from the inlet far back into the pond. Here again these channels are important features for anglers. They are home to fish moving in and out of the pond, as well as generally being a place to reside and ambush bait. The largest fish that enter the pond, which can be good-size ones, stay near this deeper water.

Water color, navigation markers, and charts help you locate the position and path of the channel. If you are going to fish the pond from the shore or by wading, be sure to note places where you can get within fly-rod range of this deeper water. Sinking flies and maybe even sinking fly lines are in order to properly probe these depths, particularly where the channel has considerable current. Be especially attentive as your fly nears the edge of the dropoff.

Salt ponds frequently have extensive shallow flats. A boat gives you access to all of these areas, but if the bottom is hard enough, you can wade and search for fish as well. On a falling tide, some of these shallow areas may have a fair amount of current as water drains off them toward the channel. The stronger the current, the better your chances of meeting up with some action. Dark and overcast days are better bets than bright, sunny ones.

The point at which the pond narrows or necks down even slightly as it heads toward the outflow is often a good place to swim a fly. Here on an ebbing tide the water suddenly picks up speed, and constricting banks make this area a collection point for baitfish and other forms of marine life caught in the current. It is also a good place on the first of the incoming tide, when baitfish feeding in the inlet are flushed by here on their way into the pond.

The most consistent action for both large and small fish in a salt pond seems to occur at night. Under the cover of darkness, stripers and bluefish spread out into the shallow flats and hunt baitfish. Here again, banks lined with cordgrass are favorite hangouts for small baitfish, especially during higher stages of the tide. Look for stripers and blues to cruise these edges. Also pay attention to areas of the bottom covered with eelgrass. It grows well in salt ponds even when salinity is low, providing a rich habitat for baitfish and other marine life.

At high tide, baitfish such as silversides and mummichogs hide in the cord-grass along the edges of an estuary. Game fish patrol here, especially from dusk to dawn. Be sure to work a fly along points formed by the grass.

After dark, because of the shallow water and the lower noise levels, you can often hear the fish feeding. If you are looking for bragging-size fish, try fishing a dropping tide well after dark. Position yourself so that the current swings your fly from shallow water to the edge of the chan-nel. Big fish sit here waiting for the flow to carry food to them.

The shallowness of these ponds means that they warm more quickly than the open sea in the spring and provide earlier action, par-ticularly for school-size stripers. They also cool more quickly in the fall. Resident baitfish, such as silversides, sand eels, anchovies, and mullet, migrate out of the salt pond as the water temperature drops. This in turn makes for excellent fishing at the mouth of the pond and along the adjacent coastline.

THE HIDDEN ESTUARY

There are some ponds along the coast that are very tight to the sea but are rarely, if ever, open to it. These ponds generally sit elevated above sea level, perhaps on top of a scarp. Seemingly sealed off from the sea, they would not be expected to have any possible effect on coastal fishing. Yet it is my firm belief that some of these ponds are a kind of hidden estu-ary and can have a noticeable influence on the fishing nearby.

As they sit above sea level, these ponds are capable of draining through the soil and slowly leaking unseen into the salt. This leakage, however small, spurs marine growth, which in turn attracts baitfish and game fish. Fish are also incredibly sensitive to the smell of fresh water. For example, a spawning run of herring may stop here for a while, attracted by the scent of the pond. Such locations may not prove to hold consistent angling action, but nevertheless they can be highly productive at times.

To find one of these potential fishing spots, use a topographic map to locate a pond in immediate proximity to the salt. Next, visit the beach directly in front of this pond. Note the place at which the land between the pond and the sea is at its narrowest. Any leakage would likely exit to the beach from this area. In one case, by wading a shallow beach, I discovered a freshwater spring coming up from the bottom about 150 feet out from the high-tide line. I could feel the cool water through my waders. The following season I fished that spot, and a striped bass of nearly 40 inches clobbered my popper one morning. Since that time, I have talked to other anglers who have done well there too. Finding a spring is not common, however. More likely you will simply have to fish the general area in question regularly in order to find where the fish hang out.

THE WORM HATCH

When saltwater fly rodders get together in the Northeast, a subject that gets some attention is the mysterious "worm hatch." This hatch is really the spawning ritual of marine worms of the genus *Nereis,* a type of annelid. Popularly known as clam worms or sandworms, they are widely used as bait. Hit the hatch right, and you are apt to see enough striped bass feeding on these little squiggly things to make your knees shake.

New England is not alone in having hatches of marine worms. They exist all along the coast, although they may not be the exact same ones. Differences include size, shape, color, preferred habitat, and mating schedule, so local knowledge is important. In the Florida Keys, for instance, there is a similar worm hatch in late May and June that involves a different creature know as the palolo worm. Hit it right, and you can expect some fantastic tarpon fishing.

For many New England anglers, their first experience with a worm hatch comes as an accident. It usually goes like this: Fishing on a spring night, they find themselves in front of a whole school of quietly sipping bass. The fishing should be great, but much to their chagrin, these fish refuse every fly thrown their way. Later someone turns on his light to see what is in the water, and the worms are discovered.

The best worm hatches take place in the lower ends of small coastal creeks, streams, and salt ponds. The finest action might be upstream inside the creek or pond, or it could be right at the mouth where it spills into the sea. You will have to hunt around. But when the moment is right, thousands of small, red worms emerge from the sand or mud and swim about seeking a mate. Striped bass have an uncanny way of knowing that the hatch is about to take place and will be lurking in the shadows.

Nature has a way of helping its members survive. Most worms begin their spawn on the crest of the high tides during several days around the new moon. These spring tides give the worms maximum room to maneuver as deep water floods into the shallow estuaries. They also produce strong currents that allow the worms to spread themselves out and "seed" a good deal of area. Since the time of high tide during the new moon varies according to geographic location, the hatch may happen either in the light, usually late afternoon, or after dark.

For example, in Lake Tashmoo on Martha's Vineyard, I have seen the hatch begin at 6 P.M. during a new moon period in early June. At

Typical worms from a hatch in New England. These range in size from 1 to about 4 inches.

this time of year, light fall is nearly three hours off, so the action takes place in full view. In Connecticut, that same high tide would crest around two and a half hours later, right at dark, and the hatch takes place during the night.

The exact species of Nereis involved in my fishing is, I believe, *Nereis limbata*. In their spawning dress, these worms are 1 to 4 inches long and appear reddish brown. If viewed closely, however, the head and tail are darker, almost black, and there is an off-white patch behind the head. Overall, it is very close in appearance to its much larger cousin, *Nereis virens,* the big sand or clam worm so commonly used by bait fishermen. Unfortunately, this worm appears to spawn in late winter and early spring, before the arrival of striped bass. Too bad. Imagine what a feeding frenzy worms up to eighteen inches long would cause.

The clam worms swim in short, erratic bursts and appear to be jet propelled. If you are in a location with minimal current, you can see the worms swimming just under the surface, making occasional darts to the top. As the tide begins to drop, swarms of worms appear just under the surface. At night you can see them very clearly by flashlight, and the water may even appear red with their bodies if the hatch is thick.

Striped bass love these little creatures and are sure to be in the wings as the action starts. They hit these guys with gentle swirls, and you will have no trouble knowing that bass are about. But you could have trouble bringing them to the hook. These worms are so numerous that a fly is lost in their midst. And it is likely that the bass sometimes swallow bunches of the naturals at a time. Furthermore, the worms swim in an odd circular motion that is nearly impossible to duplicate with a fly. Where the current is very strong, the worms tend to move less erratically and instead fall with the tide. Here a dead-drifted fly is more apt to draw a strike.

These hatches start with the first new moon after the second week of May and reoccur on the new moons of July and August. They last for only a few nights each time and may be only an hour or two in length. In some locations, there may also be a weaker hatch on the full moon. The first and last nights of a given hatch, the worms are less numerous. This can mean better fishing, since your fly has less competition from naturals. The strongest part of the hatch is most often on the exact day of the new moon. Like all marine life, these hatches seem to have cycles of boom and bust. Some years the worms are plentiful, and other years the hatches are very sparse.

Oddly enough, the only game fish I have seen feeding on these worms is the striped bass, although I have heard rumors of bonito and bluefish taking part. But regardless of what species you find feeding on these worms, the fishing will be a challenge. For one thing, no fly pattern seems to be a guaranteed killer. Standard deceivers and other saltwater streamers are too big to accurately imitate the worms, so you will need to tie something considerably smaller. A 1½ to 2 inch long Woolly Worm tied with a thin red chenille body and a short red marabou tail is a good bet for hatches that take place in the light. At night that same fly should be all black. A number 2 hook is about right. I also suggest that you tie a few droppers on your leader and fish up to three flies at a time. Use a slow to moderate strip retrieve, and try to keep the flies close to the surface.

When all else fails, tie on the biggest fly in your box. Here is why. Besides striped bass, other marine life feeds on the worms. Eels, squid, and small fish get in on the act. The larger stripers lurking in the area are tuned in to that fact and ready to nail these members of the crowd as well. By switching to a large fly, you might trigger a strike from one of these big bass. This same type of thing happens during a mayfly hatch. Sometimes a streamer fished through the hatch takes the best trout in the pool.

Work where there is current. Not only will it be easier to make the fly act like the natural, but you can expect the bass to be more aggressive. Conversely, move away from areas where the water is dead calm, particularly if the hatch is taking place in the light. Here bass have ample time to inspect the fly, and that leads to more refusals. Since the hatch takes place during the ebb, both the fish and the worms tend to drop away from shore as the water level diminishes. Consequently, wherever possible you should wade forward to follow the action. And above all, be patient and persistent.

NAUTICAL CHARTS

Once you understand how to read shorelines, you can use nautical charts as an additional source of information. Nautical charts are produced by the National Oceanic and Atmospheric Administration, which is part of the Department of Commerce. These charts are designed for the purpose of safe navigation and are sold mainly through marinas and tackle shops. If you fish from a boat, you should be already using them for that reason. But whether you fish from a boat or the shore, charts can be a real

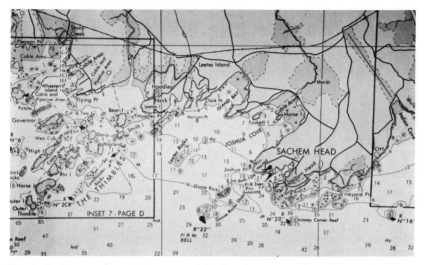

Nautical charts can provide a way of finding important shoreline and bottom structure.

angling aid too, showing you the locations of important fishing structure, including points of land, reefs, inlets, bottom composition, dropoffs, tidal rips, and much more.

First you need to identify which chart or charts cover the area you want to investigate. All charts are numbered and keyed to an index that indicates which geographical area is covered by which chart. Informed marinas and tackle shops can quickly help you identify the right charts if you simply tell them what specific stretch of the coast you wish to fish.

Pick the chart that shows the area in the greatest detail. Charts are produced on scales ranging from 1:20,000 to 1:80,000. On the 1:80,000 scale, a nautical mile is represented by less than 2 inches of chart; on a scale of 1:20,000, a nautical mile covers nearly 4 inches. The latter shows finer detail and gives a more in-depth look at the structure. Be sure to get the most recent chart, as structure is apt to change over time, especially with sandy bottoms.

Once you have obtained the right chart, lay it out on a table. The chart uses a simple color scheme to visually identify things. The land is beige, tidal flats and marsh areas are green, shallow water is blue, and deeper water is white. Water depths are indicated by contour lines and expressed in feet at mean low water (expect charts to go metric in the future). To approximate the normal high-tide depth, simply add the tidal range for that area. Besides telling you about depth, contour lines also indicate the grade of the bottom, as well as giving other information about various structures.

As on a topographic map of the land, any place where contour lines stack up tightly next to one another indicates a steep slope. Where contour lines are spread out, the slope of the bottom is gradual. This will help you spot dropoffs and flats. Along a shallow shoreline, note wherever contour lines indicate pockets of deeper water swinging close to the beach. Also use the contour lines to identify the edges, size, shape, and location of any submerged structure such as a reef or bar.

Charts use the following abbreviations to denote the bottom composition: RK, rock; M, mud; S, sand; G, gravel; rky, rocky; sft, soft; stk, sticky; and hrd, hard. Many times these abbreviations are used in conjunction with one another; for instance, hrd S means a hard sand bottom. Patches of large boulders in the water tight to the shore are frequently shown by asterisks. These spots usually hold excellent striped bass potential. Look for them especially near the terminal end of a point of land.

6

Reading Man-made Structures

There was a 15- to 20-knot wind coming out of the northwest, and although the air temperature was in the low seventies, it felt far cooler. Phil Farnsworth, Dave Foley, and I stood at the end of the Menemsha jetty on the west side. The ebbing tide was exiting the inlet, pulling the rich waters of the salt pond out into the sea. Beyond the jetties, the flow spread out into open waters, curving northwest, right into the face of swells coming off Menemsha Bight. The result was a heavy, rolling sea.

Gulls swooped and squawked as a large school of bluefish ripped into silversides and sand eels, which were present in unbelievably thick schools. Along the wall of the jetty, we could see bands of bait 1½ feet wide and 2 feet deep. Some groups stretched for more than 400 feet in length. They were using the shallow water at the edge of the rock jetty as a safe route in and out of the harbor in their quest for food. But the bluefish had others of their kind balled up both outside and in between the jetty walls. Occasionally we would look back up inside the harbor where the waters widened, leading to Menemsha Pond, and see other eruptions of wild-eyed blues.

A weighted fly, cast from the tip of the jetty and allowed to swing out the mouth with the falling tide, brought instant results. We could see bluefish rocketing up from below to chase and clobber our flies. For a

The tip of a jetty can supply fast action.

brief second, the fish would hang sideways in the blue-green swells just behind the fly as if frozen in an oil painting. These were not big blues, up to 6 pounds at best. Yet they fought with strong runs and unrelenting pressure, instantly earning our respect.

Once we subdued a blue, it would be lying 8 feet below us in the waves against the jetty wall. The trick was to get down there and release the fish without either breaking the rod or taking a fall. It can happen. One autumn I witnessed an angler who was trying to land a bass here slip headfirst into the inlet. Luckily he was not hurt, and two jetty companions pulled him out, although the striper made good on its escape in the confusion. I always plan a good route down to the water before I even make my first cast. And I use it with care and never in a hurry.

JETTIES AND BREACHWAYS

Mankind is forever altering the coast. And regrettably, many things we have done have not been in the best interests of the environment. Still, man-made structures do attract fish and in some cases actually improve the fishery. They accomplish this by either altering the habitat in a positive way or creating habitat where none existed. Concrete, rock, wood, and steel when submerged all can create currents, offer a foothold for marine life, and generally supply shelter.

Jetties are man-made structures of rock and concrete that have earned a place in the hearts of coastal anglers. They are frequently built at the mouths of medium to large estuaries and are commonly constructed in opposing pairs. The water between them is called an *inlet* or *breachway*. In common usage, there seems to be little difference between these two terms. Both are used to describe the path by which the inland waters are allowed to flow to the sea. Some might suggest that inlet generally refers to the entrance of a large coastal estuary, and breachway to the entrance of a smaller body of water, such as a salt pond.

In many estuaries, the entire exiting flow is funneled between two jetties. In other locations, especially large rivers, only a portion of the flow, usually the main channel, is protected by jetties. In both situations, the jetties serve to keep the channel open and navigable by concentrating the flushing action of the current. This discourages the formation of sandbars or other accumulations of sediment in the mouth.

Because of their location and function, jetties differ from other man-made structures such as breakwaters, groins, and bridges. A breakwater, though identical in construction, is meant to function as a barrier beach or barrier island. It sits off the shore of a beach or cove and protects things inside, such as moored boats, from the full forces of wind and wave. Groins are structures made of wood, rock, or concrete that jut out from a beach in an effort to slow the transport of sand by longshore currents. These are very often found along sandy shorelines dotted with cottages, each groin being an attempt by a landowner to preserve his or her section of the beach.

Jetties are rarely easy places to fish, and frequently they are crowded. Anglers are poised high above the water, perched on uneven, often slippery rock. It is hard to work a fly well and even harder to land a fish. So why bother? Because fishing off a jetty offers a chance to hook large numbers of fish, including trophy-size ones. As a result, some jetties have a fanatical following.

There are many productive jetties along the coast. Among the most widely known jetties in fly-rod circles are the two at Menemsha Inlet on Martha's Vineyard. During the annual Fishing Derby, these piles of rocks are apt to be swarming with anglers, a fair percentage of whom have fly rods glued to their hands. The scene can be very hectic. And to make matters worse, this fairly narrow inlet is regularly used by boaters as they enter and exit Menemsha Harbor. Still, though jetty fishing is a little crazy at times, these stone piles give up more than their share of striped bass, bluefish, bonito, and little tunny on a fly.

Fishing a Jetty

For the purposes of examination, a jetty can be divided into three sections: the outermost tip, the middle stretch, and the mainland point of origin, or shore end.

The Tip

As with a point of land, the tip of a jetty is generally the most desirable place to be. It has excellent rips and currents and is close to deeper holding water. Frequently the tip gives up the most and largest fish. When the tide is ebbing, many fish lie immediately outside the jetty tip, feeding in the exiting flow. Atlantic bonito and little tunny commonly do this, but bass and blues do it as well. The only place on the jetty you can reach these guys from is the tip. There are even more advantages. From the tip, you can cast in a number of directions and therefore cover more different types of water than from the middle of the jetty. And if you hook a big fish off the tip, the fish will likely stay outside in deep water, giving you plenty of safe room in which to wage the fight.

Still, the tip of the jetty is no rose garden. There may be extremely limited room, considering the many anglers who would like to fish it. So you had best get there early and be ready to endure close quarters with other anglers who may or may not be happy to share space with a fly rodder. Also, the tip receives the most wave action, which at times may be too much to handle for even a confirmed jetty surf caster. Because of that wave action, the tip is the slipperiest spot, and it can be the most broken-down part of the jetty too, because of the relentless pounding it gets. Some are more suited to mountain goats than to anglers. If you want to land a fish here, you must climb down a steep, jagged, and sometimes slick wall of rocks to reach the fish. This is where a sturdy, long-handled net comes in mighty handy.

Most experienced anglers wear foul-weather gear when fishing the tip of a jetty because of the wetness of these locations. In the warmer summer months, this is not as much of a concern. You can wear your waders too, although jetties do take a toll on them. Sneakers are used by many jetty anglers, but they offer little help on the algae-covered rocks. I strongly recommend felt soles or metal cleats for good traction. You may not need them standing up top, but when you have to climb down the side of the jetty to land a fish, you will be glad you have them on. For eyeglass wearers, I strongly encourage a strap to keep your glasses from falling off. If you drop them on these rocks, they will likely break.

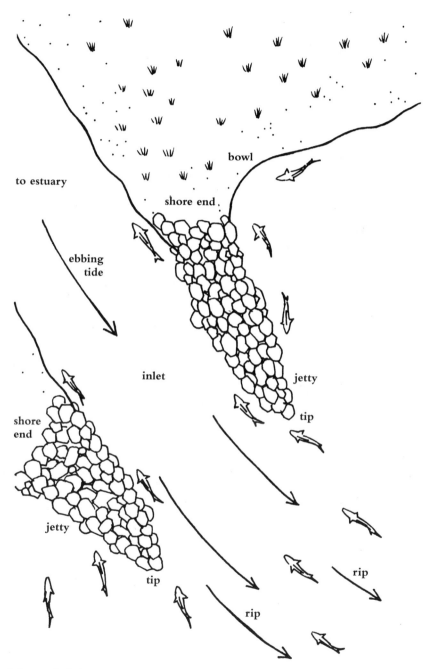

Inlets and their accompanying jetties have plenty of structure, current, and bait.

I also recommend that you bring a small amount of extra gear with you. That might include some spare leader material, a spare spool with a sinking fly line, extra flies, sunglasses, and a camera. If you plan to keep the fish you catch, you need a long-handled gaff or net.

After you reach the tip, look around for a comfortable place to fish. A dry, flat rock is ideal. Be very careful where you set down your extra gear. Place it where it is unlikely to be blown in the water or slip down in a deep, narrow crevice between the rocks. Before you wet a line, study the water for potential trouble. Are there lobster pot buoys anywhere nearby? Usually they are close to the jetty wall. A strong fish has a way of wrapping your line around those things. Little tunny are notorious for this behavior. Is there a navigation marker behind you on top of the jetty? Does it interfere with your backcast? Move around until you are in the absolute best possible situation. Now one last thing before you cast: Where will you land the fish you hope to hook? Try to figure out a good spot and a path to get down there.

Start with a short cast directly across the current of the inlet. I recommend beginning with an intermediate fly line and a streamer. As soon as the cast lands, point the rod tip down toward the water. This helps you keep in contact with the fly. Slowly retrieve the fly as it swings with the flow, all the while keeping an eye out for fish that may

When the action is hot, anglers work both the jetty and the adjoining beach.

come up to inspect it. Try a few casts parallel to the jetty, making the fly swim tight to the jetty wall. Game fish, especially stripers, frequently hide just off the edge of the rocks where the water becomes dark. During the day, these fish sit deep enough to be out of sight. At night, however, a striper may have its nose within inches of the wall.

If after several casts you get no response, make a slightly longer throw, allowing the fly to swing through a new path. Pay special attention to the edge of any rip line. Repeat that cast several times, and then lengthen the cast further. Keep up this procedure until you have reached your maximum casting distance. If none of this works, switch to a sinking line. Game fish are reluctant at times to come up through a fast current, simply because it takes so much energy to do so. The answer is to get the fly down to the right level. A fast-sinking line is in order, and perhaps even a weighted fly or a piece of twist-on lead for the leader. Repeat the same casts as with the first fly line. Also try allowing the fly to sink deeper by casting upcurrent and delaying the retrieve.

If this does not work, consider moving. Keep a sharp eye on the water next to the jetty wall for signs of baitfish. Silversides, sand eels, and bay anchovies moving through an inlet frequently travel within a foot of the jetty. Wherever they are concentrated, the fishing will be better. Be sure at some point to go around to the other side of the tip and work the outside of the jetty wall.

As with a point of land, fish feeding in the currents near the tip may be out of fly-casting range. This is especially true with bonito and little tunny, but also may be the case with bluefish and bass. Free lining a fly, as described in chapter 4, works here too. The idea is to allow the current to drag the fly line out farther than you could ever cast.

When you hook a fish here, most of the time it runs in an offshore direction away from the jetty. This is especially true when the tide is ebbing, as the fish can use the exiting current to its advantage. On an incoming tide, expect a hooked fish to run the other way, up inside the inlet. If there are lobster buoys or channel markers nearby, try to use side pressure with the rod to steer the fish away from these obstructions. Then, as the fish tires, lead it to your predetermined landing spot. If you have a friend with you, he can put down his rod and help you at this point.

On a short jetty, especially when few other anglers are around, consider landing a very large fish by walking it around the tip and then along the outside wall back to the beach. This is only possible, of course, when the outside wall is not lined with lobster pots. Wait until the fish is tired, then move around the tip, taking the fish outside the jetty walls away from the current. Slow and easy does it. Walk the fish down the wall, maintaining a tight line. Then, when possible, step off the wall onto the beach. Now you can land the fish right at your feet.

Occasionally you will encounter a fish that swims against the ebbing flow and heads up into the inlet. It seems to be the bigger fish that employ this game plan. But regardless of big or small, when it happens, expect trouble. There are more places here to snag your fly line, and believe it or not, the possibility of a passing boat cutting you off exists too. If at all possible, move down the jetty, keeping the rod high, and try to get upcurrent of the fish and apply pressure. This usually makes the fish turn and run out to where you can wage a safer fight. No matter how excited you are, do not run. It is far too easy to fall.

On an incoming tide, as the water rounds the tip of the jetty, it may form a back eddy next to the jetty wall. Immediately downcurrent of this eddy, you are apt to find a small pocket of slack water very tight to the rocks. Often large stripers hold in this water, although they may be holding 5 or more feet down. Using a sinking fly and a sinking line, let your fly sink in the back eddy. Impart action by using occasional twitches of the rod tip. A really big fish could rise from the depths and nail it.

The Middle Section

Overall, the fishing you find in the middle section of the jetty is not up to the fishing at the tip. Still, there are several reasons why you should try it. First, the tip may already be occupied. Or maybe you have fished the tip and it did not produce. Also, at times, fish are busting on the surface along this part of the jetty, making it for the moment the most desirable place to be.

Not all jetty walls are straight. Some are designed with one or more well-defined angles, or "kicks," in them. These spots are better producers of action than the straighter parts of the wall. Like irregularities in the shape of a beach, these kicks have changes in current and structure associated with them. Consider fishing near one. As you walk along the middle of any jetty, also be on the lookout for schools of baitfish. Wherever they congregate, you should fish there.

Once you have picked a general area to fish, study the water for a place free of obstacles. The fewer moorings, lobster pot buoys, and channel markers in front of you, the better. Select a dry, level place to cast from and store any gear bag you have along. Then check for a safe place to land a fish. Use the same basic techniques to cover the water as at the tip, with both intermediate and sinking lines.

In many instances, the bottom of the inlet is sand. Here many fish are apt to be found along the edge where the sand bottom meets the rock wall of the jetty. At lower stages of the tide, you usually can see where that transition takes place. This edge is similar to that found on some rocky beaches. Game fish as well as baitfish commonly follow this line when traveling in and out of the inlet, so be sure to try casting parallel to the jetty, working your fly close to the wall. There also may be hidden pockets along the edges of the wall. These spots are relatively free of current and make ideal holding spots for game fish.

If you hook a fish inside the inlet, nine times out of ten it runs with the current. If the fish feels small and controllable, hold your ground. With a strong, heavy fish, however, consider following it. Always remember to keep a tight line and to move cautiously over the rocks. It is conceivable that you could end up all the way out at the tip. On an incoming tide, that same fish would lead you all the way inside to the shore end of the jetty. As always, steer the fish away from obstacles.

The Shore End

The tip and the middle of the jetty get the most fishing pressure. What few anglers realize is that good fishing potential exists right where the jetty begins, at the shore end. Basically, this is a transition point between the natural flow of the river, salt pond, or lagoon and the constricted and controlled area of the inlet. The area around which this happens has considerable current, as well as back eddies and bottom structure.

The shore end is often a good place for small to medium-size fish on the dropping tide. It does not have the reputation the tip has, but it does not get the intense fishing pressure, either. Therefore, you have better access and more freedom to move around—things that improve the angling experience. The best time to fish here is usually on the flood, and especially at night for stripers and blues. With the incoming water, the shore end of the jetty is not unlike the tip on the ebb. The current takes everything past it. Look for a place from which you can swing a fly into the deeper holes and along the rip lines.

Baitfish often travel tight to the jetty wall. This is a school of bay anchovies.

Other Considerations

In most locations where you find a pair of jetties, one jetty is more productive than the other. This has to do with the bottom structure and the prevailing direction of a falling tide. When an ebbing tide exits the mouth of an inlet, it does not necessarily head straight out to sea. Because tides move along the coast, the rip often favors one jetty over the other. Therefore, one jetty is closer to the best current and frequently the deepest bottom. This means that the fishing is superior there on most days. There will be days, however, when the wall that is ordinarily the less desirable of the two hosts the hottest action. That is the nature of fishing.

When fishing a jetty, remember that the water along the outside of the jetty wall holds promise too. Baitfish that have exited the inlet to feed frequently visit here, especially in the bowl formed by the jetty and the adjoining beach. You can fish it from either the jetty or the beach, whichever is more convenient. Pay special attention to this spot on days when the wind and waves are pushing into the bowl. This will concentrate plankton here, drawing the bait. Unfortunately, it may also be a collecting point for seaweed and floating debris, but do not let that stop you.

Tides for Jetty Fishing

If striped bass and bluefish are your goal, the ebb is generally the most productive tide. During the middle hours of the drop, when the flow is strongest, the fish may stay on the bottom or hang outside the inlet in the rip. During the start of the ebb, currents are weaker and surface activity is often at its best. It can be an excellent time to work a popper. On the flood, do not forget to try up inside the inlet.

If you are fishing for Atlantic bonito and little tunny, the incoming tide is likely your best bet, because it draws the fish inside the inlet and therefore inside fly-casting range. On the ebb, they often hang too far outside to reach. This is especially the case where the exiting flow has a high freshwater content. As the salty sea water enters the inlet on the flood, expect these guys to ride in with tide.

Remember that the time of tide in an inlet often differs substantially from the time of tide of even nearby beaches. It is common to find the tide still entering the inlet for one or more hours after the tide has crested on nearby beaches. The reverse is true too. The tide may be dead low on neighboring shorelines while the inlet is still dropping. Look for a tide book with specific information for the inlet or ask local experts.

READING BRIDGES

Jetties are not the only man-made structures that play a significant role in our coastal fisheries. All along the coast, you will come across other structures to which fish and fishermen have long since adapted. Bridges are a fine example. On the coast, bridges vary in size from a footbridge crossing a tidal creek to a massive concrete and steel span carrying a major highway.

Game fish are drawn to bridges for several reasons. The primary attraction is the presence of rips created by the piers or abutments where they constrict the flow. At the same time, these parts of the bridge produce pockets of slack water where predators can hold. This close proximity of fast and slow waters results in excellent feeding opportunities. Also look for whirlpools to form on the downstream side, allowing suspended nutrients to settle out, further enriching the habitat. It is an ideal spot for a big bass to dine. Furthermore, shadows made by the bridge overhead both aid game fish in ambushing bait and supply cooling shade.

Though the largest bridges get most of the notoriety, smaller bridges offer some surprisingly good fishing, particularly for anglers without boats. Look for a bridge that forces the tide to enter and exit a cove, salt pond, or tidal stream through a narrow opening. In these situations, a considerable number of baitfish hang near the bridge, especially on a moving tide. If you are fishing on foot, generally the idea is to work your way down to the base of the bridge abutment where it meets the shoreline. This is not always possible, but very often it is. From here you can cover the currents. Study both sides and both ends of the bridge for the best and safest areas to fish from.

Fishing a Bridge

Many times when working around a small bridge, you will find that casting room is at a real premium. Where that turns out to be the case, use a shooting head rather than a full-length fly line. Heads require less of a backcast. You can expect fish on both the upcurrent and downcurrent sides of the bridge, so fish each, although occasionally swirls or feeding noises may tell you which side is hot. Regardless of which side you fish, pay close attention to the rip lines and especially to the pockets of slower water near the abutments just off the current. These are where many of the fish are holding.

If you are on the upcurrent, or uptide, side of the bridge, try to cast

Even small bridges have good fishing potential. This angler works the exiting currents.

roughly forward and at 45 degrees to the face of the bridge. In this way, the current swings your fly back toward the bridge on a tight line. Gauge your cast so as to work the areas around the piers and abutments. And do not forget the rip line closest to you. There may well be fish right at your feet.

When fishing the downcurrent side, try casting 45 degrees up under the bridge and allowing the fly to be swept back in the flow. Take care to control any slack line in order to remain in contact with the fly at all times. Measure your cast so that it is close to the abutments but does not hit them. You do not want to break off the hook point or snag the fly. Also work the water and rip lines below the bridge. If the current is very swift and the water fairly deep, try using a sinking line as well.

If the bridge is low to the water, you may even want to cast directly off the top side. Be very careful with your backcast. Cars, electrical wires, and pedestrians may be in the line of fire. If the bridge is low and long, you can cast parallel to the bridge and then walk the fly along the bridge's face without retrieving. It is a little too much like trolling for some anglers, but it is deadly, allowing you to maximize your coverage of the best water. Be warned that if a hooked fish shoots under the bridge, you could face problems. Never under any circumstances try to hoist a fish up to your position using the rod as a crane. It will surely snap.

Larger bridges, such as a highway bridge, are best covered from a boat, because this is big water and the better holding spots are often well out in the middle. Working a fly here is a bit of a specialized art. It involves boatmanship, an understanding of tides, and refined tackle.

The first step is locating the fish. Both striped bass and bluefish commonly hold in these waters, although other game fish like bonito may show up if the salinity is high enough. All of these predators may be working either the upstream or the downstream side of the bridge. But as a rule, expect to find them in close association with the bridge structure. In this way, they can slipstream the current yet be ready to pounce on anything that gets swept by. The exception would be when a full-scale blitz is under way. Then the action could take place out from the bridge structure.

Position the boat in such a way that you can deliver a fly to the holding areas. Never in any way block the flow of a navigable part of the channel. When working the upstream side of a bridge, hold the boat ahead of the abutment. The distance cannot be greater than the range of

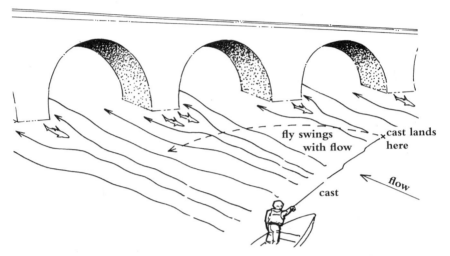

fly swings
with flow

cast lands
here

cast

flow

Many fish hold in the pockets of slower current around the bridge abutments.

the longest possible cast. The boat can be held in location by using the
motor to stem the tidal flow. Anchoring is another solution, but this can
have its problems. In some spots, the bottom alongside the bridge holds
communication cables and debris from the construction of the bridge.
An anchor could easily tangle. Also, if a large fish takes the fly and bolts
downstream under the bridge, you will be in a tough situation.

A large streamer is an excellent fly with which to search this water.
The fish are likely down below the surface a good way, however. For
that reason, many experienced bridge fishermen use the fastest-sinking
line available and weight the fly too. Cast the fly across the current, and
allow it to sink as much as possible in the heavy flow. The strike is apt to
come as the line straightens below you, sending the streamer in front of
the pier. Be prepared to apply maximum pressure immediately. Piers are
rough and loaded with sharp things, such as barnacles and mussel shells.
A big fish can cut you off in an instant if given its head.

In this kind of situation, consider attaching a 2-foot section of
30-pound test monofilament as a shock tippet between the fly and the
breaking class tippet. I have also found these long shock tippets helpful
on rocky beaches and in rocky rips. This modification does hamper
your casting and certainly is not up to IGFA regulations, but it is preferable to letting a fish swim off with the fly dangling from its mouth.

And besides, I am not looking to get my name in the record books. If, however, you are interested in records, be aware that the IGFA only allows a foot of shock leader.

Fishing from a boat positioned on the downstream side of the bridge is harder, because you cannot use the current to direct the fly as well. Here again you want the fly to move naturally with the current and travel past the pier closely. A spot directly downriver of the pier is one possibility. From there a cast can be made up under the bridge tight to the pier. Since the fly is moving toward you in this case, it is important to maintain contact by stripping in slack. You may also be able to position the boat so that you can try a few casts parallel with the bridge. This will give you an opportunity to keep the fly longer in the prime waters on the downstream side of the pier. In either case, a fish hooked on the downstream side of the bridge is much easier to handle.

When you fish a bridge pool in a trout stream, the current always flows in the same direction. In the salt, however, this is simply not so. The upstream and downstream sides of the bridge are tide-dependent, and you need to adjust to changes in the flow. The exact stage of the tide determines the water depth and rate of flow. This can affect the fishing to a considerable degree.

The first part of the dropping tide is one of the best bets for the larger fish, but the increased water depth makes it hard to get a fly to the fish. Furthermore, when the tide is high, the feeding lies are more extensive and the fish can be spread out. The last few hours of the ebb will reduce the water depth and restrict the prime feeding lies. This may not be the best time for a trophy fish, but it could well be the best time for fly tackle overall. The fish are more concentrated and easier to serve a fly to.

Fishing Bridges at Night

Fishing at night from bridges both large and small is a time-honored tradition. Bridges with streetlights that spill over onto the water are especially productive. The lights attract baitfish to the vicinity, and game fish follow. Tides are just as important at night as they are in the day, but another factor creeps into play as the sun goes down. The streetlights cause the bridge to cast a shadow on the water. This shadow line frequently becomes a prime feeding station for game fish in their attempt to ambush a meal. Expect to find fish on the upstream side sitting just inside the dark edge of the shadow line.

These fish are often near the surface as well. From a low bridge, you might even be able to see these fish holding in the current. Lean over the side and use your hands to shield your eyes from the light. Allow your eyes a chance to adjust, while paying strict attention to any movement toward the outer edge of the shadow. I have used this technique to watch stripers working along a lit dock at night. The fish appear jet black against the charcoal gray surface of the water. They will be facing forward into the flow.

7

Reading the Weather

Weather is an integral part of coastal fishing. On an immediate level, it affects our comfort. When skies are bright and temperatures warm, we feel our best. Conversely, casting into a whistling wind or fishing in a cold, driving rain is hardly pleasant. This is about as far as some anglers ever make the connection between the weather and fishing, however. Many become essentially fair-weather fly fishermen, rarely venturing out unless the elements fully cooperate. What they fail to understand is that there is more than personal comfort involved in choosing the right weather.

Changes in the weather produce changes in the fish. Fish are wild creatures whose survival depends on their ability to adapt to environmental conditions. Therefore, they are very sensitive to their surroundings and are ready to react as required. Therefore, it is easy to see that changes in the weather must also produce changes in the quality of the fishing.

Over the years, I have found this to be very true. In fact, I am convinced that fish are able to react even before a change in the weather fully arrives. Fish feel alterations in barometric pressure, which are the precursors of shifts in the weather. The more suddenly the weather

Many times the worst weather holds the best fishing. Here anglers work the edge of a dropoff as a rainstorm approaches.

changes, the more dramatically the fish respond to it. Unfortunately, there is no guarantee that one kind of weather automatically creates good fishing. Still, there are trends that are extremely helpful in deciding when to wet a line.

HOW TO STAY IN TOUCH WITH WEATHER CONDITIONS

Before figuring in the weather, you have to know what it is going to do. Newspapers and television provide forecasts, but there is a better way. Electronics stores sell small, portable weather radios. These battery-operated radios are pretuned to stations that broadcast weather twenty-four hours a day. The better ones have good reception and feature up to three stations to choose from, so that you can travel the coast and still get the nearest and strongest signal. The reports come from the National Weather Bureau and include the all-important marine conditions such as wind strength and direction. Often local television and newspaper accounts do not touch on coastal conditions, particularly if you live inland. That in itself is enough to warrant the purchase price.

A supplement to radios and meteorologists is a keen sense of the signs Mother Nature herself provides. This is the way our ancestors did it, and it is still a valid method today. The reason it works is simple: The weather follows patterns. If you develop an awareness of those patterns, you can usually predict the outcome of a change in the clouds, a shift in the wind, or any one of numerous signs.

FRONTS

What meteorologists call *fronts* are responsible for the majority of the changes in the weather. Simply put, a front is a meeting of two air masses with dissimilar temperatures. The greater the difference in temperature between the air masses, the more intense the weather change will be. Over the coast, the results of a weather front are exaggerated by the existing temperature and humidity differences between land and sea. For that reason, the weather can alter more quickly and forcefully over the water than over the inland. Mariners are well aware of this fact, and wise ones keep one eye on the sky.

Cold Fronts

Of all the weather patterns an angler faces on the coast, none affects fishing more radically than a cold front. Cold fronts can travel in excess of 25 miles per hour, producing sudden changes in both the temperature and the fish. They can either shut the fishing totally down or rip it wide open, depending on time of year, water temperatures, and whether you fish just before and during the front's passage or wait until it has gone by.

In New England, cold fronts generally start with an increase in southerly winds, but as the front nears, the wind swings around and comes out of the north or northwest. This is a good clue to remember. Just before and during the passage of a cold front, the fishing can be red hot for a short time. It appears that the fish, sensing the falling barometric pressure, decide to do a bit of last-minute feeding.

After the front passes, the barometer rises and the weather stabilizes, but the fishing is not apt to be very good for a day or two. This is particularly true with cold fronts in the spring. The fish seem to drop away from the shoreline and sit deep where water temperatures are more stable. This also temporarily slows the progress of any fish migrating northward. Survival demands, however, that they return inshore to feed soon. Therefore, if the weather remains fixed, expect the fishing to pick up in a day or two.

Cold fronts that hit during the summer seem to produce less drastic results. By this time, most game fish have already reached their summer feeding grounds. And nearshore water temperatures are high enough that the fish can withstand a short cold spell. Still, I prefer to fish while the front is passing rather than immediately after it has moved through. In the summer, however, cold fronts are sometimes preceded by strong thunderstorms, so caution is necessary. A common indicator of this weather pattern is the towering cumulonimbus cloud often called a *thunderhead*.

Cold fronts in the fall are dynamite. They lower the water temperature, which, coupled with the shortened days, triggers the migration feeding frenzies that are legendary on the coast. In most southern New England locations, the critical moment comes when the surf temperature is pushed near or just below 60 degrees. Once things get cranked up, the fish tend to stay in high gear, blitzing beaches all along the coast until colder weather and the migration of important baitfish such as menhaden force them southward. So fishing in the fall will not drop off after the front passes, but instead remains good for a considerable time. You should make every effort to get to the coast during these periods no matter how gray and miserable the day may seem.

Northeasters
Northeasters are not just ordinary cold fronts, but strong coastal storms that occur in the late fall or early winter as cold air situated over the land moves southward and hits the still-warm waters of the Gulf Stream. Here the two opposing forces mix and create a powerful storm with winds from the northeast, giving these storms their name.

Scientists say that northeasters, like their summertime cousins hurricanes, are cyclones by definition. Hurricanes are briefer and more powerful weather events that tend to be focused on narrow sections of the coast. Northeasters, in contrast, can last for three days at a time and rock thousands of miles of seaboard with a single storm. Both types of storms can be responsible for severe coastal erosion and flooding.

Northeasters have the effect of pushing large amounts of colder offshore waters in to the coast, quickly lowering temperatures near shore. Even in warm years, when inshore waters are still very warm into the late fall, one big storm can cool things off practically overnight. This in turn triggers the southerly coastal migration of blues, bass, bonito, and little tunny, as well as baitfish such as menhaden and mullet.

If the fall migration down the coast is not already under way and a northeaster hits the coast, get out there with your fly rod. I realize that many readers will straighten up in their seats at this suggestion. Fly-fish in a cyclone? You gotta be kidding. The fact is that the best fishing of your life may be about to happen, not only for numbers of fish, but for true trophy fish as well.

Although I am telling you to cast a fly into the wind, I am not suggesting that you throw all caution with it. High surf and rolling seas are no time for carelessness on the beach, on a jetty, or in a boat. So a healthy dash of common sense is required to judge the conditions. Northeasters come in various strengths, from a class one, or a weak storm, to a class five, which is extremely powerful. History shows that half the northeasters are of the weak variety and fully three-quarters of them are weak to moderate. The weaker storms make it easier to fish, but they last on average only about half a day. The stronger storms will hang in for several days and give anglers a chance to respond.

Since the winds are likely very strong, it is best to pick a location with the wind coming at your back, or at least not opposing your casting arm. In many cases, the fish will be within two dozen feet of the water's edge. And I have seen fish in the teens and up swirling within 5 feet of the shoreline. So if you can launch even a short cast, you could be all set. Tidal inlets, rips, and points of land are the prime spots to consider. Remember to use extreme caution.

If the storm has been under way for a time, water conditions will likely be poor, making fishing difficult. Make a quick call to a shoreline tackle shop for information about present coastal conditions before you head out. But do not tell them you are fly fishing! Many shops unfamiliar with saltwater fly fishing's potential will automatically tell you that it is too rough for such equipment.

Warm Fronts

When a cooler mass of air is being shoved out by a warmer air mass, this creates a warm front. Warm fronts tend to arrive slowly and hence do not produce the strong winds or rapid changes in barometric pressure commonly associated with cold fronts. Nevertheless, a warm front can affect the quality of fishing you encounter on the coast.

Warm fronts often start with winds from the east. The clouds are cirrus or cirrostratus, which is to say high, wispy, and transparent. As the front nears, these clouds fill the sky, gradually getting lower to the ground. There is a good chance for rain until the actual front moves through and the barometric pressure starts to rise. A warm front that arrives in early spring is likely to help the fishing. With marginal water temperatures, the increased air temperatures will accelerate the warming of the water and thereby improve your chances in two ways: Warmer water makes fish feed more actively and stirs the northerly advance of migrating fish. Warm fronts in summer are a mixed blessing. If the front becomes stationary, it can have a stagnating effect on both the fish and the fisherman. These are the "dog days." Fish tend to drop away from shore and seek the cool water found in deeper quarters. Often there is little fishing action until very late at night as darkness slowly lowers the heat of the day. On the positive side, warm fronts often provide cloud cover. This encourages some fish to feed nearer to the surface during the daytime.

A summer with a greater than average amount of warm fronts creates some long-range benefits for the angler. The inshore waters will be warmer than normal, which means that they will take longer to cool in the fall. That promises to extend the season, perhaps even by several weeks. The warm water also increases the spawning ability of some bait-fish, and the more bait you have, the more game fish are apt to show up.

CLOUDS AND FOG

Without a doubt, cloud cover and fog can improve your fishing. Both reduce light on the water, encouraging fish to stay longer in the shallows and feed nearer to the surface, where fly fishing is most effective. Here is an example. At dawn, the action generally is hot until the first rays of sunlight strike the morning surf. Then, as if someone has flipped a switch, the fishing can shut off. Morning clouds or fog, however, can delay the sun's first appearance. This is called a *high dawn* and often allows the fishing action to last considerably longer into the morning.

Under cloud cover or fog, not only do fish seem to hit surface flies such as sliders and poppers more often, but they do so with fewer misses. In short, you hook up better. Likely it is easier for the fish to look up into a subdued sky than a bright one, and the fly is better outlined. A cloudy or foggy day is therefore a better day to fish than when the sun shines. Save those bright days for lounging around or getting a tan on the beach.

Another benefit of clouds has to do with your ability to read the water. Bright, sunny days make it difficult to look at the sea because of the strong glare. On dark days, on the other hand, it is much easier to see and identify those subtle changes in the surface of the water that

Dave Foley holds proof that fog or overcast skies can improve the fishing.

help anglers find fish. Small rip lines, swirls, and even jumping baitfish fleeing a predator can be picked up more readily when the surface of the water is dull.

LIGHTNING STORMS

Though your chances of being hit by lightning are extremely low, lightning deserves your utmost respect. Lightning kills more than one hundred people a year in this country, a high percentage of them either near or on open water. Clearly coastal fly fishing is a sport that exposes an individual to such situations. The majority of lightning storms happen during the summer months, and New England gets about two dozen a year.

If the present weather affords you good visibility, you will be able to see a storm coming on the horizon. But on a hot, hazy day or wherever visibility is poor, a storm could come upon you without much warning. These storms are frequently caused by cold fronts that can move over 25 miles per hour. Portable weather radios are a good way to find out about approaching thunderstorms.

If you see lightning approaching, get out of the water immediately. Next, break down your rod (I do not know how good a conductor a graphite rod is, but I do not want to find out the hard way) and get back from the water. If you are on a jetty, retreat to solid ground. Getting indoors is the best idea, but short of that, your car with its rubber tires is a fine alternative. If you are a long way from your car or any building, seek low ground inland away from the water. Never just stand on a wide open beach. You will be a very inviting target. And never stand near metal objects such as navigation markers or high-masted boats, or handle metal objects like rod tubes or fly reels.

Those individuals who have been hit and survived or had lightning strike very near them report that just before the lightning bolt struck they felt a strong tingling sensation. Often their hair stood on end. If this happens, you must act immediately. Drop down into a squatting position, and place your hands over your head. This position will help diffuse the charge of the bolt and increase your chances of survival.

WIND

The ocean is home to the wind. And the presence of wind has played a crucial role in how man and sea have interacted over the centuries. Over the land, winds are forced against the changing terrain, which shapes their speed and course. But winds at sea face no mountains or valleys, instead blowing free and wild over its vast open reaches.

During most of the fishing season, the prevailing wind in the Northeast is from the southwest, and its usual strength is between 5 and 15 knots. This wind pattern starts around April and continues throughout the summer months. The only dramatic variations are associated with the passage of weather fronts. In late October, the wind begins to shift to the north and strengthen.

Sea Breezes

There is a daily rhythm to the breezes along the coast. These patterns of air movement are weaker than the conditions imposed by weather fronts and therefore are easily overridden by them. Still, these breezes are common along the shore and figure into the fishing picture. Like so many coastal weather events, sea breezes are the result of the differences in the way the land and sea are able to absorb the heat of the daytime sun. Being in tune with the pattern of these breezes helps fly rodders anticipate the conditions they must fish in.

During the day, the land warms rapidly—far faster than the sea. As the hot air rises above the land, cooler air off the water is drawn inland to replace it. The net result is an onshore movement of air called a *sea breeze.* Anyone who has driven to the coast on a very hot day has felt these cooling winds as they neared the water. Naturally, fly casting from the shore is made a bit more difficult by a sea breeze, while those casting toward the shoreline from a boat find conditions ideal.

As the sun sets, the coastal breezes often die down. This gives fly rodders a period of calm in which to cast their wares. Those who like to cast large saltwater poppers at this time of day find it made easier by the still air. As night takes over, the land cools faster than the sea. Now the breezes reverse themselves, with a gentle offshore breeze coming from the land. Shore-based fly rodders now find the wind at their backs as they fish under the stars.

The Wind and the Tide

Wind can have a real effect on the coming and going of the sea. It can alter both the time of the tide and its strength. If the compass direction of the wind is similar to that of the tide, the wind helps the tide on its way. For example, if a flooding tide moves from east to west and a strong wind is accompanying it, the wind prolongs the duration of the tide, forcing additional waters in toward the beach. Therefore, the tide crests later than scheduled, and the water level is considerably higher than expected.

As a general rule, in New England, winds from the east or south that occur during the time of incoming tide have this effect, and winds from the north or west during an ebbing tide do the same. The amount of change depends on both the strength of the wind and how closely its direction matches the direction of the tide.

Winds moving against the tide have the opposite effect. They reduce the movement of the water and shorten the tide's duration. Expect the tide to finish earlier than scheduled and the tidal range to be less. In New England waters, commonly winds from the north or west can be expected to do this during the flood, whereas winds from the south or east will oppose a dropping tide.

How much can this phenomenon affect your fishing? In certain circumstances, plenty. Let me give you a case in point. One night, I headed out to fish a rip, planning to get there at the crest of high tide and fish the first part of the drop. These are the best hours here, as the rip is so shallow. By the middle of the ebb, the fish are largely gone. When I arrived, the ebb was already under way and the water level was extremely low. A strong daylong wind from the southwest had stalled the flooding tide, forcing it to crest early and reducing the tidal range.

That same wind was now also speeding up the ebb tide. And I was out of luck.

Wind and Weed

Prolonged days of onshore wind can drive tremendous amounts of seaweed in to shore. This is particularly noticeable along rocky shores, as they have more vegetation on the bottom. A quick walk down to the water's edge will generally reveal just how bad the situation is. If you want to fish in the stuff, try using a weedless fly. If you do not have a weedless fly, try leaving one knot in the butt section of the leader untrimmed. Weeds slipping down the fly line will now tend to get caught on the upper part of the leader rather than traveling down to the fly.

The worse type of weed I have come across is what anglers call "mung." It is a soft, reddish clump that accumulates during the warmer months. Where this weed is thick, it produces a wide, reddish brown band in the water next to the shore. You can also see it suspended in each wave. On every cast, the mung clings to your line, the fly, and even the guides on the rod as you retrieve. Your only course is to leave until the wind and tide are able to pull the stuff off the beach.

8

Matching the Marine: Baitfish and Beyond

For fly fishermen who love trout, mayflies and caddis have long been magic words. It is something that nonanglers will never understand. Why could anyone be that interested in bugs? It is not that the mayflies or caddis are in themselves so terribly fascinating; rather, it is their integral part in one of nature's cycles. To witness a hatch and see the insects riding the currents as trout rise is to be in the presence of one of the complex workings of nature. And to have and cast the right fly allows us to actively enter and take part in this complex elemental scheme.

In salt water, the names are different, but not the feeling. On the coast, new magic words ring in the ears of fly fishermen and conjure similar images of nature's eternal order. Here the mayfly and the caddis give way to coastal forage fish such as sand eels and silversides. These small baitfish are critical cogs around which our coastal fly fishing revolves. And nonanglers will never understand.

There is also a more practical twist to this fascination with the food chain. Every experienced angler realizes that there is a direct connection between knowing what fish eat and success in catching them. Spend a day on the water with a skilled bait fisherman and you will come away convinced. Fly rodders, of course, are keenly aware of this relationship too. Before selecting a fly, expert trout anglers often turn over stones in a stream to see what food is available.

In the salt, the connection between forage and fishing goes far beyond just choosing the right fly. The type, size, and abundance of baitfish along any stretch of shoreline determine to a great extent the character of the fishing you will encounter. Where big schools of forage fish congregate expect high numbers of predators, too. If the baitfish are both numerous and large, your chances of hooking a big fish greatly increase. Conversely, where baitfish are scarce and small, the fishing may be poor. Therefore, an understanding of local baitfish, including where and when they are apt to appear, is a significant part of angling success.

A fairly comprehensive list of common coastal baitfish would include silversides, sand eels, bay anchovy, sticklebacks, butterfish, mummichogs, mullet, and Atlantic mackerel, as well as members of the herring family: Atlantic herring, blueback herring, alewives, and menhaden. Now that is quite a few fish to pattern flies after, and to date we do not have a wealth of specific flies to do so, although I expect it to happen before long. One problem confronting coastal tiers is that a number of these baitfish as adults are as big as the largest trout in many streams. Members of the herring family can reach a foot or more in length. Obviously, making a fly to match that could still be cast would be difficult. One solution is to focus on the immature stages of these larger baitfish. For example, a herring in the first summer of life would likely be under 4 inches overall and is a bait greedily sought after by hungry game fish. At that size, it is easily matched with a fly.

Of the baitfish mentioned above, a few stand out as extremely important for coastal fly rodders to understand, not only because they are fed upon by many fish anglers seek to catch, but also because of their extensive range and frequent abundance. These are the silversides, the sand eels, and several members of the herring family.

A meaningful understanding of these forage fish is more than a simple awareness of their existence. Consider this: Any self-respecting trout fly fisherman not only can identify the mayflies most common to the area, but also knows when and where to expect them. In salt water, a veteran coastal fly rodder knows what baitfish to expect and when and where to expect them. Only then can an angler hope to be consistently successful.

The silverside is one of the most important baitfish on the coast.

THE ATLANTIC SILVERSIDE

In the shallow waters of the Atlantic from the chilly reaches of Prince Edward Sound to the ever-warm Florida shores, the silverside *(Menidia menidia)* is an ecologically important baitfish. It spends the majority of its life tight to the coastline or swimming the rich tidal estuaries that adjoin them. Here, where land meets sea, the silverside is one of the most numerous inhabitants. Given that abundance, you can bet that it has a prominent place on the menu of many fine game fish. And all coastal fly rodders would do well to be informed.

In shape and appearance, the Atlantic silverside, sometimes called spearing or sperling, is not unlike the common freshwater shiner. Its maximum length is about 6 inches, and it is often found in smaller sizes of 2 to 3 inches, making it one of several coastal baitfish that are easy to imitate with a fly. The coloration is pale and somewhat translucent, with a faint tint of olive green along the back. As its name implies, a single prominent bright band of silver runs down each side. Overall, the silverside has a robust appearance, being fuller and thicker than a sand eel, for instance. The two dorsal fins are separate and occupy only a small percentage of the entire back (another difference between it and the sand eel). Its mouth is upturned and extends back to reach the midline of the eye. The eye is large and the tail is forked, proving the silverside a sight feeder and a powerful swimmer.

Silversides can spawn from March through August, water temperature being an important determinant. Although some spawning may take place in waters below 60 degrees, 60 seems to be a reliable minimum. Water closer to 68 degrees is optimum. In the northern end of its range, silverside spawning starts around June; farther south, spawning can be under way two or three months earlier.

The spawning occurs in tidal estuaries and happens at dawn on high tides, especially those of the new and full moons. If you would like to see this event, be aware that silversides use only the intertidal zone (the area between high- and low-tide marks) for reproduction and like marshy areas with cordgrass. The exact location can often be pinned down by looking for active terns, cormorants, and gulls. Silversides can spawn many times in one season. Therefore, warmer than normal years will likely trigger larger year classes by enabling the spawning to get an early start.

There are several ways in which silversides generate action for the coastal fly rodder. The most obvious way is simply by attracting fish like striped bass to certain areas of the shoreline where this baitfish is concentrated. Anglers often can see a lot of action by working a fly during the actual spawn. Striped bass and bluefish shadow these events, and your best bet is probably a high tide that crests shortly after daybreak. Under lower light, the bigger fish are much more likely to cruise into shallow waters. I suggest you cover the area just offshore of the spawning with a good silverside imitation.

In the two most common scenarios, which occur across the season, large schools of silversides are attacked in a classic blitz during the day, or small pods of silversides are pinned against the shoreline and picked off one by one at night. Both are excellent opportunities to work a fly, although they call for different strategies.

When the sun is up, silversides form schools, often swimming within a few feet of the water line. They cruise salt marshes and the adjacent coastal waters, feeding on copepods, shrimp, crab larvae, and other fish. Two of the best places to find them are around the mouths of estuaries and near points of land on a moving tide. These places generally have currents associated with them, which funnel nutrients to these hungry baitfish.

These currents or rips are also ideal spots for game fish like stripers, bluefish, and bonito to set ambushes. As a general rule, anglers look for this type of activity on the second, third, and fourth hours of the dropping tide or the first two hours of the incoming. The game fish attack the school of bait by first schooling themselves. For example, a gang of bluefish will first attempt to herd the bait. Some will swim underneath the silversides and push them up against the surface, while other bluefish push the school of bait laterally into a strong current. There the bluefish's powerful swimming ability will give them a firm advantage. Then, when the moment is right, a few blues will rocket up through the bait, disorienting the silversides and fracturing their formation. When the action gets really hot, the surface commotion will give the location away. The trick is to get there quickly and place your fly immediately upcurrent of the scene. Allow the flow to swing your silverside fly back into the mayhem, and be ready for an instant strike.

Since silversides are strong swimmers, you can use a moderately fast retrieve to imitate them. The only exception is at night, when silversides tend to move very slowly. A slow or medium-speed sinking line, such as a weight-forward intermediate, often is the best bet. It will get the fly down a bit. Predators like to key on strays that have been separated from the baitfish's main school, so a fly moving underneath or just to the side of the school will get quicker attention than a fly moving through the middle or over the top.

As good as these daylight blitzes are, they also have some drawbacks. First, they are often short-lived, providing only limited fishing, and are notoriously unpredictable. Furthermore, your fly has to compete with potentially thousands of naturals. Anyone who has fished a size 24 Trico in the midst of a thick hatch knows that this can lead to frustration. For these and other reasons, fishing at night is more productive.

As light levels fall, silversides no longer have the necessary visual contact with one another to continue their schooling strategy. Therefore, as evening descends, they split up into small pods containing as few as a handful of fish and spread out along the beach. Once split up, they seem to alternate their time between resting and slowly cruising near the surface, feeding on plankton. Striped bass and bluefish will also break up into small groups and be actively on the prowl. They are on high alert for the least bit of movement that might signal a lone baitfish. If your fly is within reach of their acute senses, they will come after it.

On a productive beach, this type of fly fishing can provide hours of steady action and often some of the biggest fish you are apt to catch during any season.

The best fly for night purposes is generally one that stays near the surface and pushes a small wake. Size and silhouette are important, and the best color is black. Both striped bass and bluefish have excellent overhead vision and are highly alert to things passing across the surface. My favorite fly for this type of fishing is a slider. It stays in the surface film and pushes a gentle wake that imitates a cruising silverside extremely well. Whatever you use, try a slow, steady retrieve. And remember that many times at night, even very big fish will pick up the fly as lightly as a trout sucking in a nymph. It is only when you set the hook that all hell breaks loose.

THE SAND EEL

The presence of sand eels is always a hopeful sign to the fly rodders of the North Atlantic coast. Many fine game fish love to devour these little creatures and are never far away. And sand eels are easy to match with a fly. Unlike some of the other baitfish, sand eels are small, slender, and narrow. Their basic body shape and size are perfectly suited to a dressed hook. Many of the first stripers I caught on a fly were a direct result of

Sand eels are fed upon by a great many game fish and are easy to match with a fly.

the presence of these small baitfish, and I have loved them for it ever since.

Sand eels, also known as sand launces or sand lances, are not eels at all. Rather, they are fish whose elongated shape and long dorsal and anal fins give them an eel-like appearance. There are two species in the salt waters of New England: *Ammodytes americanus* and *Ammodytes dubius*. Both are extremely valuable members of our marine ecosystem, a rich food source for both larger fish and birds. *A. dubius* is strictly an offshore species and as such is of only passing interest to the fly rodder. *A. Americanus,* on the other hand, is a common resident of our estuaries and coastline, as well as deeper waters of the continental shelf.

A sand eel is a slim, attractive fish. The head is slightly long for the body, with a pointed snout and large eyes. The back is dark, varying from olive to brown to bluish green. In contrast, its flanks are bright silver with a beautiful iridescent sheen, and the belly is white. The dorsal and anal fins are long and run nearly the entire length of the body, stopping just short of the tail.

A. Americanus spawns widely over the North Atlantic, covering thousands of miles from Cape Hatteras to the Canadian Maritime Provinces. Offshore they reach a maximum length of 9 inches, but inshore, where anglers most often encounter them, they are only occasionally greater than 6 inches, and more commonly 4 inches or less. Locality plays a role too. In Long Island Sound, a short fly of 2 to 3 inches is appropriate. Studies have failed to find sand eels greater than three years of age in these waters. In fact, fully three-quarters of the population is one year or younger. Apparently the Sound is rarely conducive to older adults.

Farther north, from the open coast of Cape Cod, on up to Maine, the sand eels reach six years of age. Consequently, they are on average larger by about a full inch. Anglers in these waters would be wise to carry patterns at least 4 inches in length, and 5- or 6-inch flies are not out of the question. At any location along the coast, the time of year and the severity of the previous winter affect the size of the sand eels. In the spring, schools may be largely small young-of-the-year. If the winter has been very cold, these juveniles will be even tinier than normal, hardly bigger than a toothpick. By late summer, the general population of sand eels in all locations has grown and will be larger than in the spring.

Sand eels prefer to travel in large schools. Primarily plankton feeders, they spend much of their time relatively high in the water column. Research does show some deep bottom feeding for small snails and small clams, but this probably takes place at times when plankton is scarce. Sand eels likely are sight feeders, and they dine mainly during the light of day. As evening approaches, schools will bury themselves in the sand, often very near the water's edge. This is a defense mechanism against night hunters, such as stripers and bluefish. Depending on the softness of the location, they will be from 1 to 6 inches down. Sand eels avoid rock bottoms, where they could not dig in on a moment's notice.

Once dug in for the night, sand eels for the most part will stay put. Still, you can always expect a few of them to come out and search for a late-night snack. This is especially so on very dark nights around the new moon, at which time plankton tends to surface in large numbers to take advantage of what little light there is near the top. Sand eels can then cruise slowly and gather a nice meal. Expect stripers to be on the lookout for these late-night wanderers and ready to pick them off. As the faintest glow of light begins in the eastern sky, the sand eels emerge from the sand and re-form their school for the day's feeding.

Spawning starts in the fall and peaks around December, ending by February. Sand eels can be prolific. Each female, depending on her size, can carry two thousand to fourteen thousand eggs. Hatching takes place from December right on through to March, ending just before the first plankton blooms of the year. Sand eels, like so many marine fish, go through periods of population boom and bust. These cycles are not fully understood. Generally, when Atlantic mackerel and herring are on the upswing, sand eels are down in number, and vice versa. There are many factors that might play a role in this process, including local water temperatures, predation, winter weather patterns, and variations in salinity.

When and Where to Find Sand Eels

Anglers should begin looking for activity around June in New England, although around the warm-water releases of shoreline power plants, sand eels may arrive earlier. Once sand eels are in an area, they will likely be around for the summer. Any estuary or river mouth or beach with a sandy bottom is a potential sand eel location. Short of actually seeing schools, there are a number of common tip-offs to be alert for. Terns diving hard along the shoreline at dawn or dusk is number one. If they seem to be catching something small and difficult to see, suspect sand eels. A flock of very noisy gulls digging at the immediate water's edge during a quickly retreating tide at sunrise or sunset is another possible sign. In this case, the sand eels have become stranded under the sand by a fast-moving tide. If the birds are able to get them, the sand eels are just below the surface of the wet sand. You can walk over and dig, and with a little luck you will find a handful of sand eels.

Specially designed rakes are made for the purpose of digging up sand eels. These rakes are commonly used by anglers seeking bait for striped bass. But fly rodders who fish from a boat may want to rake up a bucketload of sand eels too. Sand eels make excellent chum for any number of species, including bonito. If you do not care to dig up your own, tackle stores sell frozen sand eels by the bag.

On rare occasions, you may come across a situation involving sand eels that can lead to some fantastic fishing. When sand eel populations are heavy along a sandy beach, stripers will come in with a rising night tide and use their blunt snouts to dig for their supper. In shallow water about 2 feet deep, I have seen hundreds of stripers with their tails and backs out of the water, rooting like bonefish. At that time, you can wade over slowly, and every cast into their midst will get you a quick hookup. If the water is a bit deeper, you may not see tails breaking the surface, but swirls and dorsal fins often are still visible. These fish will not spook easily, and they will let you get very close. Even if you bump into one, it will just shoot forward a few yards and resume feeding.

In this situation, use a weighted fly. A Clouser Minnow or any sparsely dressed weighted fly of the right size should work. Remember that the bass have their heads down and are paying strict attention to the bottom directly in front of them as they dig. A fly that passes high overhead will go unnoticed. A fly bouncing on the bottom, or at least near the bottom, will be found and gobbled up rapidly.

Fishing with Sand Eel Flies

Once you are reasonably certain that sand eels are in a given location, the next step is to determine when the game fish will arrive. Atlantic bonito, little tunny, stripers, and bluefish all can be found at one time or another hunting down these schools of sand eels right in the middle of the day. Although it is nearly impossible to constantly predict when and where this action will take place, once you are on to it the fishing is very good.

At dawn, sand eels face another defenseless moment as they emerge from the bottom before forming a school. This is without a doubt the best time to cast a fly, although the action may be brief, lasting only thirty to forty-five minutes. Note that sand eels come up before the scheduled sunrise. Therefore it is extremely important that you arrive while the beach is still in total darkness. This allows you to get into position before things get rolling.

As the first faint glows of light emanate from the east, expect swirls to start as striped bass greet the emerging eels. Quickly move to the spot where the swirls are most numerous and begin casting. The number of feeding bass you encounter is directly related to the number of sand eels present. If the schools are small, you may see only a limited amount of action. When sand eels are very thick in a location, however, I have seen hundreds of stripers swirling, porpoising, and even jumping clear of the water. It is an experience you do not forget. Regardless of the number of bass present, expect the action to taper off quickly as the light level increases. By the time the sun is above the horizon, the bite is usually over.

It is not uncommon for sand eels to bed down in the same area for days, weeks, or even a month or two. When you are lucky enough to find such a location, you can expect fairly consistent fishing every dawn. Anglers who live near the water might be able to catch a few fish, head home for breakfast, and never miss a day of work. Record such a place in your fishing log book because sand eels can return to the same beach or general vicinity for several seasons in a row.

Night fishing, especially during the warmer months, can be productive too, as striped bass and bluefish patrol areas looking for stray sand eels. Frequently, these late-night eels will be found cruising near the surface, and a slow-moving fly on top is deadly. Do not expect a striper or blue to wallop the fraud. Instead, at night they might just slowly overtake it and continue swimming straight toward you. You must be alert to a modest change in resistance in the fly line. Keep the rod tip down and as much slack out of the line as possible. If, however, there is a fair current working along the beach, things will be different. Here the fly will swing with the flow, and generally any predator will tend to hit the fly much harder.

When sand eels bed down on a tidal flat, a high tide at dusk can lead to excellent fishing late at night, during the ebb. At sundown many of these slender baitfish will have buried themselves far up on the flat in places that are fully exposed during low tide. Late at night, some of these sand eels sense the falling water levels and, not wanting to be stranded, come up and move to deeper water. The bass will be ready for them. As the tide turns and floods back over exposed parts of the flat, sand eels that were stranded by the ebb have another opportunity to relocate. Here again, expect stripers to be on the alert.

THE HERRING FAMILY

Compared to silversides and sand eels, herring (family Clupeidae) might be thought of as giants of the baitfish world, often reaching well in excess of a foot in length. Though their size does make matching adult herring with a fly difficult to do, it also gives herring the power to entice the very largest striped bass and bluefish. The trade-off is a fair one. What it means is that when and where herring are found in number, fly-fishing opportunities for big fish exist.

The two largest members of the family, American shad and the hickory shad, are actually game fish in their own right. Although striped bass and bluefish do feed on these fish, especially the juveniles, they are not usually a significant part of their diet. Four other members of the family are more important for anglers to be aware of: the alewife, the blueback herring, the Atlantic herring, and the menhaden. All of them are big, silvery fish that annually make an important contribution to the coastal forage base.

The alewife and the blueback are nearly identical. Both are about

A group of herring ranging in size from near full-grown to juvenile.

10 inches as adults, although they can grow upward of 15 inches. Even at these lengths, however, like all herring, they are thin in cross section. Both have deeply forked tails, greenish to blue-green backs, and a single dorsal fin positioned halfway down the back between head and tail. They both have a single black spot high on the body immediately behind the gill plate. This distinguishes them from the Atlantic herring, which does not have such a spot. The ventral fin is directly below the dorsal fin and looks odd at this midpoint on the body. The scales are large and shiny, and these fish lack a lateral line. These two are closely related to the American shad and look very similar, although smaller in size.

The alewife *(Alosa pseudoharengus),* or buckie, as it is sometimes called, ranges from Nova Scotia to North or South Carolina. This bait-fish tolerates fresh water very well and can exist in totally landlocked situations. On the coast, it ascends tidal rivers and streams a considerable distance in early spring to reach ponds and upstream coves where spawning takes place. Alewives do not need much in the way of an estuary and run up things as small as a brook. In southern New England the run starts in April, but farther north it begins later, going into May and June.

Stripers love to follow these alewife runs up the coastal rivers. So closely are these two fish tied that in a good many locations the first appearance of striper bass each year pretty much coincides with the arrival of alewives. There are locations, however, where the run takes place before migratory stocks of bass reach that part of the coast. Where stripers and alewives do meet, fly rodders should know which streams and rivers host the best runs. This is an important bit of angling information.

The blueback herring *(Alosa aestivalis),* also called the glut herring or blackback, has a more southerly range, from northern Florida to southern New England, occasionally reaching into the Gulf of Maine. They usually appear about a month after the alewife run begins, and they do not ascend estuaries as far inland. In Connecticut, it is not only stripers that get to cash in on this herring; by then the first bluefish of the year have also arrived in time to dine.

Before entering an estuary, alewives and bluebacks first stage in large numbers near the mouth. The most likely time for them to start upstream is near high tide, when current direction and water level are most advantageous. It also makes sense for the herring to move at night rather than in daylight when predators can see them. Therefore, look for the strongest part of the run to begin on a high tide that occurs after dark, especially around the new and full moons.

Both alewives and bluebacks seem quite sensitive to light. During the day, expect them to stay deep, whereas under the stars, they rise to the surface and move closer to shore. In part this may be a defensive tactic, but along the open coast it is also an attempt to follow the movements up and down of their main food source, plankton.

Herring move upstream in schools. In a large estuary, they frequently stage a second time in the mouth of a tributary or cove where spawning will take place. Here the herring wait for water conditions to be right before traveling on. These staging points hold the best fishing. Striped bass shadow the herring schools, and the action can go on for weeks in some locations. Generally it is somewhat tide-dependent, and you must learn which part of the tide produces your best chances. A sinking fly line and a large white streamer are the right rig in most of these situations.

Later in the year, the young-of-the-year descend the coastal estuaries of their birth and head out to sea. This migration of juveniles produces fishing opportunities, but rarely as concentrated or as predictable as during the initial influx of spawning adults. These young herring are commonly as large as 6 to 8 inches in length. Along the Connecticut and Rhode Island shores, they can be found near the mouths of estuaries from midsummer to early November. If they exit to sea late in the year, their presence is responsible for some of the last major blitzes of the season.

The Atlantic herring (Clupea harengus harengus), which is considered the most economically important food fish in the world, is longer and more slender than either the blueback or the alewife. It is a northern fish, common in the Gulf of Maine but not south of New Jersey. It averages about a foot long and has a deeply forked tail, a blue-green back, and silvery flanks. The Atlantic herring lacks the single dark spot of the two river herrings. This fish is mainly found in open waters, more so than the alewives and bluebacks. They do approach shore, however, often congregating in bays and river mouths. The exact timing of these events varies widely. I have never seen them in Long Island Sound before late October, by which time the fishing season is almost over. But farther north, spring, summer, and even fall spawning runs are possible. In Maine, the young-of-the-year enter the coastal rivers in the spring and are responsible for drawing great crowds of hungry striped bass.

The Atlantic menhaden *(Brevoortia tyrannus),* often referred to as the bunker or pogy, populates the coast all the way from Nova Scotia to southeastern Florida. This fish is, on average, longer than the alewife or blueback and noticeably heavier set. Its tail is deeply forked, its back greenish blue, and its flanks silvery, often with a coppery sheen. Like the alewife and the blueback, the menhaden has a black spot high and just behind its gill plate; unlike the others, however, it usually sports numerous other smaller spots along the midsection.

Many Atlantic menhaden winter over offshore of the Carolinas. As the winter subsides, the menhaden begin migrating northward along the coast, arriving in southern New England waters as early as April. By summer, they have spread all along the coast to the north and are a common sight in bays, harbors, and estuaries, often feeding in vast numbers. Here they stay until the urge to head south strikes in late fall. To some degree, it is their long inshore residency that makes menhaden such an easy target for game fish.

Big stripers and big bluefish go nuts for these oily creatures, making live or even dead menhaden the preferred bait of many saltwater anglers. When bass and bluefish are locked on adult menhaden, or for that matter any big herring, conventional-size flies often prove worthless. They simply do not have the length needed to make a convincing fraud. Therefore, experienced fly rodders resort to large poppers, sliders, and streamers measuring at least 5 inches long.

Note that chopped or ground-up menhaden makes possibly the best chum on earth, calling every hungry predator for miles around. Boat anglers can hang a mesh bag containing the chum over the transom, allowing the natural rocking action of the boat to stir the contents. They can also ladle the chum overboard from a pail. As with all forms of chumming, some current is necessary to broadcast the scent over a sufficient area.

Menhaden oil is available in squeeze bottles from some tackle stores. It is convenient to carry, and very powerful. A few drops over the side of the boat create a wide slick on the surface of the water. Unlike ground or chopped chum, which actually supply the fish with something to eat, the oil offers just the smell of food. Therefore fish cannot possibly get overfed while seeking the source of the chum. Fly fishermen on shore can use the oil in a rip or inlet, but only when they are out of the water. You do not want to be in the middle of a bunch of hungry bluefish with the smell of menhaden on your waders. Anglers can also apply a tiny drop of menhaden oil directly onto a fly.

Immature Menhaden: A Fall Bonanza

Menhaden are spawning someplace during almost every month of the year. In New England, it happens mainly offshore during the summer. Slowly the larvae are pushed back in toward the coast by the waves and wind. The young-of-the-year start showing up along the shore from Massachusetts to Connecticut in mid-August as 1½-inch-long silvery baitfish. Often they hang around coastal estuaries and their adjoining beaches in thick schools. These schools look very dark from above because the tightly packed formations reveal only their backs. If you watch a school long enough, however, individual fish will twist and turn, producing silver flashes. By late fall, these baby menhaden, or bunker, will be 3 to 5 inches long.

These schools of immature herring make an immense forage base for game fish. If you can find the baby bunker, you generally will have found the predators too. Gulls and cormorants also follow the schools and frequently reveal a school's position to the observant angler. For that reason, in the fall I pay special attention to places where cormorants

Young-of-the-year menhaden cruise very close to shore and provoke game fish into wild feeding frenzies.

congregate and scan the horizon for packs of gulls sitting idly on the water. Often they are sitting over the herring, waiting for game fish to attack so that they can get their share.

Baby bunker are relatively easy to imitate in length with a fly. Capturing the wide silhouette of this forage fish is another matter, however. In terms of coloration, any fly to match should have an electric blue topping and a good deal of flash to both sides. Some patterns have been developed specifically for matching this baitfish. The very first one I ever heard of was made by Joe D'Allesandro of Bridgeport, Connecticut. Today we have a number of other flies.

OTHER COMMON BAITFISH

Though the above varieties of baitfish make a large contribution to the forage base along the coast, there are numerous other baitfish to be found. To examine all of them would be outside the scope of this book, however; among the more common ones are American eels, mummichogs, bay anchovies, and butterfish.

American Eels

Ask a serious bait fisherman to name the best two things to use for trophy bass, and likely one of them will be an eel. No doubt about it, eels are something big bass, and for that matter blues, go nuts for. So it is little wonder that many a fly tier has sat down at the vise trying to create something long and slinky.

The eel in question is not the marine conger eel, but its smaller freshwater cousin the American eel *(Anguilla rostrata)*. This eel is common along the entire Atlantic coast in both fresh and brackish water. It is a nocturnal fish and is not commonly seen during the day. An average adult is about 2 to 3 feet in length, too long to actually mimic with a fly. Small adults, however, especially in estuaries, range down to a foot, and immature eels can be found less than half that length. In general, coloration is yellowish to greenish brown, but eels are able to change their body color to match their surroundings. Therefore, over mud bottoms they are quite dark, and over sand, much lighter.

The American eel is catadromous, making a long journey each autumn from its freshwater home to spawn in the salt waters of the Sargasso Seas southeast of Bermuda. As the mature eels head downstream on their migration, their coloration become more silvery. In the lower estuaries, they wait for the best conditions to exit to sea, usually leaving at night under a dark moon. Larval eels make an even more remarkable yearlong journey, swimming all the way back to the coast from the open ocean. Arriving in early spring, they enter our coastal rivers in large schools under the cover of darkness.

As they near land, the larvae are transparent and are referred to as glass eels. Upon reaching brackish water, they take on a dark to black pigmentation. At this point, they are called elvers and measure about 2 to 3 inches in length, easy to match with a fly. Some of them will ascend rivers a great distance inland; others choose a home in an estuary, brackish bay, or harbor.

Mummichogs

Mummichogs *(Fundulus heteroclitus)* are small, dark minnows that live very tight to shore in protected waters. You'll find them in salt ponds, harbors, and estuaries. They are extremely rugged, able to exist in salt, brackish, and even fresh water. Not only are they common residents of our nearshore waters, mummichogs are found from the Gulf of Saint Lawrence to the Gulf of Mexico. Other names for this fish in New England are killifish, mummichubs, and simply mummies. The striped mummichog *(Fundulus majalis)* is closely related and very similar in appearance. For the purposes of this discussion, they will be considered as one and the same.

Mummichogs are numerous in salt ponds, marshes, and brackish water areas.

Mummichogs reach a maximum size of about 6 inches but are more commonly found in the 2- to 3-inch range. They are thick, robust little fish, with a much sturdier-looking body than either a silverside or a sand eel. A 4-inch specimen would likely stand 1 inch from belly to back. Striped mummichogs are a bit more slender. Their hardiness is legendary, allowing them to survive in warm and even polluted water with little oxygen. This toughness makes them a favorite of many anglers, who use them as live bait.

The coloration of mummichogs differs considerably between males and females and changes with the time of year. Overall, they tend to be noticeably darker than silversides or sand eels. The back is often a deep olive green to dark brown or even black. The flanks are paler and usually have a distinct series of vertical bands or stripes. The belly of the fish is much lighter, ranging from white to yellow or even orange.

Bay Anchovies

Bay anchovies *(Anchoa mitchilli)* are the smallest of all the forage fish considered here, but their size in no way reflects their importance. What they lack in length, they more than make up for in sheer numbers. Whereas silversides may congregate in groups as small as four or five, anchovies are usually found in schools of several hundred to several

The bay anchovy is perhaps the most abundant baitfish on the entire coast.

thousand. For that reason, these tiny fish are a major part of the food chain. In some locations, they are the primary invertebrate eaten by striped bass, especially late in the season.

Unlike sand eels, silversides, and herring, bay anchovies are not found throughout New England. Instead, they prefer the waters from Cape Cod southward to Florida, avoiding the chilly waters of the Gulf of Maine.

The bay anchovies I have seen near shore are generally only 1 to 1½ inches long and ¼ inch high. Likely these are juveniles that will grow up to greater size later in life after they move offshore. Reference books on marine life report that bay anchovies are 3 inches in length and silvery. Yet the anchovies I find are much smaller and translucent with a pale yellowish brown tinge. The difference, I believe, is that the anchovies I see are juveniles and therefore are not full grown and lack complete pigmentation.

The anchovy's stomach, which is low and forward of center, contrasts with the rest of the body and is a silver-white ball. The head, from the gill plate forward, can also have a silver sheen. There is a thin, faint, broken midline running from head to tail. Along the back and belly, there are numerous tiny dark dots that extend out onto the fins. In overall appearance, the bay anchovy could be mistaken for a young-of-the-year silverside. The shape and position of the anchovy's mouth is a good clue. It is wide and underslung, extending well back of the eye. The silverside has a much smaller mouth that is far forward of the eye. Also, anchovies have one dorsal fin, silversides two.

Here in the Northeast, the importance of bay anchovies for fly fishermen comes mainly in a short time window each fall. At that time of year, bay anchovies form tightly packed schools with millions of members. This happens around the middle of September in southern New England. The schools start out tight to shore, particularly over sand bottoms. Look for them in bays and the lower ends of estuaries. These fish slowly move out to sea and by early October they are well away from shore over reefs and rips.

Anchovy schools are so dense that they color the water. Nearshore small schools appear as tan clouds, but large schools in deeper water can actually make the water appear reddish brown. Bluefish, bonito, little tunny, and stripers devour these tiny guys. Because anchovies are not powerful swimmers, game fish have little trouble catching them. That makes them doubly attractive to predators. Once a school of anchovies is pinned against the beach, striped bass seem to just wallow in them, sucking in huge mouthfuls.

Now the bad news. Fish feeding on bay anchovies can be frustratingly hard to hook. Not only are they selective to fly size, but given the numbers of naturals in the water, even the most realistic fly can go totally ignored. Therefore, in most situations it is imperative that you get your fly under the bait, where predators can see it separated from the school. Simply casting into the school is largely a waste of time. Stay cool.

Butterfish

Atlantic butterfish *(Poronotus triacanthus)* are a schooling baitfish found from Florida to Newfoundland. Within that range, they are most plentiful from North Carolina to Cape Cod. Here, they frequently exhibit a seasonal migration, moving inshore and northward in late spring or early summer. In Rhode Island, for example, adult butterfish appear close to the coast in early May, while it will be mid-May or early June before they do so in the waters of southern Massachusetts. Come late fall, butterfish return offshore for the winter. This cycle from shallow to deep water exposes butterfish to a long list of predators, from bluefish to swordfish.

Butterfish are thin, oval-shaped, and about half as tall from belly to back as they are long. They have a small mouth, which does not extend back under the eye. Their dorsal and anal fins are long, extending all the way back to the tail, which is deeply forked. Adult butterfish reach 6 to 9 inches in length by their second or third year of life, but a few survive to be six years old and a foot long. Butterfish are silvery with a bluish or greenish tinge along the back. Their sides may show large, irregular spots.

Like menhaden, butterfish are often seen near the surface; unlike menhaden, the schools are small and not tightly knit. A knowledgeable tackle shop owner should be able to tell you where schools of butterfish are found locally because some recreational anglers catch butterfish for food. Generally, look for butterfish in harbors, bays, estuaries, and other sheltered areas, mainly over sand bottoms.

By August, in southern New England, the young-of-the-year are 1½ to 2 inches long; by fall they are 3 inches or longer. These fish have an interesting habit of seeking protection from game fish by hanging in small groups just underneath the stinging tentacles of the reddish brown lion's mane jellyfish. As the jellyfish is pulled into a strong rip, any baitfish below it have a hard time swimming exactly into position. Game fish rise from below to intercept those that stray too far. As a result, a single jellyfish floating downcurrent through a rip may be accompanied by a series of swirls and explosions. Captain Steve Bellefleur pointed this out to me several years ago near Watch Hill Passage.

Frozen butterfish can be purchased for chum at many shoreline tackle stores. Offshore anglers regularly use it to entice large pelagics, such as bluefin and yellowfin tuna, but near the coast it can be used, like sand eels or menhaden, to attract bluefish, bonito, little tunny, and striped bass to within fly-rod range.

OTHER TYPES OF MARINE LIFE
Saltwater game fish, such as striped bass, bluefish, Atlantic bonito, and little tunny, can and do, to varying degrees, eat marine invertebrates such as amphipods, squid, shrimp, crabs, and marine worms. This is especially true of striped bass and has over the years been the reason fly tiers have developed things to match grass shrimp and squid, among others. Because baitfish are frequently a large and important part of the dietary intake of all four fish, however, the most widely used and commonly known flies mimic schooling baitfish.

Although invertebrates, animals without backbones, definitely are on the menu of many species of game fish, generally speaking, their importance to fly fishermen is more limited than the role played by baitfish. Still, having some insight into these food sources helps a fly fisherman catch more fish and better understand the fishery. Consider, for example, that in some locations, invertebrates constitute from 35 to 85 percent of the dietary intake of striped bass.

Amphipods
One June night while fishing along a sandy beach, we came across a large number of stripers feeding in the quiet waters of a shallow bowl. They fed slowly and determinedly for hours, often no more than 4 feet from us. It looked like a piece of cake. Yet these fish steadfastly refused nearly every fly we cast to them. After a while I turned on a small flashlight and investigated the water, fully expecting to find sand eels and silversides. Much to my surprise, the water contained only a few baitfish but was loaded with amphipods. Hundreds of them swam through the beam.

Amphipods are tiny marine crustaceans. Found under rocks, among seaweed, or buried in the sand, they live in the intertidal zone everywhere along the coast. Although they are individually small, their numbers along a stretch of shoreline can be staggering. It is a silent and little observed part of the food chain. Research done on the diet of striped bass on the south side of Long Island in the spring revealed just how significant amphipods are. In this location, amphipods were found to be the dominant invertebrate fed upon and made up as much as 43 percent of the total diet of small stripers! They were eaten in large numbers by big bass as well. It is likely that they also reach this level of importance elsewhere along sandy shorelines.

Of the various marine amphipods, the sand hopper, or sand flea, is best known by beachgoers. Unlike other amphipods, these creatures are nearly terrestrial, preferring to live on wet sand but not totally underwater. Kick over a clump of damp seaweed by the water's edge, and these little guys go jumping all over the place. Even though sand hoppers do not go into the water directly, fish do feed on them. Striped bass accomplish this by cruising the surf line, watching for sand hoppers that have been sucked off the beach by the force of the waves.

In appearance, most marine amphipods look a great deal like their freshwater relative, the scud. Their bodies are flattened from side to side but appear somewhat round in cross section. The surface is smooth looking, and they are clearly segmented with short legs hanging underneath. They could be also be confused for tiny translucent shrimp, although they lack a well-defined head. They range from less than ½ inch to members of the genus *Gammarus,* which can be a full 1½ inches in length. Color varies from grayish white to reddish or olive brown. On the June night I told you about, the amphipods were probably in a mating swarm. Next time I will have the right fly.

Crabs

Crabs are common in shallow water along the coast. You will see them out on the open beaches and even more frequently in estuaries such as salt ponds and coastal marshes. Some are found mainly over soft bottoms; others like a rocky home. The crabs commonly found on our coast include the spider, the green, the rock, the fiddler, the blue, and the lady or calico.

Crabs certainly play a role in the diet of striped bass and to some degree bluefish. And adult crabs can be imitated by creative fly tiers. Making a fly behave like a crab is more problematic, however. Adult crabs spend their time moving right over the bottom or even burrowing into it. Dragging a fly over the bottom, especially in rocky locations, can lead to trouble. I rarely try it. Two crabs, the blue crab and the lady crab, are fair swimmers and can travel above the bottom for short distances when provoked. A floating or suspending crab fly could be effective in imitating them. Use it over sand bottoms only, since this is where these two crabs are usually found. The fly should be retrieved at a slow to moderate pace. In a rip or current you may want to try a dead-drift presentation too.

Another opportunity to use a crab fly arrives in mid to late summer after crabs have spawned. At first the young-of-the-year are found in estuaries and often around marinas and pilings. But sooner or later, large clouds of these small crabs will drift out into open waters. I have seen clouds of tens of thousands of baby crabs as small as the fingernail on your pinkie moving with the tide. I believe these to be juvenile lady crabs *(Ovalipes ocellatus)*.

Where fish are feeding on these clouds of young-of-the-year, getting a fly to work can be a frustrating experience because the naturals are so numerous and fish are sucking them in by the mouthful. Perhaps a lightly weighted crab fly suspended underneath a strike indicator, in the way a trout angler presents a nymph, might work, although I have yet to try it. Captain Greg Weatherby of Newport tells me that as an alternative to matching these tiny crustaceans, a popper fished over the top of the crabs can get the attention of a striper or two.

Shrimp

Several types of shrimp inhabit our waters. Of them, the grass shrimp and the sand shrimp are of some interest to anglers. The sand shrimp reaches about 2 inches in length and is a translucent sandy color with a hint of olive green. The grass shrimp reaches only half that size. It is also transparent but has brownish spots. The grass shrimp can be completely dark brown when living over an equally dark bottom, however, so there must be some variation based on locale or diet. Both of these varieties live in shallow water, often very close to shore. And like crabs, they are very common in our coastal estuaries.

Shrimp are poor swimmers and therefore are forced to travel in and out of estuaries at the mercy of the tide. For that reason, one of the best places to use a shrimp fly is in a rip exiting an estuary. The fly should be swung downcurrent like a wet fly or fished dead-drift. Another excellent way to use a shrimp pattern is to cast it up against the bank of an estuary. Retrieve it back slowly as you might with a nymph in fresh water. This method is effective in the springtime for schoolie stripers.

Squid

Squid are both hunters and hunted. Swimming in schools, they attack small baitfish with a vengeance. I have seen them repeatedly strike a fly, although because of their small mouths, they were impossible to hook. Striped bass are so fond of them that anglers once called stripers "squid hounds." But you can bet that bluefish, bonito, and little tunny get in on this act too. There are two types of squid, but both look and act much the same.

Adult squid reach lengths of over a foot. Typically, they range in color from milky white to light reddish brown, but squid can change their color to adapt to various situations. Expect them to migrate inshore in the spring and summer to feed, especially where they can dine on baby herring, sand eels, or small mackerel. While inshore, one species, usually referred to as the long-finned squid, will spawn in or near estuaries. In Long Island Sound, this happens in June, particularly during low moon tides. As winter approaches, squid migrate back off-shore to deep water.

Squid are active both day and night. They can swim with great speed, but just as often they cruise slowly about. Other times they sit on the bottom and simply wait for prey to come by. After the sun goes down, they are especially drawn to areas where artificial light strikes the water, such as around marinas and bridges. So voracious are they that sometimes in hot pursuit of baitfish near the water's edge, they shoot right up onto the beach. This happens particularly on nights when the moon is extremely bright.

9

Saltwater Flies: A Selection for New England

When I used to fish for trout exclusively, I wore a chest fly box. It was a metal contraption with five large compartmentalized trays in which to organize my offerings. Dry flies, spinners, nymphs, wets, and streamers in assorted colors, sizes, and styles made up this vast collection. So deep were they piled that I dared not open a tray without turning my back to the wind. Some were favorite patterns that had proven themselves in many a streamside situation and I could not do without. Others were rarely used. They sat as new as the day they were tied, eagerly awaiting a call to active duty. A third group of flies was so worn and matted down as to be hardly recognizable and clearly ready for the scrap heap, although I could never bring myself to carry out that order.

Flies are at the heart of our sport. And no fly fisherman ever thinks he has too many. Our bulging trout vests are a clear testimonial to that fact and are seen by our fellow anglers as a sign of both our competence and our preparedness to do battle. So deep runs this philosophical bent that often the most dreaded and recurring nightmare is to find oneself in the midst of rising trout without the fly that works.

The history and development of patterns for the saltwater angler are brief in comparison with their freshwater counterparts. Nevertheless, there are many excellent flies to choose from, and the number of patterns coming to light each season is greatly increasing. This is in part because of the increased numbers of fly rodders venturing into the salt, as well as the availability of new materials. But most exciting is the growing awareness that saltwater fishing is every bit as complex as freshwater angling and therefore deserves the same spirit of experimentation that has for so long surrounded freshwater fly creations.

Putting together a good selection of saltwater flies involves matching the most common forage found along the coast in the same way that a trout angler seeks to imitate stream aquatic life. You might say that one tries to "match the marine." Saltwater flies are designed to do so either in an impressionistic fashion or with a higher degree of realism. These two approaches are familiar carryovers from freshwater and form the backbone behind all attempts at fly tying.

Though some fly tiers may claim that only one approach is correct, in truth both ideas work. Many fine saltwater patterns are highly impressionistic, mimicking a variety of small baitfish. They work well in many situations. Some coastal flies, on the other hand, are developed with one specific natural in mind, attempting to match them in nearly every aspect of size and color. These work too and are especially effective in clear water or wherever fish are fussy.

Like trout, coastal game fish are generally opportunistic feeders, which means that they are able to feed on a variety of different things. It is a survival mechanism that allows predators to cope with the difficulties of life in the brine. It does not mean, as some would have you believe, that saltwater fish are never selective. Far from it. If striped bass are feeding on a school of sand eels, a fly that is not the right size, shape, and color may go untouched. Of those three criteria, size is the single most critical element in correctly imitating the natural. Shape is next, followed by color. Why is color the least important? Because while a baitfish may look very colorful in your hand, underwater colors tend to be highly muted or subdued.

Matching the size of some baitfish is not an easy task. Adult herring, for instance, reach a foot or more in length, making them as big as the trout in some streams. The solution is to use lightweight materials that breathe in the water to give the illusion of greater volume. Ideally the material should not soak up water, for the added weight will make a large fly extremely difficult to cast. Another solution is to focus only on the immature stages of these bigger baitfish. For example, a herring in the first summer of life would likely be under 4 inches in length.

The color plates in this book show numerous flies for the coastal angler. Many represent baitfish examined in the previous chapter, particularly the three most important ones: sand eels, silversides, and herring. Remember that menhaden are members of the herring family and are commonly called bunker or pogy. Juvenile menhaden are often referred to as baby bunker. Other flies imitate invertebrates: grass shrimp, marine worms, crabs, and squid.

In fresh water, anglers categorize flies as dries, wets, nymphs, or streamers, each of which has its own job. Along the Atlantic seaboard, patterns are classified as saltwater streamers, saltwater poppers, or saltwater sliders. Each of these three types of saltwater flies has its own special character, allowing anglers to cover a variety of situations from top to bottom.

Poppers are clearly the most exciting type of fly to use, because the strike is visible. This same kind of sentiment is often expressed about the beauty of dry-fly fishing, but believe me, you will rarely see any dainty rises in the salt. When a fish of 10 pounds or better hits a saltwater popper, it can rattle you from your baseball cap down into your waders.

Streamers in the brine are what streamers have always been in fresh water: seductive subsurface baitfish frauds. The only immediate difference is size. A trout angler might pick a #8 streamer, but the saltwater standard streamer rides a 1/0 hook.

Sliders are the least well known of the group. They are essentially floating streamers whose performance lies midway between the noisy presentation of a popper and the silent glide of a streamer. Riding near the surface, sliders push a small wake during the retrieve. This strategy can drive game fish nuts, and when you think about it, "waking" flies have a strong track record with steelhead and salmon.

SALTWATER STREAMERS

Versatile, easy to tie, and highly effective, streamers are also the oldest and most commonly used fly on the coast. With their record of success, no angler should go to sea without them. The word *streamer* in its strictest sense implies a very particular construction, wing placement, and use of traditional materials. In normal practice, however, the word is frequently used in a looser sense to cover bucktails and other streamerlike flies. On the coast that is true as well. Anglers use the term for flies tied with bucktail, artificial hair, and a host of modern synthetics.

In recent years, the term has expanded to include flies with bodies of epoxy and hot glue, as well as other unconventional materials. This is in large part because of the efforts of fly tiers like Eric Petersen, Bob Popovics, and Page Rogers. These hard synthetic materials are often used to form rigid bodies. Although they often require slightly more time at the vise to construct, these flies can be quite realistic. Materials such as epoxy give the flies a high degree of transparency while affording the tier good control of the shape of the resulting fly. Others are designed to incorporate special features of silhouette, flash, and sink rate.

The primary characteristics of a streamer, and for that matter any saltwater fly, are size, shape, and color. Size refers to the overall length of the fly, and shape to the fly's profile and bulk.

Your decision on the size and shape of a streamer is guided by one of two concepts. You can pick something that matches the prevailing baitfish in the area, or you can select a large fly regardless of whether it looks like the present bait, in the hope that it will attract more and bigger fish. Both ideas are useful.

Matching the marine makes sense when fish are actively feeding on one specific baitfish. You do it by tying on a streamer whose length, height from top to bottom, and thickness from side to side closely approximate the natural. Where the water is clear, matching the color of the natural makes sense too.

While a fly's length is always a consideration in matching the natural, the importance of a fly's height or a fly's thickness may vary, depending on the situation. When you fish in shallow water, game fish are apt to view your streamer from the side. They can see the fly's height, yet its thickness is harder to judge. In deep water, game fish frequently see a fly from underneath. Viewed in this manner, the fly's thickness is very apparent, but its height is not. This is extremely helpful when adult menhaden are swimming near the surface. In this case your fly need not mimic the menhaden's considerable height, only its length and thickness.

The "bigger is better" tactic is sound advice when searching large stretches of water or a swift current. Not only is a bigger fly easier to see, but fish are more apt to move a distance to get it. Big flies are also useful in situations where the prevailing bait has amassed in tremendous numbers. Here a matching fly becomes anonymous and may reduce your chances of a hookup. Beyond sheer size, bulk is another attention-grabbing feature. A thick head on a fly pushes a good deal of water as you retrieve it. This sends out shock waves through the immediate area, which game fish sense with their lateral line radar. Therefore, in discolored water or at night, a bulky streamer can be easier for a fish to locate.

Color does several things. First, like size and shape, it can help you more closely match the baitfish. For that very reason, streamers usually follow a basic color scheme that mimics the essential nature of most baitfish. Dark hues are common along the top half of the fly, and lighter hues along the bottom. Equally important, color plays a role in how visible your fly is in the water. Because many game fish are primarily sight feeders, this is a significant factor, made even greater in times of low light or murky water.

Flies constructed from highly transparent materials are not a good choice when water clarity is poor. They simply are not visible enough. This also might be a consideration for clear water situations in which the fish are spread out and must find your offering from a great distance. Hot fluorescent colors, on the other hand, are extremely visible even in murky water. Tests have shown that chartreuse is one of the most visible colors underwater.

For general night fishing, black flies are the answer. Since fish generally view the fly from below, black makes a very distinct silhouette against the faint glow of the water's surface. There are even situations where black is the most visible color during the day. When the sun is high, a black fly traveling overhead is easier to see than a white fly. I might, however, use a white fly at night when the moon is very bright and the game fish are feeding right on the surface. Then a white fly can prove its worth by reflecting the moonlight to predators that are swimming at the same level as the fly.

Three more things that play a role in the effectiveness of a streamer are flash, eyes, and action. Many baitfish have reflective sides that flash brightly when they turn or twist near the surface. By dressing a fly with flash materials such as Flashabou or Krystal Flash, you mimic that reflectivity and help draw attention to the fly.

One of the most striking features of all baitfish is their relatively large, prominent eyes. The sharp contrast of the darker pupil against the lighter eye stands out boldly underwater compared with the muted transitions found elsewhere on the body. These eyes are a visual target for prowling game fish. As a result, many fly tiers incorporate some type of eye on their streamer patterns. It is a good idea.

Another consideration is action, or how a fly behaves in the water. Compared with surf-casting plugs, few saltwater flies truly wiggle, dive, or shimmy. Flies do have enticing action, however. Soft materials like hackle and marabou wave very seductively during the retrieve. Flies with lead eyes can be made to rise and fall like a jig. And there are even attempts to make a lipped fly to imitate the famous action of deadly lipped plugs like the Hellcat and the Bomber.

SALTWATER POPPERS

As wonderful as saltwater poppers are, they can also be the most difficult flies to use well in the entire saltwater angler's arsenal. Your success or failure heavily depends not only on the proper design of the popper, but also on your ability to manipulate it effectively. In short, these things are not foolproof. The fly itself must be light enough to cast yet big enough to produce a healthy *pop* on command. In addition, it should have good hooking capabilities, be easy to lift from the water, and be durable.

On the angler's side of the equation, you must be able to wield a 9- or 10-pound rod and toss these babies a fair distance come wind or wave. Next, you need to be able to vary the retrieve to match the desires of your quarry, and you must have the right technique to drive the point home when the opportunity arises. All in all, there is plenty to learn.

Popper bodies are made of cork or foam for the most part. Cork was the traditional material for the job, but today both closed- and open-cell foam have taken over the task. The desired result is a fly that sits down a bit in the film, which is crucial in bringing the fly face in contact with the water, and at rest sinks slightly toward the bend of the hook. These two considerations create a fly that drives water on the retrieve and when stopped tilts its face skyward, allowing for an easy pickup by the caster.

Regardless of the body material you pick, the size and shape of the popper's face play an important role in the fly's effectiveness, because this surface is largely responsible for the fly's ability to create the commotion that attracts fish in the first place. A popper with a ½-inch diameter or less can result in poor performance. Such a small face may be all right for schoolies, but it has a hard time producing the kind of commotion that attracts a big striper or blue. An increase in diameter to ⅝-inch results in a nearly 50 percent gain in surface area, making a much more effective saltwater popper without a tremendous trade-off in castability. At times, an even larger popper face is necessary. When fish are feeding on adult menhaden, a popper with a face of ⅞-inch may catch considerably more fish, although it is difficult to cast.

Some anglers may argue that too much noise has the opposite of the desired effect—it scares fish. This is true, yet given the personality of two main quarries, large-faced poppers are more successful. Bluefish want the louder insistent *pop,* and anglers can deliver. For stripers, by

varying the amount of force used in stripping the fly, anglers can produce either loud or soft *pops* at lower speeds. The net result is a more
versatile fly. There are even two ways tiers can increase the surface area
of the face without increasing body diameter. One is by slanting the
face to an elliptical shape, and the other is to cup the face.

Color, eyes, and flash are all of less concern than with a streamer.
Most anglers seem to prefer a hot color such as orange or chartreuse.
My experience tends to agree, although a strong case can be make for
black, since it is the easiest color for a fish to see moving overhead. Eyes
on a popper are fun but not functional: They are there to attract anglers,
not fish. Flash is unlikely to be of any real value when the fly is traveling
fast. To entice a bass, however, you may have to stop the popper occasionally. As a striper sits under the fly, a bit of flash might turn the tide,
convincing the fish to inhale your offering.

SALTWATER SLIDERS

Each type of fly has its own personality. Poppers are loud and assertive
extroverts that never fail to make themselves known; streamers are
the silent types that move along quietly, minding their own business.
Between these two extremes, there is a third character: the slider. In
approach, it lacks the noisy presentation of the saltwater popper, but at
the same time, it is not content to be as diplomatic as the streamer.

Sliders are flies that swim in or near the film and push a small wake
as they glide ever forward. You can think of them as a kind of cross
between the popper and the streamer. The wake they create alerts fish
to their presence in much the same manner as the popper's *pop* signals
its position, but at the same time a slider's relatively slim silhouette
suggests a baitfish with a relatively narrow body in the manner of a
streamer.

I like sliders with a balsa wood body, like the Farnsworth Fly, but
foam does work too. Either should ride a long-shank stainless popper
hook. The body is blunt in front and tapers a bit toward the rear. The
tail is usually made from either bucktail or a synthetic product such as
FisHair.

Sliders come in the same color schemes as streamer patterns. Expect
to see two-tone models with green or blue over white and others in hot
fluorescent dress. Black is also the answer for a slider intended for night
use. Flash can be incorporated into either the tail or the body of the fly
by the use of mylar tape, now widely available to fly tiers.

The length and diameter of the cylindrical body can be varied to match different baitfish. A sand eel slider might have a very small diameter, between ⅛ and ¼ inch. Naturally, the overall length should also reflect the size of the sand eels in the area you intend to fish. A good general-purpose slider is one with a diameter closer to a full ⅜ inch. This increased size allows the slider to produce a bigger wake and simulate a wider range of small baitfish. For this standard model, the body would run about 1⅜ inches; with the tail, the total length reaches 3½ inches. This overall length is very similar to most saltwater streamers. To match a large adult menhaden, you should go to what Phil Farnsworth calls a mega-slider. The body is at least ⅜ inch in diameter, and the overall length extends to 5½ inches. Traveling overhead, it looks to your quarry like a large, thin-bodied fish.

You can change the action of a slider by slanting its face forward. When done correctly, the fly will dive and even wiggle a bit during the retrieve. The slant starts on top of the body about ¾ inch back from the front end and extends downward toward the eye of the hook. This in effect creates a lip that forces the fly down during the retrieve.

To use this type of fly, cast it out, and after it lands on the water, give the fly line a strong pull. This initial yank forces the diver under the surface of the water. Now retrieve normally. If you wish the fly to go deeper, hold the rod tip underwater and speed up the retrieve a bit. When you want to pick up the fly to start another cast, you must wait a second for the fly to float up near the surface. Otherwise, if you simply lift on the line with the fly deep, the fly may just go deeper and resist your attempt to lift the line.

SALTWATER HOOKS

Freshwater fly tiers have long enjoyed having a great selection of hooks at their disposal. Unfortunately, in the salt that luxury has been lacking for some time. Ten years ago, we had so little it was really a sad joke, but that has started to change in recent years. And today we have more and better hooks designed for the coastal angler than ever before. With luck, that trend will continue.

In New England, saltwater fly fisherman use hooks from roughly #4 to #3/0. Ninety percent of the time they are straight-eye hooks with a standard-length shank and a forged O'Shaughnessy bend. Commonly the point of the hook is formed in a traditional triangular shape, sometimes called a cut or knife point. Recently, conical points, also called needle points, have come to rival this design. Both types work, but there is some controversy as to which is superior.

Common streamers and bucktails. Flies range from 3½ to 4 inches in length. Left row top to bottom: Salty Beady Eye, tied by Page Rogers; Bend Back, tied by the author; Clouser Deep Minnow, tied by the author. Right row top to bottom: Strawberry Blonde, tied by the author; Lefty's Deceiver, tied by Mark Lewchik; HieTie, tied by the author. *(Color plates by Gary Mirando)*

Assorted flies. Flies range from 2 to 4 inches in length, except for the crab, which has a body approximately ¼-inch square. Left row top to bottom: Mark's Worm Fly, tied by Mark Lewchik; Page's Shimmering Shrimp, tied by Page Rogers; Skeeter, tied by Glen Mikkleson; Rogers' Spartina Flats Crab, tied by Page Rogers. Right row top to bottom: Tabory's Sea Rat, tied by Lou Tabory; Page's Menemsha Minnow, tied by Page Rogers; Popovics' Bonito Candy, Umpqua; Eric's Epoxy Minnow, tied by Eric Peterson.

Sand eel flies. Flies range from 2¾ to 4 inches in length. Left row top to bottom: Eric's Mono Sand Eel, tied by Eric Peterson; Gartside's Sand Eel, tied by Cooper Gilkes; QT Eel, tied by the author; A. J. Hand's Sand Eel, tied by Page Rogers; Harris's Sand Eel, tied by Page Rogers. Right row top to bottom: Page's Pearly Bait, tied by Page Rogers; Page's Sand Eel (olive/pearl), tied by Page Rogers; Page's Sand Eel (black/pearl), tied by Page Rogers; Tabory's Mono Sand Eel, tied by Page Rogers; Morning Star, tied by the author.

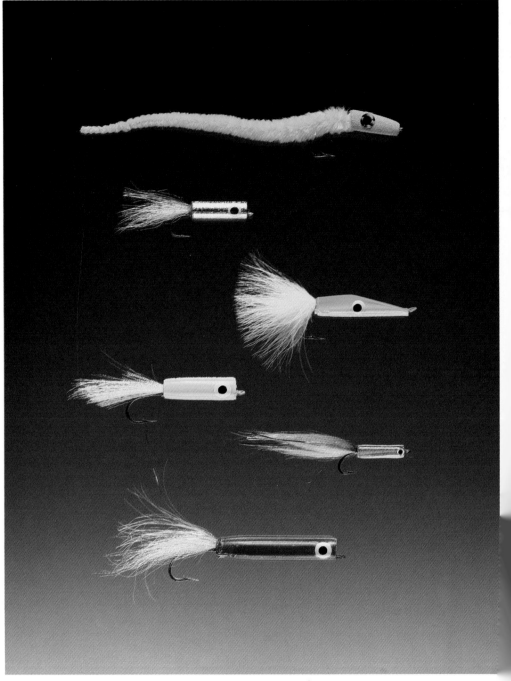

Saltwater sliders. Flies range from 3 to 7 inches in length. Top to bottom: Rat Tail Slider, Edgewater Flies; Farnsworth Mini Slider, tied by Phil Farnsworth; Farnsworth Diver, tied by Phil Farnsworth; Farnsworth Fly, tied by Phil Farnsworth; Rogers' Slim Jim, tied by Page Rogers; Farnsworth Mega Slider, tied by Phil Farnsworth.

Saltwater poppers. Flies range from 3½ to 4½ inches in length. Top to bottom: Master Blaster, Edgewater Flies; Ka Boom Boom, tied by "Terp" Terpenning; Sparkle Bug, Mystic Bay Flies; Bob's Banger, Umpqua; Skipping Bug, The Gaines Company; Rattle-N-Pop, Edgewater Flies.

Night flies. Flies range from 4 to 6 inches in length. Top to bottom: Black Mega Diver, tied by Phil Farnsworth; Black Lefty's Deceiver, tied by Mark Lewchik; Night Train, tied by the author; Black Clouser Deep Minnow, Umpqua; Black Angus, tied by Eric Leiser; Brian's Black Velvet Eel, tied by Brian Owens; Rabbit Eel, tied by Phil Farnsworth.

Assorted flies. Flies range from 3 to 6 inches in length. Top: Tabory's Slab Fly, tied by Lou Tabory. First row, left to right: Eric's Baby Bunker, tied by Eric Peterson; Mark's Baby Bunker, tied by Mark Lewchik. Center: Page's Big Eyed Baitfish (mackerel), tied by Page Rogers. Bottom row, left to right: Pic-a-Bomber, tied by Tom Piccolo; Page's Simple Squid, tied by Page Rogers.

King Kong flies. Flies range from 7 to 12 inches in length. Top to bottom: Brad's Bunker, tied by Brad Burns; Popovics' Shady Lady Squid, tied by Page Rogers; Big Bait, tied by Jim Slater; Tom's Herring, tied by Tom Piccolo; Page's Big Eyed Baitfish (herring), tied by Page Rogers; Pogy, tied by Bill Catherwood.

A conical point, like the point of a sewing needle, is only sharp at the extreme tip. Tests have shown that this style of point requires less force than the cut point to initially penetrate the flesh of a fish's mouth. But these tests also reveal that conical pointed hooks require more force than cut points to drive in all the way pass the barb—one more difference to consider. Be aware too that conical points require a different approach to resharpening (see "Sharpening Hooks" in chapter 13).

When choosing a hook, you should also consider its composition. Bronze hooks, the mainstays of freshwater fly fishing, are rarely used in the salt. They simply rust too quickly. Stainless steel hooks are popular because they are resistant to saltwater corrosion. The amount of resistance is related to the specific stainless steel alloy used by the manufacturer, the tempering process, and the smoothness of the hook's finished surface. Corrosion not only shortens the useful life of a hook, it can also discolor the fly tied on it and perhaps even other flies next to it in your fly box. Here is one more reason to pick stainless steel: Should you accidentally hook yourself, a stainless steel hook offers a measure of protection against tetanus.

Cadmium-plated hooks are the only other type in general use by saltwater fly fishermen. They do slowly corrode, yet they also have some advantages over stainless steel. Cadmium hooks hold a better point and are considerably less expensive. Some folks have even argued that cadmium is better from a conservation standpoint, because it would rust out of a fish's mouth, unlike stainless steel. Recent research, however, indicates that most hooks, with the possible exception of bronze, do not rust out of a fish very quickly. And the type of hook used seems to have a marked effect on the survival of the fish. Cadmium has been found to poison a percentage of fish when left in their mouths. So mortality is likely much higher with cadmium rather than lower.

The most popular hook size for a saltwater streamer is #1/0, although you will find flies in sizes from #2 to #3/0 in wide use. Over many years, the Mustad 34007 has become the most popular hook for this purpose. It is a forged, stainless steel hook with a straight eye and an O'Shaughnessy bend. The 34007 comes in a wide range of sizes, from #8 up to a mighty #11/0. Mustad offers this style hook in a cadmium plate. It is model 3407. Both the 34007 and the 3407 employ a cut point.

Mustad has recently introduced two new hooks that are similar to the 34007. The 34044SS is a stainless steel hook with a conical point. The 34043BLN is a black nickel-coated hook with a conical point. Both are forged hooks with an O'Shaughnessy bend and a straight eye.

They are available in sizes from #2 to #9/0. Another recent hook from Mustad is their 9174S, a stainless steel hook available in #5/0, #4/0, and #3/0 sizes. It is constructed with 1X strong wire and has a 3X short shank. All three of these hooks are part of Mustad's new "Premium-Range" line of hooks.

Eagle Claw's 254SS is another stainless steel hook that deserves your attention. The 254SS has slightly thicker wire, a shorter shank, and a larger eye than the Mustad 34007. It has an O'Shaughnessy forged bend, comes in sizes from #2 to #11/0, and is priced attractively. Another hook manufactured by Eagle Claw is the D067F. This is also called the Pate Tarpon hook for its designer, Billy Pate. This is a very strong-looking hook with a small barb and a nice point. It is found in sizes from #6 to #5/0. The D067F is not stainless steel, but it is plated with what the manufacturer calls a Sea Guard finish to slow corrosion. Unfortunately, this finish can be chipped off by some fly vises. Both hooks use cut points.

The Tiemco 800 series consists of extremely nice stainless steel hooks, although they are expensive. They look very tough and are formed from wire that seems to be 1X or 2X strong. These hooks have straight eyes, forged bends, and points that angle upward toward the eyes. Unlike most other hooks discussed so far, the 800 series uses a conical point. It is very sharp but does not have any of the conventional cutting edges on the side of the point leading to the barb. One problem I have noticed with this line of hooks is a tendency to develop spots of surface rust after use.

Daiichi makes a fine general-purpose saltwater hook for fly tiers. It is model 2546 and comes in sizes #6 to #8/0. This stainless steel hook has a forged O'Shaughnessy bend, a straight eye, and like the Tiemco, a conical point. The wire is strong and the barbs nicely shaped.

Partridge, the well-known English hook manufacturer, distributes a line of stainless steel saltwater hooks, models CS11, CS51, CS52, and CS53. These are very well made and use some of the heaviest wire around. All incorporate conical points. The CS11, the J. S. Sea Streamer, is a long-shanked hook that comes in sizes from #10 to #2. The CS51, the Homasassa Tarpon hook, comes in sizes #2/0 to #5/0. The CS52, the Sea Prince, is available in a wider range of sizes, from #4 to #6/0. And model CS53, the Sea Lord, comes in #1/0 to #4/0.

VMC, a French company, makes hooks for the salt too. The two most likely to be used by fly fishermen are the 7255SS and the 9255.

These two hooks appear to be identical except for their finish. The 7255SS is a stainless steel hook, and the 9255 has what the manufacturer calls a "perma-steel" finish, which is dull and looks to me like some kind of galvanization. Both hooks have straight eyes and a forged O'Shaughnessy bend, although neither hook appears to be constructed of very strong wire. One unique thing about these two hooks is the shape of the point, a combination of a conical point and a conventional or cut point. As far as I know these are the only hooks to do so.

There are two special-purpose hooks designed for bent-back type flies, the Mustad AC 34005 and the Tiemco 411S. Both hooks are prebent and ready for the vise. Bent-back flies ride point up and are therefore relatively weedless. It can be a real help wherever you need to work a fly over a weedy bottom. At one time stainless steel Keel Hooks were available for tying patterns that rode hook point up, but they went out of production some time ago. I used them when they were around. If you come across one, offset the point of the hook slightly. You will get better hookups.

Saltwater streamer patterns, unlike those for fresh water, are only occasionally tied on long-shank hooks, for several good reasons. First, saltwater game fish tend to be aggressive and quickly overrun anything they wish to eat. So even if the point of the hook is well forward in the fly, you still get a solid strike. Second, in the larger-size flies, the long shank adds additional weight and is therefore less desirable. Finally, the bend on a long-shank hook is quicker to open up during an extended fight. As the angler pressures the fish, the long shank becomes, in effect, a lever that exerts increased force on the bend of the hook. Once the gap is widened, the fish has a greater chance of getting free. It is not an everyday problem, but nonetheless it can happen.

The long-shank hook used most often for coastal streamers is the Mustad 34011. It is about 1XL. This hook is a Mustad 34007 with a slightly longer shank. The Mustad 92608 is another long-shank stainless hook, although generally much harder to find. It is considerably longer than the 34011. The point of this hook is offset, but I recommend that you straighten it so that the fly will track better in the water. Rumor has it that Mustad is going to stop making this hook in the near future. This hook is also available in a nickel-plated version as model 92611. Eagle Claw makes a long-shank stainless steel hook that is worth a close look. Like the Mustad 92608, this hook, model 66SS, is offset. You can also get it in bronze, nickel, and Sea Guard finishes.

Popper Hooks

Whether you buy commercially finished poppers or plan to tie your own, the hook in common use is the Mustad 9082S. It is a #2/0 stainless steel, straight-eye model with a kinked long shank and a forged bend. Specially designed for big poppers, this hook has the length and gap for the job. This long-shank hook can be noticeably bent, however, during the battle with a particularly strong fish or by the pressures applied from an overly zealous fly rodder. It has a lot to do with the angle of pull, too, so the relationship between the angler and fish at the moment of the strike is sometimes to blame. Do not attempt to fix the hook. Once bent, the shank should be considered weakened and retired, no matter how good the rest of the popper looks. Failure to do so will result in lost fish.

Mystic Bay Flies designed its own popper hook and had it manufactured by Eagle Claw. It too is a stainless steel, straight-eye hook with a kinked shank. But there are some differences worth noting. The point is better shaped, although straight from the box it does not seem quite as sharp as the Mustad. Also, tiers will find that the overall hook shank is shorter by about ¼ inch and made of slightly lighter-gauge wire. This will lighten the weight of the finished fly. Finally, whereas the Mustad hook is formed with what appears to be a modified round bend, the Eagle Claw appears to be more like a limerick. Tiemco recently released a kinked-shank saltwater popper hook, model 511S. It is stainless and is available in #2/0, #1/0, and #2. Like Tiemco's other hooks, it has a conical point and nicely formed barb. It looks like a good hook, but I have not yet had a chance to use it.

Hooks for Sliders

Sliders are built on a variety of hooks, depending on their length and design. Some use long-shank stainless steel hooks. Like poppers, they are prone to having their hooks opened up by heavy fish. Those sliders, however, have a much slimmer body, and a kinked shank is not an absolute requirement. So one solution is to use long-shank cadmium hooks, which are much tougher. Other sliders, such as the Edgewater Rat Tail, use standard-length stainless steel hooks.

10

Saltwater Tackle

Knowing your quarry and understanding the conditions under which you will find them are crucial parts of the sport, but having the correct tackle is no less important. When a little tunny smokes off into the backing, a quality drag earns its keep. When stripers sit deep in the strong currents of an inlet, only the right fly line is able to get the fly down to them. And once you hook one up, a well-designed rod goes a long way in helping you land that fish. Whatever the circumstances, having the right equipment can make the difference between success and failure.

Until fairly recently, much saltwater fly fishing tackle was simply freshwater gear dressed up for a day at the beach. Today that is not true. Most saltwater fly equipment is specifically designed with the brine in mind, and the selection has never been better. Nevertheless, be aware that in the rush to bring new products to market, a significant number of products were not adequately field tested. This can lead to trouble on the water. I suggest you seek the advice of experienced saltwater anglers before you open your wallet.

At the end of this chapter is a list of what a basic outfit should contain, along with some highly recommended but optional gear. True, taken together, these two lists are more than bare bones, but I doubt you will be comfortable with much less.

The first step in assembling any outfit is deciding exactly what you plan to use it for: What size fish do you want to catch with it, and under what types of conditions will you fish most often for them? Once you have established that, picking the best fly-line weight is relatively easy. From there, the rest falls neatly into place.

LINE WEIGHTS

A 7- or 8-weight line is ideal for casting flies from 1 to 3 inches long using leaders ranging from 8- to 12-pound test. Match it with an appropriate rod and reel, and you have an exciting light tackle outfit for school-size stripers or blues. An 8-weight also works well with bonito, especially where they run less than 10 pounds. Use it in shallow, protected waters, including salt ponds, tidal flats, and embayments. This is not the right choice, however, for fishing in heavy surf, swift currents, or rocky areas.

A 9- or 10-weight line handles flies up to 5 or so inches in length, including saltwater poppers. Leaders can test from 10 to 15 pounds in strength. With the right rod and reel, you have a fine general-purpose saltwater rig for light to medium duty. This rig is at home in both protected and open water. Use it for striped bass, bluefish, bonito, and little tunny, from school-size to trophy. An 11- or 12-weight line casts large saltwater flies up to 7 or so inches in length. Use them with leaders testing from 15 to 20 pounds. With the correct size rod and reel, you have a heavy-duty rig capable of handling large fish sitting in deep and swift currents.

RODS

Once you have decided what line weight to use, you will want to pick out a rod. Though I do own and use saltwater fly rods made of bamboo and fiberglass, today graphite is king, and with good reason. In many ways, it is ideally suited to the salt, producing a long, powerful, yet lightweight rod. But never forget that it is more than simply a matter of material; fine fly rods have always been first the result of fine fly-rod design. That fact has become clouded in an era when new generations of graphite seem to come along every few years.

Forget the modulus numbers, forget the scientific claims, and instead pick it up and cast it. It is ultimately more important to know how an individual rod performs when you use it than what type of graphite it is made of. Be sure to test the rod with the exact type of fly line you intend to use with it most often. A rod's material, its design, the fly line, and the caster's ability are all factors in casting performance.

The most popular rod length for the salt is 9 feet, a very effective length for a wide range of situations. Longer rods often prove tiring for most individuals. If you have above-average upper-body strength, however, you might consider using a 9-foot, 6-inch model. It will help keep your backcast high when wading deep. Anglers who work strictly from a boat may find that 9-foot rods are too long and less effective at pumping fish. Here, an 8-foot or 8-foot, 6-inch rod is likely a superior fishing tool. These lengths are hard to find, however.

Most saltwater anglers want a two-piece rod for general duty. These work fine. If you need a rod that packs down into a tight space, I recommend three-piece rods over four-piece models. They are easier to assemble, likely stronger, have one less ferrule to worry about, and still fit into small car trunks and most airplane overhead compartments.

The size and shape of a rod grip are more important than most

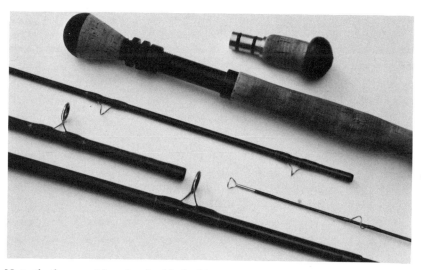

Note the large guides, the double-locking reel seat, and either a permanent butt extension or a detachable one.

people think, and it always surprises me how little attention this rod feature is given. First and foremost, a saltwater grip must be comfortable in your hand. Too small a diameter forces you to close your hand more tightly around the grip and as a result is more fatiguing. A grip that is too large for your hand makes it difficult to hold the rod securely.

Equally important is the shape of the grip. It must put your hand in the most favorable position to deliver power to these bigger rods. A full Wells-style grip is ideal. The only other grip shape that is designed with larger rods and longer casts in mind is the now rarely seen Ritz grip developed by the late Charles Ritz for tournament casting. This grip is widest at the winding check and progressively tapers toward the reel seat.

Double up or down locking metal reel seats are the standard in the brine. Some come with a rubber O-ring between the locking nuts to ensure that nothing slips or binds. It is a good feature. Look for an all-metal reel seat with an anodized finish or a combination of metal and graphite. Unfortunately, the tackle industry does not currently have a standard for reel foot dimensions, and consequently they vary. For that reason, you cannot expect every reel seat to hold every reel equally well. If you already own a saltwater reel and are in the market for a rod to use with it, be very careful to see that the reel seat holds your reel of choice firmly and without wobble.

Nothing more quickly identifies a fly rod as a big-game tool than a butt extension. These extensions are usually constructed of several cork rings, often with the addition of a soft rubber or plastic end cap. Today extensions are much shorter, with 2 inches being a common size. I like them even a hair shorter. In practice, these extensions allow you to force the handle end of the rod into your stomach, chest, or side during the fight. In this way, you can gain extra support and leverage while still maintaining some clearance between the reel and your body. This clearance helps prevent having a whirring reel handle become entangled. If you are using a rim control reel, the clearance also gives the rim some room to revolve freely.

Today's saltwater fly rods should come with large, high-quality guides. As an example, on the wall above me at this moment is an older 10-weight rod. The first stripping guide is only 9 millimeters, hardly big enough to be called a pea shooter. Nowadays the first stripping guide on a 9- or 10-weight rod could be 18 to 20 millimeters in size and sport a ceramic oxide or silicon carbide ring. Snake guides and tip-tops should be large too, and hard chrome plated. This change toward new materials and especially larger guides has noticeably helped the casting performance of saltwater rods. The larger diameters not only allow a freer passage of the fly line during the cast but also permit some fly-line tangles to pass out the rod rather than becoming jammed in a guide.

REELS

Choose a saltwater fly reel carefully. It must have a drag capable of smoothly and consistently releasing long lengths of line. It must stand up to the rigors of saltwater corrosion. It must be solidly constructed so as not to come apart under heavy-duty use, and it should hold ample backing. Such reels range from under $100 to over $500.

How much backing should a reel hold? Experience tells me that most striped bass and bluefish can be landed with 100 yards of backing. Still, a very large bass or blue can go over 100 yards where aided by a strong current. Furthermore, pound for pound, bonito and little tunny make even longer runs. For that reason, I recommend a bare minimum of 150 yards of 20-pound backing, but 250 yards is preferable. If the reel takes 250 yards of 30-pound backing, all the better.

Manufacturers are glad to tell you how much backing their reels hold, but it pays to be a little skeptical. For one thing, the amount of backing a reel is capable of holding depends on which fly line you use. Floating lines take up the most space, and sinking lines the least. Just as important, fly lines are not all the same length. Some are under 100 feet and others over. So to be truly helpful, manufacturers should inform you exactly which fly line was used in making their calculations. Unfortunately, that is not always the case.

Under no circumstances should you load a reel to the point that the last few turns of the fly line are nearly touching the pillars of the frame. This is an invitation to trouble. When fighting a fish, it is difficult to retrieve the fly line so that it loads perfectly onto the spool. If the spool has been filled quite full under normal conditions, when the fly line stacks unevenly it could well jam against the pillars of the frame, stopping you from retrieving any further. When all is wound on evenly, I like to see about a ¼-inch gap between the fly line and spool. This much space allows room for error during the closing moments with a good fish. If, after loading your reel with the desired amount of backing, you do not have enough room to accommodate your fly line, consider trimming the rear of the fly line rather than reducing the backing.

Drag Characteristics

Every drag has three important properties: continuity, drag range, and start-up inertia. Continuity refers to the drag's ability to maintain an even amount of pressure at all drag settings. It should not slip or bind. This ensures that the drag pressure does not vary suddenly as the line is going out. Drag range refers to the difference between the least pressure and the maximum possible resistance the drag is capable of applying. You will find a good deal of difference between reels in this regard. Inertia, or start-up force, relates to how much additional pressure is needed to initiate the drag to begin releasing line. If you have ever been in the unfortunate position of having to push your car by hand, you have experienced something very similar. It takes a good deal of force to get the car rolling, but once under way, things become a lot easier.

How much drag pressure is actually required in the field depends on the breaking strength of your tippet and the kind of conditions or places in which you fish. With the common tippet strength being 12 to 15 pounds, you would likely need no more than about 2 pounds of maximum resistance at the reel. Even if you planned on using a 20-pound tippet, the maximum allowed by the International Game Fish Association, you would not likely set more than 3 or 4 pounds of drag at the reel.

Does that mean that anything over 5 pounds of drag resistance is wasted? Not really. When a reel is brand new, the drag is usually stronger in the total amount of resistance it is capable of creating. That maximum level comes down noticeably as the drag gets worn. Just how much depends on the specific reel and how hard it is used. Therefore, a reel with a monstrous amount of drag right out of the box may feel quite different after a season on the water. The smoothness and start-up inertia of the drag will deteriorate over time as well.

Here are a few hints about caring for drags. Get in the habit of always backing the drag off to the zero or free-spool position when the reel is not in use, and resetting it carefully before heading out. Learn how the drag in your reel can be taken apart and reassembled. (Note, however, that some reels cannot be disassembled by the user.) Learn how to do it correctly before you ever have to do any service in the field. Improper assembly causes very serious performance problems, from slipping to freezing solid. Consult your instructions or the manufacturer about the best way to service your drag. Drag washers wear and, like the brake shoes in your car, need to be replaced when performance drops.

LINES

The ordinary weight-forward line is usually the best taper for most salt-water situations and is especially good for anglers new to the salt. These lines are easy to cast even into the wind, handle big flies fairly well, and can be thrown a good distance. Furthermore, nearly everyone has had experience casting one at some point in his or her fishing career. Double-taper fly lines, on the other hand, are out. They simply are not effective into the wind and take up too much room on your reel, stealing precious backing capacity.

Saltwater tapers are specially designed weight-forward lines with shorter, more abrupt forward heads. In the hands of an experienced caster, they are easier to lift from the water and can be cast more quickly than conventional weight-forward lines. They are often harder for a novice to adjust to, however, because the timing of the cast is faster. Still, you may want to add one of these lines to your arsenal as you get more advanced.

The specific gravity of a fly line determines where in the water column it will ride and hence where the fly will be. Therefore, picking the right density is an essential consideration in purchasing any fly line. If you plan to regularly fish shallow beaches, light surf, or wherever the fish are lying close to the surface in fairly protected waters, a weight-forward intermediate is your best line. This slow-sinking line is extremely versatile. It can be dressed with fly line floatant to stay on top for use with poppers or allowed to sink slowly to get the fly down a bit. You can expect it to go down at a rate of about 1½ inches per second. Floating lines sit on top of the water and therefore take on the shape of the waves. This results in a great deal of slack between you and the fly, enough that feeling the strikes and setting the hook are interfered with. Intermediate lines lie just under the surface and make for a straighter connection between you and the fly.

If, on the other hand, you are fishing in places of moderate to heavy surf or out of a boat over deep water, a faster-sinking line is a better bet. True, it will never allow you to work a popper, but poppers are not the most versatile flies in your box; streamers are. Therefore, a line that works a streamer well in large swells or over fish lying deep may be the best single line for your fishing. Try a weight-forward line with a moderately fast sink rate of 2½ to 3 inches per second. Owning both an intermediate fly line and a moderately fast-sinking line will enable you to cover most fishing situations you will face on the coast.

If you have ever seen how deadly a lead jig or trolling a lure on wire line is, you know that many times the fish are sitting deep in 15 or more feet of water. Frequently compounding the problem of getting an offering to these fish is the fact that they are often lying below a swift current. A fly line that sinks at 2½ inches per second is simply not practical for reaching those fish. But there are some extremely fast-sinking lines available that can do the job. These fly lines head to the bottom at 5, 6, or more inches per second. With them a fly rodder can score against seemingly impossible odds.

Shooting Heads

As an alternative to full-length fly lines, some coastal anglers opt for shooting heads. These 30- to 40-foot lines are essentially just the forward taper of a conventional full-length fly line. This is connected to a thin running line, which in turn connects to the backing.

Shooting heads have several advantages. They are cheaper than full-length lines. They are more compact and therefore take less room to transport. Anglers generally can cast farther with them than they can with full-length lines. They are ideally suited to situations where a long backcast is not possible. And finally, since shooting heads can be attached by a loop to the running line, you can swap one head for another to avoid the necessity for a spare spool.

So why doesn't everyone use heads rather than full-length lines? First off, shooting heads do not cast heavy flies as well as full-length lines. Thus, casting a large saltwater popper or even a large streamer that absorbs water is made more difficult. Second, the running line used with a shooting head tends to tangle a bit more frequently in a stripping basket than an equal length of fly line. Another thing anglers dislike about shooting heads is handling the running line during the retrieve. These lines can be so thin and slick that they are difficult to grip. And when it comes time to set the hook, I prefer something more solid to grasp.

Running Lines for Shooting Heads

Running lines come in three styles: flat mono, braided mono, and conventional level running lines. Flat mono has gone out of favor, although it is the distance champ. Level running lines are still in use and come in two types: floating and intermediate to match different style heads. Both are usually 100 feet long. Braided mono running lines are the most popular style today. They come in 100-foot lengths in either 20- or 30-pound test.

Backing

For many years the backing of choice has been Cortland Micron, a braided line very similar in its properties to braided Dacron. Both lines handle easily and knot reasonably well, but they are subject to wear. Note that once Micron or Dacron has been nicked or abraded, it is significantly weaker. Saltwater fly rodders use Micron in either 20-pound or 30-pound strengths. For 7-weight on up to 9-weight outfits, the 20-pound Micron is fine. For 10-, 11-, or 12-weight outfits, I suggest 30-pound.

Recently, Cortland announced a new type of backing constructed of a different material. It is called Micronite and has a smaller diameter for its breaking strength than Micron. This decrease in diameter effectively increases the backing capacity of any reel. It might also allow anglers to use a smaller reel, one that previously appeared unable to hold the necessary amount of backing. Like Micron, Micronite comes in either 20-pound or 30-pound test.

Beyond Micronite, there are other new materials that are sometimes used as backing, including Stren Kevlar and Fenwick Iron Thread. These lines were developed primarily for spin- or plug-casting gear as super-strong, superthin diameter replacements for conventional monofilament. Generally, they are constructed of Kevlar or gel-spun polyethylene. While these products may eventually enjoy widespread use, they are not without drawbacks. Unlike Micron or Micronite, they require special knotting techniques. More importantly, they could present a real danger to anglers who are fighting a fish. If you accidentally touch conventional Dacron or Micron backing as it exits the spool at high speed, it can burn your hand; these new lines would likely cut you like a buzz saw.

STRIPPING BASKETS

Coastal anglers consider stripping baskets a necessary evil. These contraptions hold the retrieved line in a confined area at about waist height, allowing the caster to shoot the maximum amount of line on the cast. Simply dropping the retrieved line into the water, as is so commonly done in fresh water, does not work. Not only will the line be difficult to pick up when you want to cast it, it will also tangle in things such as seaweed. If you are working in a location with current, any line left in the water drifts away from you, causing even more problems. And sinking lines are the most trouble, because they grab everything on the bottom. Boaters, of course, have the option of simply letting the line accumulate on deck. Still, care is needed to be sure that the line does not catch on your foot or another obstacle. For these reasons, I use a stripping basket at times in a boat.

A simple yet practical stripping basket can be made from a plastic dishpan. Color makes little real difference for day fishing; however, a light-colored stripping basket is easier to work with at night. It will reflect the beam of your flashlight, making it easier to use the interior of the basket as a place to change flies. Dishpans seem to come in a standard width and length: 12 by 14 inches. They come in two depths, however: 5½ inches and 7½ inches. The shallower one makes a lighter and more comfortable stripping basket, but it is less useful in windy conditions, as the wind can actually lift your line out of the basket. The deeper variety allows you to keep the line in the basket when the winds really howl.

It is important that your stripping basket fit firmly against your body. A commercial stripping basket will have an adjustable belt for that purpose. If you make your own stripping basket from a dishpan, there are two solutions. Some anglers cut two slots to act as belt loops in the basket. These slots are made along one long side of the dishpan. Make them at least 8 inches apart to produce a more stable grip for the belt. The belt and the buckle must be entirely synthetic so that the salt water does not affect them.

Another, better, system is to use a bungee cord as your strap. Hardware stores often carry them. They come in a variety of lengths and have hooks on both ends. For most anglers, a 24-inch length is fine. Drill two holes along one long edge of the stripping basket, just in from the corners and down from the rim a short distance. Determine the exact distance down by matching it to the gap on the hook of the bungee cord. Hook one end of the cord to the basket, lift it into position, and reach around for the other end of the cord. Hook that end into the other hole. Be sure to have the ends of the hooks down. If they are up, the fly line will catch on them.

Do not drill any other holes in the basket. Some people think that holes in the bottom would help release water that sometimes floods over the rim in surf conditions. True, but it also allows water to enter from underneath. This water sloshes around and causes the fly line to tangle in the stripping basket. The result can be a major headache. So do not cut holes in the bottom, regardless of what you see others doing. Also note that stripping baskets made from open-mesh material are notoriously difficult to use in the surf for this very reason. When water needs to be removed from the basket, place your rod under your arm, reach down with both hands to the far rim of the stripping basket and pull the rim to your chest. The water is quickly spilled harmlessly over the front of your waders.

Orvis sells a stripping basket with a specially shaped interior. The bottom is covered with a series of knobs that are a molded part of the basket. These knobs help keep the loops of fly line separated and stop much of the movement problem.

If you prefer to alter your own stripping basket, here is an idea that works. For many years, coastal anglers have been gluing pieces of Astroturf to the bottom of the basket with either epoxy or hot glue. Do not use a piece big enough to cover the entire surface; it will add a lot of weight to the basket. Instead, cut a few strips, no more than four, about 1¼ inches wide and just shorter than the width of the basket. Space them evenly in the bottom of the basket.

WADERS AND CLEATS

Chest waders are an essential part of the surf caster's uniform. And some of the same thinking that anglers use in fresh water applies. Felt soles are mandatory, with only one exception: If you fish strictly on sand beaches, plain rubber cleated waders will work fine. Beyond felts, you might want a set of metal cleats, or studs. These are highly recommended on slick rocks and jetties. They are an accessory item worn as a sandal over your wader boot. Korkers are one such product. The last option is a combination sole that incorporates both felt and metal cleats. These are now available as replacement kits and make a versatile sole.

There are some other things about coastal work that require a slight adjustment to your wader thinking. Although stocking-foot waders, with their accompanying wading shoes, are great in the trout stream, they are a poor idea in the surf. Sand works its way into the wader shoe with the relentless forces of the waves. Not only is this uncomfortable, it wears out the stocking-foot part of the wader. Next, the eyelets used in the standard wading shoe are not resistant to salt. They corrode and cut through your laces. And finally, zippers on some gaiters are quickly jammed with fine sand.

For the saltwater angler, boot-foot waders are the only game in town. They do not allow sand to enter, have no metal eyelets to corrode, and are much easier to get on and off. Traditional cotton-over-rubber construction does not stand up well to salt water. Nylon and other synthetics are definitely superior in this regard and will give a lot more service. Neoprene has long been used in salt water in divers' wet suits. It makes a fine wader, although this is not the perfect warm-weather wader. Since it is common to get hit with a wave in the chest, make sure you get a pair of waders that fits you as high up under the arms as possible. You will be glad you did.

WADING JACKETS OR RAINCOATS
Practically every angler has either a water-repellent wading jacket or raincoat tucked away in the back of his or her trout vest, ready for the first sign of foul weather. In salt water, they are used far more frequently, not because it rains more along the shore, but to ward off waves. It takes just one wave over the top of your waders to convince you of the value of a good coat. They are also valuable as windbreakers.

Be sure to avoid short wading jackets, as they are not effective in this game. You need something at least long enough to reach below your waist. Wear it outside your waders so that water running down the jacket does not enter your boots. Put on your jacket before mounting your stripping basket. As the bungee cord for the stripping basket goes around you, allow it to belt down your jacket too. This will prevent waves from coming up under the hem of the jacket. Look for a jacket that has good, tight cuffs so that water cannot enter the sleeves. Otherwise, water will work its way up inside, particularly on your casting arm, causing discomfort.

VESTS VERSUS CHEST PACKS
A vest is the ultimate garment for the freshwater angler. In one sophisticated, neat design, a great deal of tackle can be stored. But down by the sea, vests are not so effective. For one thing, coastal fly rodders do not carry the amount of gear found on the average trout addict. And given the fog, spray, and waves, even the shortest vest is soon soaked and heavy. Furthermore, casting in the surf is more physically demanding, and the weight of a loaded vest on the shoulders is not helpful.

Steelhead anglers and float-tube fanatics enjoy the virtues of a chest pack as an alternative means to carry gear in a more comfortable and

Chest pack with assorted items.

drier fashion. Some packs have recently been designed with the coastal angler in mind. The first I saw was made by Elite, now Buck's Bag, and others have joined in. Though float tubers like a chest pack with only a front compartment so that they can lean back in their crafts, a chest pack with both front and back compartments is preferable for the surf caster. The front should be able to carry two large, plastic fly boxes. I also use the front compartments to hold a small waterproof camera, stainless steel pliers, a small focusing flashlight, a hook file, and some tippet material. There is just about enough room in the back for a spare spool with another line, a measuring tape, a plastic sealable bag with spare batteries for my light, and a compass. Make sure the chest pack is all plastic and other synthetic materials. Metal buckles or zippers will not withstand the exposure to salt water.

HATS

A hat with a fairly long brim is a real friend on the coast, shielding your head from the dampness associated with fog and spray while reducing glare off the water. The brim should be dark underneath, and for summer use the hat should be ventilated. Make sure the hat fits snugly on your head so that the wind will have a hard time stealing it. The hat should be made from a material that does not shrink. Today, some hats are even made out of material that is both water repellent and breathable. They are expensive but worth a look.

POLARIZED SUNGLASSES

The sea, with its powerful glare and wind-blown sand, is extremely tough on your eyes. Polarized sunglasses help protect them and improve your vision, allowing you to see into the water. Do not go to sea without them. Pick amber or brown lenses for near-shore work. For anglers who work both near-shore and offshore, gray lenses are a compromise. Glass lenses hold up far better than plastic.

Anglers with prescription lenses can opt for clip-ons, although I find them a nuisance. An alternative is fully framed plastic polarized glasses designed to be worn over your existing frames. Unlike clip-ons, they offer side shields. They are relatively cheap, and they stay on your head better and are less likely to be blown off by the wind. Vision Products is one company that makes them; this model even has replaceable lenses. Be sure to find a pair that fits comfortably and has ventilation holes to reduce fogging in the summer heat.

Last but not least are prescription sunglasses. These things cost, yet clearly they are the best. They are the most comfortable and often have the most features, including removable side shields and lanyards. I have a pair made by Specialized Eyewear that even has a special coating on the lenses to repel water.

PLIERS

A pair of pliers is one of those essential things in the salt that always seem to give you a little bit of trouble. Pliers rust, become frozen up, have poor cutters, or are too short to reach that deep hook. I have owned many different pairs and can honestly say that none of them are without their shortcomings.

Basically, you need the following in a pair of pliers: They must be able to grasp a hook firmly and tightly so that you can free it from a fish. The jaws should come to a fine enough point to allow you to pinch down a barb. They must be able to easily cut the gauge of wire you use for shock tippets without weakening or chipping the cutter. They should be able to snip monofilament too. And the cutters should be positioned so that you can trim a knot closely. They should not rust quickly or freeze up from corrosion. And they should fit inside a chest pack, feel comfortable in your hand, have nonslip grips on the handles, and cost under $60.

Does it sound like I am asking a lot? I must be, because I have not been able to find such a pair. To tell you the truth, in an ideal pair of pliers, I would ask for even more features. For the occasional fish that gets hooked deeply or the blue that barely opens its mouth, I want a long, needle-nose pliers. I also prefer a pair whose jaws are not heavily serrated. I think the serration can weaken a hook when you clamp down on it. I also like a pliers with cutters strong enough to snip off a hook cleanly at the bend. Should you or a friend accidentally get hooked, you will quickly see the advantage. And finally, I would like a place to attach a slit ring so that a lanyard could be used.

The pair that comes closest, in my opinion, is the English-made "G" plier sold by Nu-Mark. It is a coated, stainless steel model, spring-loaded with a fairly long nose and a side cutter. I recommend that you wrap the handles with waterproof tape to improve the grip. The G plier sells for around $40.

HOOK REMOVERS

Hook removers are tools specifically designed for only one task: removing a hook from the mouth of a fish. So unlike pliers, these things cannot be used to also cut wire or monofilament or to pinch down a barb. Still, they are handy items. The one I like is a pistol-shaped tool called a

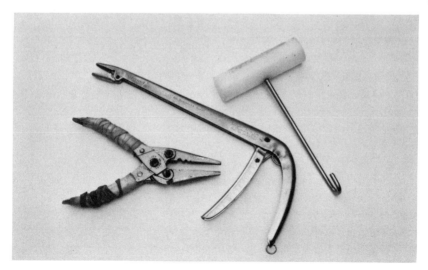

Pliers and release tools. From left to right: stainless steel pliers (note rubber bands wrapped around handle to improve grip), stainless steel hookout, and a stainless dehooker.

hookout. Be sure to choose the stainless steel version. It comes in two lengths, the standard 9-inch model and a 6-inch "shorty." The shorter one is fine, fits in a chest pack so that you can carry it in the surf, and sells for under $15.

FLASHLIGHTS

You need a small, waterproof flashlight with a focusing beam. The mini Mag-Lite is one that is well liked by many anglers. I have used them for years in all kinds of weather and have never had one problem.

To accompany it, I also recommend a Bite-A-Lite, a small plastic cap that fits tightly over the back end of the Mag-Lite. It costs under $2. This cap has two grooves designed to allow you to comfortably grip the flashlight with your teeth, leaving both hands free to work. The cap covers the spot where you can attach a slip ring to the flashlight, however, so you can no longer use it to attach a lanyard. To get around this, I simply use waterproof tape to fasten a strong loop of heavy Dacron to the middle of the light. Then I put a clip on my lanyard and slip the loop into it.

HOOK SHARPENERS

You absolutely must have a good hook sharpener, and you should own at least one that can be carried easily in the field. That eliminates electric battery–operated models, although they do work well for some types of hooks. You should also avoid small pocket- or pen-size hook hones. These are mainly intended to sharpen trout-size hooks and have little use in the salt. Try stacking one of these things up against a #3/0 cadmium-plated hook and you will see what I mean.

Many anglers like the Luhr Jensen file. I agree. Pick the 4-inch model, and get one with the handle already molded on. It is cheap and really works well. This file will rust a bit, however, so be sure to occasionally spray it with a product like WD-40. I also use and like a product called a Shur Sharp, which is constructed with two chain saw files placed side by side. When I purchased this item years ago, it was the only one of its kind. Since then I have come across at least one other manufacturer. Not only is this kind of sharpener lightning fast, you can even use it in the dark, because the hook tracks in a groove. Pick the smaller model. The offshore one is for hooks larger than a saltwater fly fisherman normally uses.

Both the Luhr Jensen file and the Shur Sharp might be called

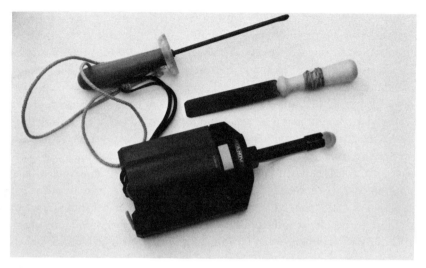

Three different types of hook sharpeners. From top to bottom: a double round file made by Shur Sharp, a flat file by Luhr Jensen, and an electric sharpener called a Hook-Hone-R II for hooks with conical points.

"aggressive" files—with each pass over the hook, they quickly remove a fair amount of metal. If you would like a slower, less aggressive hook sharpener, try the finer NorMark File. Another less aggressive hook sharpener is the electric battery–operated Hook-Hone-R II. The Hone-R sharpens only the extreme tip of the hook. It does not sharpen any other cutting edge in the way a file does. It is a bulky object, but it has its value, as many new saltwater hooks do not have any other cutting edge other than the point itself. These are the hooks with conical or needle points, such as the Tiemco 800 series and the Daiichi 2546. These hooks are not easy to sharpen with a file, but the Hook-Hone-R does the job.

HELPING YOUR TACKLE SURVIVE

There is not one piece of equipment you will use in the salt that can be expected to last as long as a comparable piece of freshwater equipment. This is sad but true. Poor equipment care can greatly accelerate the damage, and a few simple procedures can ensure a more productive life.

The reasons for this rapid equipment wear are threefold. The most obvious is the corrosive effect of salt water. It can prove devastating, especially to fly reels. Next is the considerable strain placed on equipment by prolonged slugfests with powerful fish and by the continual casting of heavy fly lines and heavy flies. Also, the cumulative effects of sunlight, sand, barnacle-covered rocks, and rocking boats take their toll.

Saltwater fly reels require the most attention. This is largely because of their metal construction, which is vulnerable to the corrosive powers of salt water. The amount of attention a reel needs is to some degree a factor of its design. Stamped parts require screws to hold them together. The screw heads provide places for salt to lodge. Furthermore, since the screws are likely made from a different type of metal than the body parts of the reel, a phenomenon known as electrolysis takes place. This problem is well recognized by owners of outboard motors used in the salt. Two dissimilar metals in proximity when submerged into salt water set up a batterylike condition. The salt water becomes the battery fluid, and the two metals produce a negative and a positive terminal. As a weak current flows from one terminal pole to the other, some metal is lost, resulting in the pitting of one terminal.

To best maintain your reel, lightly clean it off after every use, and follow that up periodically with a thorough going over. Never put a wet reel away in a case; that is a sure invitation for trouble. Years ago, I used to hose my reels off after each trip to the coast. And then I would carefully dry the entire thing. My efforts produced poor results. It is now common knowledge that hosing reels off simply drives the salt deeper into various hiding spots.

A better procedure is to first wipe the reel down with a damp cloth to remove external salt and grit. Follow that by spraying the reel frame with a moisture-displacing oil such as WD-40. Wipe the excess oil off, but allow a fine coat to remain. The oil will pick up and trap the salt water, and will protect the metal for the next journey into the surf. Take care not to allow the oil to reach the drag washers, especially where cork or leather is used. The oil would greatly reduce the drag's performance. These oils might also adversely affect your fly line and backing, so take care there too. Finally, let the reel dry off in a place with good air circulation.

Back up this maintenance with an occasional complete cleaning. How often this is necessary depends on your reel's design and the amount of use it gets. Four times a season is a good average. If your reel ends up submerged even briefly, however, consider more than a once-over. First study your reel for signs of corrosion. Pay particular attention to screw heads, the line guard, the base of the reel handle, and the reel foot. Most reels are black, and salt corrosion will stand out clearly as a white powdery material on the surface of the reel's parts. Where this is found, you must clean completely. Remove screws if necessary, and oil again. Take note of wherever you found problems; they will likely recur in the same places, and these areas should be watched.

Now disassemble the reel as far as possible using simple tools, paying strict attention to the order in which you remove parts and their locations. (Remember that some reels cannot be taken apart.) It is imperative that you are able to reassemble the reel correctly, so take your time until you know your reel well. A good idea is to make a photocopy of any detailed parts diagram that came with the reel; one copy can stay home and one can travel with you. Be sure to have on hand the right tools in the right sizes for the job. A screwdriver that is too large might, for example, strip the head off or otherwise damage a screw. Check for wear or corrosion as you go. Reassemble the reel and test for correct performance. And be sure to order parts if you find extensive wear.

Fly lines are vulnerable to the salt and will also need occasional cleaning. A sure sign of trouble is a line that will not shoot well through the guides. You can bet that the line is dirty. Soak it in a bath of warm fresh water with a drop of mild soap. After the bath, rinse the line well, and dry it with a soft, clean cloth. Finally, apply a light dressing to floating lines or use one of the line dressings on the market designed to improve casting performance.

The fly line and leader must also be inspected for nicks caused by barnacles or other sharp surfaces. Replacing leaders is easy, but a nicked fly line is another matter. If the nick cuts through the outer PVC coating but does not reach the core, the fly line can be used with the knowledge that the problem will eventually get worse and there is some chance that the fly line could let go with a fish on. If the core is nicked too, you must replace the line. Monocore fly lines, which have a braided monofilament core, are prone to cracking with use. Once cracked, the coating will gradually peel off. These fly lines are weak once this happens and may break at any time.

Check the connection between the fly line and the leader, as well as the knot to the backing, for integrity. Retie if necessary. Users of shooting heads should also check the loops between the shooting head and the running line for wear. If there is any sign of trouble, refasten or replace these loops before reusing this equipment.

One piece of equipment that rarely gets any care is the backing. Most anglers have it wound on and then forget about it, but that attitude can lead to the loss of a trophy fish. When the backing is loaded onto the spool, care is taken to load it evenly. When a strong fish has taken you deep into your reel's reserves, however, the last thing on your mind as you try to reel in the backing is winding it perfectly onto the spool. As a result, the backing is often loaded unevenly and crisscrosses itself. The next time you hook a hot fish, the backing may suddenly jam. And there is little you can do about it with a fish pulling on the line. Naturally, the tippet will likely pop.

You can avoid this problem by occasionally pulling off the fly line, continuing into the backing. Check to see that it is flowing freely. Go as far as necessary until you come to where the backing is still loaded evenly and neatly on the spool. Sometimes that may mean going in as far as 100 yards. Now reload it correctly under a slight bit of pressure with the help of a friend. It is time-consuming, yet well worth the effort.

Most fly rodders realize that Micron or Dacron backing resists rotting, but few realize that once nicked it loses nearly all its strength. When you have the backing off and ready to reload, have your friend pay attention for flaws in the backing as it passes through his or her fingers on its way to the reel.

Fly rods see their own trouble in the salt. Like fly reels, they must never be put away in a case when wet. The moisture will ruin the finish. Waves, fog, and salt spray all lead to moisture on the rod. As a result, never place a rod into a rod sock or a sealed rod tube immediately after use. Instead, place the bare rod into an open tube for security from breakage, and as soon as you are home, remove the rod and allow it to air dry completely. Also dry the rod sock and tube if necessary.

Rods can be washed and protected with a light coating of wax. Be sure to get sand out of the ferrule before you attempt to reassemble the rod. Sand will cause a ferrule to wear rapidly. Also check the ferrule from time to time for signs of wear or hairline cracks. If a ferrule is starting to slip, use some candle wax on the male end to help tighten it until you can have it repaired. Hairline cracks can be detected by holding the female end up to a strong light. Inspect the inside walls for damage. Usually a crack looks like a faint white line running straight from the base of the ferrule upward toward the tip. Scratches look very similar but are usually lighter and less straight. If you suspect a crack, have it looked over by a rod builder or a knowledgeable tackle store before returning it to the manufacturer. Some cracks are the result of poor design, but many are the result of failure to properly seat the ferrule during use. Be sure to learn how to correctly join the tip and butt section. There are several ferrule types on the market, and each has its own idiosyncrasies.

Rod guides do not last forever. I have worn some of them out in a single season of saltwater fishing. This is another trouble spot that often comes as a surprise to many anglers. Begin your check of the guides by grasping the ring of each stripping guide one at a time. Apply a little pressure to see if the ring is firmly attached to the frame. Also look in the weld areas to see if any rust has developed. Next, run a nylon stocking through all the guides on the rod. If there is a crack or a burr anyplace, the stocking will quickly snag. Replace any damaged guides, as a bad guide can quickly destroy a fly line. Check to see that the snake guides are not bent. If one is misshapen, take great care in bending it back into alignment. Never use the pliers directly on the chrome surface of the guide; you will surely scratch the finish and ruin it.

Finally, check the tip-top under a strong light. This guide takes more than its share of punishment. It is here that the full weight of the line being cast comes to rest and where the line puts the most pressure

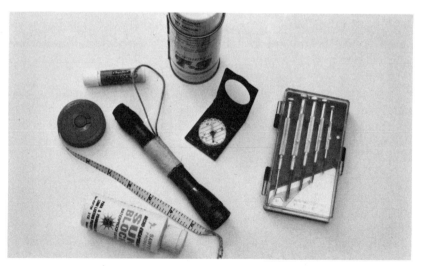

Miscellaneous items for your fishing trips include a flashlight, a plastic tape measure, a compass, waterproof reel lubricant, lip balm with sunscreen, waterproof sunblock, and small tools for repairs in the field.

during a fight. This guide is where I most often find trouble. If you see flat spots on the inside circumference, there is excessive wear. Many modern saltwater fly lines have a bumpy exterior surface that improves the speed at which the line travels through the guides. Unfortunately, these fly lines also cause rapid guide wear. If your tip-top is worn, replace it.

THE BASIC OUTFIT: A SOLID START

9-foot rod for either a 9- or 10-weight line, with a Wells grip, double-locking reel seat, extension butt, and oversize guides

Saltwater-resistant fly reel with a decent drag and the capacity to hold your fly line and at least 150 yards of 20-pound backing, preferably 200 or more yards

Intermediate weight-forward and fast-sink or sink-tip fly lines

20- or 30-pound Dacron backing (not mono backing!)

Leader materials, including wire for shock tippets

Stripping basket with belt or bungee cord

Chest waders, boot-foot with felts (if you plan to fish on rocks and jetties, see optional list below)

Chest pack or vest with one or two plastic boxes deep enough to hold saltwater flies

Selection of flies (see chapter 9 for details)

Foul-weather jacket with hood and tightly closing cuffs (no short wading jackets)

Stainless steel pliers with wire cutters

Waterproof flashlight with focusing beam and lanyard

Hook sharpener

Hat with good-size brim (one that will not shrink)

Polarized sunglasses, amber or brown for near-shore work; side shields and lanyard a plus

Tide book

OPTIONAL BUT HIGHLY RECOMMENDED

Spare reel spool

Metal cleats for anyone fishing on rocks or jetties

Sturdy **thermometer**

Coastal charts for your area (most marinas carry them)

Small portable **weather radio**

Water-resistant or waterproof **pocket compass**

Stainless steel **hook remover**

Synthetic **measuring tape** to measure your catch (available at
  sewing stores)

7- or 8-weight fly rod and reel outfit

Fly-tying vise (capable of holding saltwater-size hooks) and
  accompanying tools

Additional fly lines in various densities for your 9- or 10-
  weight outfit

Portable first-aid kit

Wader repair kit

Waterproof **binoculars**

Fingerless **gloves** for the late fall and early spring

Small weather- or waterproof **camera**

Easy Lok **rod holder** (slips over wading belt and frees up both
  hands)

Bug repellent for summer

Minnow net for collecting samples

Long-handled **landing net** for fishing off a jetty

Chatillon scale

MORE THAN YOU REALLY NEED

Spare rod (in case your main stick suddenly gets shorter)

Spare pair of waders

11- or 12-weight rod and reel outfit with lines

Frame backpack (I use one when walking down a long, open
  beach for a night's fishing. With rod tubes tied to the side, I can
  carry everything from waders to food, coffee, and even a change
  of clothes.)

5-millimeter **boot-foot neoprene waders** for late fall and early
  spring work

Portable loran or GPS, may be helpful in finding your way
  back to productive areas if you four-wheel-drive or hike long
  stretches of open beach, especially in the fog or at night

Portable side scan fish finder might be useful to wading anglers
  in calm, shallow water, although some anglers will say this is
  nothing short of cheating

Stainless steel, waterproof tide watch

Night vision scope (hand-held units cost at least $500)

11

Knots

Saltwater fly fishing does require you to learn a few new knots and handle at least one new material: solid wire. Still, much of what anglers have grown accustomed to on trout streams carries over to the surf. So the clinch knot, the blood knot, the nail knot, and the arbor knot should come as no surprise. Even the surgeon's knot is not unknown to many freshwater anglers.

Perhaps the hardest aspect of saltwater knots is the conditions under which you tie them. Frequently you must fix a leader with wet hands or in a rocking boat. You also need to be able to tie knots in low light and even at night. Furthermore, expect to find yourself, sooner or later, standing in the surf with your knees knocking as you try to tie on a fly in the middle of a blitz. These things are the true tests of your ability.

Loop connections are more commonly used in saltwater fly fishing than in freshwater. As a group, loop knots are reasonably quick and easy to tie, except for the Bimini twist, which is not essential. In the salt, you also work with much heavier monofilament. It is stiffer and harder to handle, but you will get used to it. Wire is the one thing totally foreign to trout fishing. You need to know how to connect it to the fly and how to connect the tippet to the wire.

It is beyond the scope of this book to examine every knot ever used by a saltwater angler. Rather, this chapter provides a selection of good knots with which you will be able to handle most situations in the surf.

A good knot has five characteristics. It must hold at 90 percent of the breaking strength of the material in which it is tied, unless it is a knot designed strictly for heavy mono shock tippets. It should not be complicated to tie. You must be able to tie it repeatedly and get the same results each time; anything less is a ticket to unexpected tragedy. It should not be too bulky. And it must function well for the purpose for which it is intended.

In the way of tools and supplies, you will need a toenail clipper, a fly-tying bobbin (one without a flared end on the tube), needle-nose pliers capable of cutting solid wire, Pliobond or AquaSeal, and a non-water-soluble glue such as PermaBond 102. These modern glues are so powerful that many anglers are using them as an insurance policy against knot slippage, because slippage is the primary cause of knot failure. They work on knots tied with Dacron, Micron, and monofilament, but a word of warning is in order here: This glue is not an excuse to tie knots poorly in the first place. Remember that over time, the glue may slowly break down, so a properly tied knot remains the essential foundation of any connection.

CONNECTING THE BACKING TO THE REEL

The very first knot you need in assembling a saltwater outfit is the one that attaches your backing to the reel. The most commonly used connection is the arbor knot. It works well and is very easy to tie.

Pass the end of the backing around the center pillar of the spool. Then take the end of the backing, and tie a simple overhand knot around the main line. Leave enough line at the tag end to tie a second overhand knot. The two overhand knots should be about 1½ inches apart. Tighten the knot marked B in the illustration. Snug up knot A, but do not fully tighten. Pull on the main part of the backing at C. The two overhand knots will come together and slide down to the spool. Trim off excess. After tying the arbor knot, wind on the backing under slight tension, making sure it loads evenly over the width of the spool. Do not allow it to bunch up.

If you plan on having your backing put on at the tackle store where you buy it, the store will tie the knot and load your backing with a line-winding machine. This saves you a lot of time and effort. If you plan on

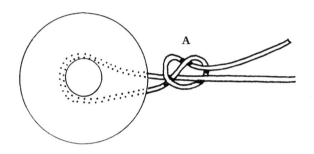

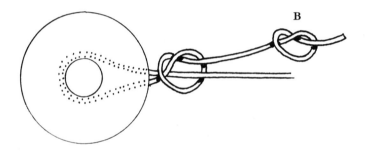

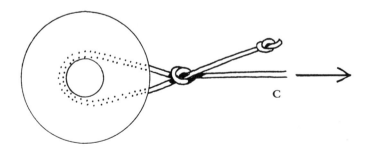

Arbor knot. **Use the arbor knot to attach your backing to the spool.**

loading the backing yourself, do it with the reel mounted on a rod, and run the backing through the guides before you start.

BACKING TO FLY LINE

If you are going to use a full-length fly line, the next step is to join the backing to it. This can be accomplished with a nail knot or by forming a loop-to-loop type of connection. Although some anglers feel that the nail knot is a risky choice for attaching the backing to the fly line, a properly tied nail knot actually holds very well. Still, I prefer to use a drop of glue on this connection. A nail knot also works to connect a monofilament leader butt to the forward end of the fly line.

To tie a nail knot, I recommend using a fly-tying bobbin instead of the traditional nail. It makes things quite a bit easier. Pick a bobbin with a tube that does not have a flared end. Next, clean any residual wax left in the tube by the tying thread. Lay the bobbin directly on top of the fly line as illustrated. Run the end of the backing or mono along the bobbin tube. Leave plenty of line to work with. Then circle it firmly around the fly line and the bobbin tube six times, winding forward toward the front end of the fly line. Keep the wraps tightly together. Insert the tag end of the backing or mono into the bobbin tube, and pass it out the far end. Be sure you have plenty left to pull on later.

Here is where things get a little harder. Pinch the wraps to the tube, and slowly cinch down on the knot by pulling them, one at a time, in the direction of the arrows. When the knot starts to close, pinch the wraps to the fly line and slide out the bobbin. Now pull carefully on the tag end (the one that came through the bobbin tube) until the wraps start to bite into the fly line. Then grab both ends of the backing or mono and pull firmly to drive the knot home. Be sure the wraps end up lying neatly alongside one another. If the wraps have jumped over one another, start again.

To see just how well a glued nail knot would hold, I tested this type of connection several times using my Chatillon scale. I used backing that had been on a reel for almost one full season, rather than brand new backing, to more accurately duplicate field conditions. With both 20- and 30-pound Micron backing, the backing itself always snapped first, and well away from the knot. The backing broke at about 70 to 75 percent of its rated strength. The 20-pound Micron reached 14 pounds, and 30-pound micron reached 23. I was surprised by that but pleased to see the strength of the traditional nail knot.

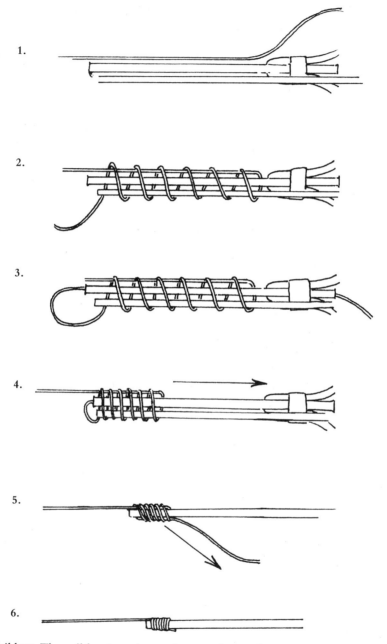

1.

2.

3.

4.

5.

6.

Nail knot. The nail knot can be used to attach your backing or the leader to the fly line.

When you use glue on a nail knot connection, use only a small drop, and apply it directly to the knot. Be very careful not to get it on the bare fly line. If you do, it makes the PVC coating very stiff. This causes the coating to crack prematurely and shortens the line's useful life.

If you are using a monofilament fly line such as the 3M bonefish taper, sometimes known as a Monocore or slime line, special attention is in order. These lines have a very slick, hard outer surface, and a nail knot does not bite into them as well as it does with a standard PVC-coated line. Here, take a cigarette lighter, and quickly pass the flame over the tip of the line. You want to melt the end into a small ball. The accent here is on the word *melt;* you do not want to burn the line. Then use your fingernail to chip off any loose excess from around the melted ball.

Tie your nail knot immediately above this ball, drawing it tight. Put a drop of glue on the nail knot with the same caution you would use on a conventional fly line. Later, cover the nail knot and ball with a thin coat of Pliobond. Repeat this process on the forward end of the line if you want to attach the leader butt with a nail knot.

The loop-to-loop idea for connecting the backing to the fly line has the advantage of allowing you to quickly disconnect one from the other. So if a fly line becomes damaged or you simply wish to use a different fly line, it is a simple matter to swap things. This is a great help for anglers who do not own a spare spool.

To facilitate this process of changing lines, make the loop in the backing large enough to pass the entire reel through. This permits you to skip the time-consuming task of pulling a long fly line through the loop in the backing to join this connection. A 6-inch-long loop will accommodate most reels.

The backing loop can be made with a surgeon's loop knot. This is a fantastic knot that every angler should know. No other knot comes even close to matching it for its ease of tying, speed, strength, and repeatability. You can use other loop knots, although you do not want one that slips down tight such as the uni-knot. The spider hitch is a candidate here, as is the Bimini twist, although the Bimini twist is a bit more bulky and harder to tie.

For insurance, when connecting the backing to the fly line, I like what is called a double surgeon's loop. This produces two loops of equal size in the end of the backing. Start by doubling a long length of backing, then fold it over to double it again. Now you are working with four strands instead of two. Finish the knot as shown.

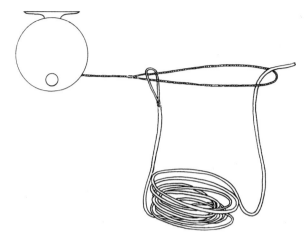

Backing loop. **The backing can be attached to the fly line via backing loops.**

To make the loop on the back end of the fly line, you have several choices. Some saltwater anglers use the braided loop connectors that have become so popular in freshwater fishing. I am a little leery of them for constant heavy-duty work, but to date the ones I have used performed reasonably well. These connectors can be bought ready-made or constructed from kits. The ready-made ones come in a couple of sizes. Pick the correct one for the size of your fly line. Included in the kit is a short sleeve that slides down over both the connector and the fly line and protects the far end of the braid from fraying. This sleeve is important; be sure to use it.

The loop system formed by these braided connectors is very neat and passes through the guides beautifully. It is not perfect, however. You must glue it carefully or it will slip, so never use these things without the glue. This is a case, however, where too much is just as bad as using none. You want only a small drop on the portion of the connector that rides over the fly line. Apply it near the fray collar so that it too will be firmly held in place. If you use several drops, the construction of the connector tends to act like a wick, soaking the entire length with glue. This makes the braid stiff and unable to squeeze down on itself in the manner in which it was designed to, and thereby weakens it. If you use a braided connector, change it each season—not a bad idea for any connection.

I ran some tests on braid connectors with my Chatillon scale and

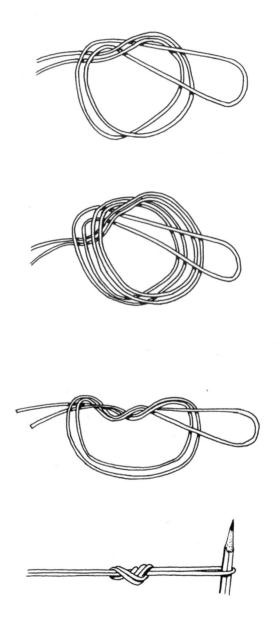

Surgeon's loop. **The surgeon's loop is a strong and easy-to-tie loop knot.**

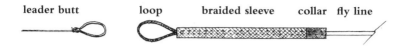

leader butt   loop   braided sleeve   collar fly line

Braided loop connector. **The braided loop connector can be used to make a loop on the end of a fly line, but put it on with care and check it periodically for wear. To put it on, force the fly line up inside the braided loop connector so at least 3 inches of line are in the sleeve to ensure a solid connection.**

found that as with the nail knot, the backing itself snapped first. I then attached the scale directly to the loop on the braided connector to see how much weight it could take. The loop finally broke at 28 pounds of pressure. Pretty good. If improperly mounted, however, these connectors will probably release at much lower weights, hence the warning about constant heavy-duty assignments.

An alternative way to create a loop in the fly line is to fold it back on itself, securing the end with two monofilament nail knots or by whipping it with Kevlar thread. For my taste, this is too bulky to be practical. Once you have loops on both the backing and the fly line, you are ready to join them. Start by pulling the backing loop off the reel, making sure it exits through the reel's line guide. Then simply pass the

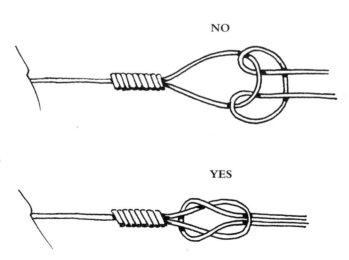

NO

YES

Loop-to-loop connection. **Loops are easy to use but should be mated correctly in a square-knot configuration.**

backing loop completely through the eye of the loop on the fly line. Pass the reel through the eye of the backing loop and slowly snug down until the two loops start to meet. Be absolutely sure that the two loops come together in a square-knot configuration.

SHOOTING HEADS: BACKING TO RUNNING LINE

If you want to make a shooting-head system, you must connect a running line rather than a full-length fly line to the backing. Since running lines are not tapered, you may connect either end to the backing. The braided mono-style running line is the most popular type. This line comes in a 100-foot spool in either 20- or 30-pound test. Purchase an inexpensive splicing needle kit too. Follow the instructions that come with the needle to splice a loop in both ends. Be sure to place a drop of glue on the splice. When you are ready, simply tie the backing to one of the running-line loops using a clinch knot.

SHOOTING HEAD TO RUNNING LINE

Shooting heads come with a preformed loop, ready to be attached to the loop on your running line. The loop connection between the running line and the head is subject to a lot of wear. If the loops are made of dissimilar material—for example, one Dacron, the other monofilament—expect trouble. The harder material will eventually wear through the softer loop. It may take several seasons, or it could happen a lot faster. So keep a close eye on things, and replace when signs of wear are evident.

FLY LINE OR SHOOTING HEAD TO LEADER

I do not recommend the braided mono connector as a means of attaching the leader to a fly line or shooting head, unless you are willing to regularly inspect and replace it. This is another connection that takes a lot of punishment, and these connectors can break down. I do use them, but I frequently inspect them for signs of weakness.

I suggest instead that you use a nail knot. Here, too, a small drop of glue is a good idea. I tested this nail knot connection for its strength and was pleased with the results. Using 40-pound leader butt section mono and a 10-weight fly line, the resulting nail knot withstood more than 35 pounds of pressure. This is more than any tippet you might use, and more than any normal fly rod could handle. Tie the nail knot using a bobbin exactly as you did with the backing.

With monofilament-type fly lines, nail knots may have trouble getting a firm bite. Melt a small ball into the end of the fly line, as described for the backing to fly line connection, to decrease the chances of the nail knot slipping off the end of the fly line. Glue the knot as well.

LEADER: SECTION BY SECTION

In salt water, leaders are kept relatively short and simple. A basic one would be between 7 and 8 feet long, with a breaking strength of 12 to 15 pounds. This leader could be made up of only three different sections, roughly following the old leader formula of 60 percent butt section, 20 percent midsection, and 20 percent tippet. Using this formula, a 7½-foot leader translates into approximately a 50-inch butt, 20-inch midsection, and 20-inch tippet.

The diameter of the leader's butt section and the breaking strength of the tippet are determined by the size of the fly line. For example, with an 8-weight fly line, I use a 30-pound butt section, followed by a midsection of 20-pound mono and a tippet of 10- or 12-pound test. For a 9- or 10-weight fly line, try a 40-pound butt, 30-pound midsection, and 12- or 15-pound tippet. With a 12-weight line, go to a 50-pound butt and taper to a 15- to 20-pound tippet.

To build this basic leader, start by connecting the butt section to the fly line or shooting head with a nail knot. Now use a blood knot to connect the midsection to the butt. In the end of the midsection, tie a surgeon's loop. Next, tie a double surgeon's loop in the end of a 2-foot piece of tippet material. Loop the tippet to the midsection. When the tippet wears back, simply replace it by looping on a new one.

A 7- or 8-foot leader is acceptable when fishing near the surface, but if you are using a sinking line, you can go even shorter. If the water is clear and you are fishing down 8 feet or so, a 5- or 6-foot leader is sufficient. If you go even deeper or find yourself fishing subsurface in murky water, your leader can be just 3 or 4 feet total.

The old standby blood knot is popular for joining two sections of a leader. The number of turns you should make is determined by the size of the monofilament. When either section is 25-pound test or greater, I prefer a 3½-turn blood knot. More turns create too much friction, producing heat when the knot is drawn tight. In smaller-diameter material, make five or six turns. Tighten either style of blood knot with a little saliva or water to ease the knot into place and reduce heat.

The surgeon's knot is also a good way to join two pieces of monofilament, and unlike the blood knot, it will join two sections of greatly

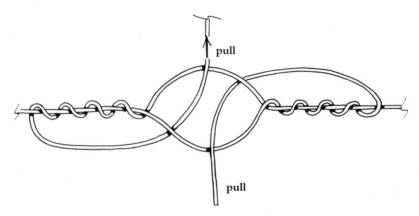

Blood knot. **The well-known blood knot is useful in building a leader.**

differing diameter and even connect braided wire to mono. Do not confuse the surgeon's knot with the surgeon's loop knot. The surgeon's knot does not create a loop; it simply connects two sections of line end to end.

If you want to loop the leader onto the fly line, you will need to form a loop in the leader butt. Here again, a surgeon's loop knot is handy. Use a single loop, not a double. Do not use a slipping loop knot like the uni-knot. I also believe that the perfection loop, so popular in fresh water, is a poor substitute for the surgeon's loop. It is far weaker, and when tied in heavy, stiff monofilament and subjected to sudden impact, it can suddenly come apart.

Many people sing the virtues of the Bimini twist as a 100 percent knot essential to all light-tackle anglers. But for the coastal fly fisherman, the Bimini twist has little practical application. Here is why: In tropical salt water, where anglers regularly encounter fish that weigh five to even ten times the breaking strength of the tippet, such a knot is clearly warranted. There, the tippet-to-weight ratio is high, and the fight may go on for hours. But fishing for striped bass, blues, and the like is different. Even a 50-pound striper on a 15-pound tippet is less than a four-to-one ratio. Furthermore, the Bimini twist is difficult to tie and even more so to tie consistently. The surgeon's loop is very close to a 100 percent knot, easy to tie even in the dark and easy to repeat consistently; it is therefore a more practical loop knot.

So where does the Bimini twist fit in? If you are actively seeking a world-record fish or heading out after a big offshore species such as a

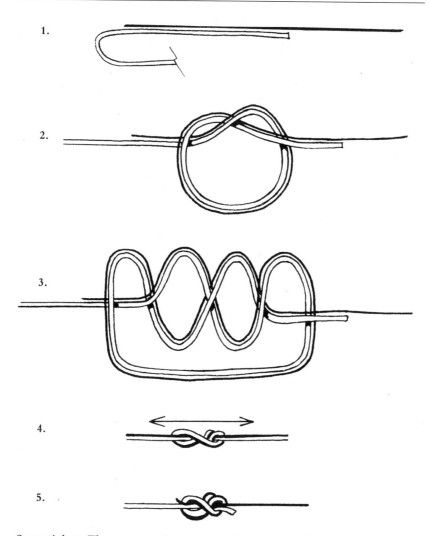

Surgeon's knot. **The surgeon's knot is a good way to attach two monofilaments of unequal size.**

tuna, the Bimini twist makes sense. And the greater the ratio between the tippet you plan on using and the weight of the fish required to set a record, the more it is imperative to use it. So, for example, if you wish to set a world record on bluefish using 2-pound test, you would need to land a blue of around 15 pounds or better, quite a task. The tippet-to-weight ratio would be nearly eight to one.

TIPPET TO LEADER

The tippet can be tied directly to the leader with a blood knot or a surgeon's knot, but I prefer to use a loop-to-loop connection. It allows me to change tippets much faster. Make a doubled surgeon's loop in the end of the tippet. Again, do not confuse the surgeon's loop with the surgeon's knot. They have different purposes. Tie a single surgeon's loop in the end of the leader and join it with the tippet. Make sure that the loops run down and mesh neatly, forming a square-knot configuration.

WIRE SHOCK TIPPET

Bluefish, especially the bigger ones, require that you use a wire shock tippet. Even heavy monofilament simply cannot do the job. And solid wire is far superior to braided. I use plain #6 tobacco-colored stainless steel leader wire. It has a breaking strength of about 60 pounds, more than needed, but thinner wire kinks too easily. To connect the wire to either the fly or the leader, use a haywire twist. This is a simple knot to form and holds exceedingly well.

The haywire begins with a series of twists and ends in a number of barrel rolls. I have never had one slip or break. If the eye of the hook is not completely closed, however, the solid wire could possibly be pulled right out of the eye. So check the eye first.

The total length of the shock tippet should be about $3\frac{1}{2}$ inches. This will protect you from getting bitten off in about 95 percent of the cases. Start by cutting a piece of wire about 6 inches long. Haywire-twist the wire to your fly, and form a second haywire loop on the other end at the appropriate distance. Break off the excess wire on either end by bending it back and forth until it snaps off. Cutting with a pliers, though faster, leaves a very sharp edge. When you reach down to release the fly from a fish's mouth, this sharp point can do some damage to your hand. And be sure to pick up and carefully discard the pieces you remove. Leaving them on the floor is dangerous to anyone in bare feet or socks.

You can now tie the monofilament tippet to the wire loop with a clinch knot. Rig several flies with wire, and keep them in your fly box ready to go. If the wire gets bent while you are fishing, be sure to straighten it, as the fly will not ride properly. If the wire cannot be straightened, change flies.

Recently, a new generation of flexible wire shock tippet material has reached the marketplace. It is convenient, easy to work with, and

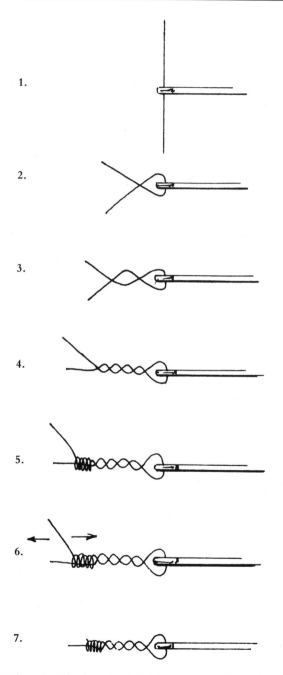

Haywire twist. **The haywire twist forms strong loops in solid wire.**

can be attached to the fly with conventional knots. Do not expect it to be inexpensive, however. Orvis makes some called Super-Flex. It comes in various strengths from 8- to 50-pound test. I think big blues will go through the lighter gauges, so I recommend you try any size from 30 pounds on up. Fenwick makes some too, referring to it as braided alloy leader material. It is available in roughly the same range of breaking strengths.

In some situations, you may want to use a 30- or 40-pound monofilament shock tippet, not to stop bluefish from biting you off but to keep from being cut off on sharp submerged objects such as barnacles or rocks. Start with a 1½-foot piece of the heavy monofilament. Using a surgeon's knot, attach it to your regular tippet. Then tie the fly to the heavy monofilament using a three-and-a-half-turn clinch so that the shock tippet is about 1 foot long. This combo is a little awkward to cast but is a lifesaver in some situations.

TIPPET TO FLY

In the salt, the clinch knot is the standard way in which anglers connect a fly to the leader. It is a very strong connection, somewhere close to 95 percent of the breaking strength of the line. Make four or five turns, except when using mono of 20 pounds or more; there, three and a half turns is all you should do. The improved clinch knot is also used, although it is not as easy to fully tighten in mono over 10-pound test.

Clinch knot. **Use the clinch knot to attach your fly to the tippet.**

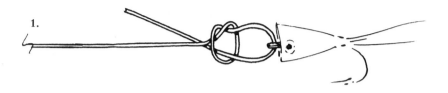

1.

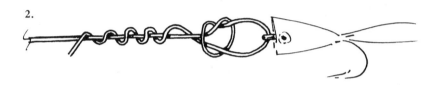

2.

3.

4.

Mono loop knot. **The mono loop knot can also be used to attach your fly to the tippet.**

For that reason, you find fewer anglers using the improved clinch in the salt.

Be sure to fully tighten the clinch knot. By doing so, you will get maximum sensitivity during the retrieve. Furthermore, failure to fully tighten opens you up to two potential problems: The knot may come undone, or it may slide to one side of the hook eye, causing the fly to track improperly.

Some anglers feel that using a clinch knot reduces the action of the fly, and therefore they prefer a loop knot. I have not, however, seen any meaningful benefit from using a loop knot to attach the fly, and because the loop knot does not attach solidly to the fly, I think you lose some sensitivity. Loop knots also tend to be weaker than clinch knots, and they can cause their own troubles. If the loop is too big, the fly may get snagged in it during the cast. And loop knots eat up your tippet a lot faster.

If you want to try one anyway, pick one that does not slide down on the eye of the hook when pressure is applied. This leaves out the uni-knot, for example. The mono loop is a fine knot when tied properly. Keep the size of the loop small. You do not want it to be anywhere near as long as the hook shank, or you run the risk of the hook fouling in the loop during the cast, which would totally ruin the action of the fly.

12

Striped Bass, Bluefish, Bonito, and Little Tunny

Anyone can learn to cast, anyone can learn to tie a fly, but until you know what makes your quarry tick, you will never truly learn to fish. Fortunately for anglers, most game fish share some universal patterns. They react in predictable ways to changes in tide and current. They follow schooling baitfish and prefer to haunt the edges of structure. And they love to feed in rips.

Other types of behavior, however, are specific to certain species and not found across the board. Each game fish has a unique blend of strengths and weaknesses. Some have relatively short lives but live extremely aggressively, seemingly always in high gear; others live longer but prefer to do things at a slower pace. Some are largely nocturnal, using their powerful eyesight to hunt in darkness; others feed only during the day and disappear at twilight. Some like relatively warm water and are active only during the hotter months of the year; others tolerate a wider range of temperatures and survive in the coastal waters year-round. Together these traits give each game fish species its distinctive character, and anglers must be prepared and ready to adapt.

Other habits are local ones, the way a species of fish reacts to conditions in a specific location. Ultimately this is the most useful knowledge of all, but it is also the most difficult to obtain. It is reserved only for observant anglers who regularly fish the same places time and again. Experience has taught them that if they catch a particular type of fish around a piece of structure at a specific tide and time of year, they are apt to find them there the next year under the same conditions. For that reason, local experts keep logs, recording every aspect of each trip from wind direction and weather to water temperature and tide. I recommend that you do this too. Eventually your log may tell you much about your home waters: where the fish go when the tide is slack, where they feed when the wind shifts, and where to get one or two fish even when the action has been slow.

Fly rodders working near shore in northeastern waters have a favorite four: striped bass, bluefish, Atlantic bonito, and little tunny. They are the most sought-after fly-rod game fish in our coastal waters, and they deserve special attention. Of course, these four are not the only saltwater fish along the coast that come to a fly. From our beaches and in our estuaries, a fly fisherman might hook Atlantic salmon, Atlantic shad, hickory shad, weakfish, fluke, drum, pollock, Atlantic mackerel, Spanish mackerel, sea-run trout, and white perch, among others. And in the briny deep, fly rodders with large boats pursue even bigger game. Blue sharks and mako sharks are two popular gamesters that take a fly, the latter being harder to hook and tougher to land. School tuna and dolphins *(Coryphaena hippurus)* are two more ideal targets for the offshore fly angler. And in the future, this brand of saltwater fly fishing is surely going to grow.

Although these four fish are presently the most popular players for the near-shore angler, fish stocks go through cycles of boom and bust. For instance, striper fishing was poor in the early eighties but now finally is showing strong signs of recovery. So the future there is bright, but now bluefish are simultaneously showing signs of possible decline. Had this book been written in the mid-seventies, we would be covering the beautiful weakfish. But stocks have been depressed now for many years. Let's hope they make a comeback soon. One way you can help is by joining an active coastal conservation organization to preserve our marine resources. Do it today.

STRIPED BASS

Of the four species, the one that has longest stirred the imagination of fly fishermen is *Morone saxatilis*—the striped bass. As early as 1849, Frank Forester was writing about the taking of stripers on a fly, and the great fly rodder Theodore Gordon also had excellent sport with them. The love affair between stripers and fly rodders has gone on ever since, passed along through such able hands as Joe Brooks and Harold Gibbs. It still burns brightly after all these years.

Striped bass, also referred to as stripers, linesiders, rockfish, or simply bass, are handsome, powerful, and sometimes elusive creatures. Along the Atlantic coast, three estuaries produce most of the stock: the Chesapeake Bay, the Hudson River, and the Roanoke River–Albemarle Sound area. In the late 1970s, because of overfishing, poor weather patterns, and lowering water quality, striper stocks slipped into a spiraling decline. Then Congress stepped in with the Atlantic Striped Bass Conservation Act of 1984. Since then, through the hard work of many organizations and individuals, striped bass stocks have recovered. And in 1993, the Chesapeake Bay finally produced another dominant year class, one larger than our wildest dreams.

The striped bass is a robust fish with a decided tendency to develop a belly with age. Its tail is wide and slightly forked, a design that, though not offering high-speed endurance, gives stripers tremendous takeoff power and rapid maneuverability. As a result, they can sit nearly motionless under your fly and then, with a flick of the tail, make an explosive strike that will shake you down into your socks. The mouth is large and shaped like a freshwater largemouth bass. Stripers do not have teeth, although the inside of the mouth is rough and hard in places. They cannot chop up their diet, and instead swallow their prey whole. The eyes are large and set high on the body. The position of the eyes gives stripers excellent overhead vision, allowing them to see and attack their prey from below; their size indicates that stripers are ideally suited to hunting the shadows of darkness and dawn.

Seven or eight black longitudinal stripes on either side make up the striper's most distinctive physical feature. The flanks are silvery, the belly is white, and the back varies from pale olive green to black. Coloration changes with location, probably an adaptation to help camouflage a striper in its environment. For example, stripers caught in discolored waters are apt to be dark with sides that are more brassy than silvery; those that inhabit the clear waters of the open surf and live over sand bottoms can be very pale along the back and their sides reduced to a milky translucency.

Stripers grow to the greatest size of the "favorite four" and likely live the longest. Most of the stripers you get on a fly are 10 pounds or under. These fish are young, ranging from about three to six years of age. They invariably travel in large schools, hence the name "schoolies." Stripers over 10 pounds do school, but much less so and in small numbers. Stripers of 10 to 20 pounds are fairly common on a fly and can really rip into backing. Big bass of 20 to 30 pounds are caught on a fly every season, providing a memorable moment for some lucky angler. And be aware that, though rare, it is possible to catch fish of 50 pounds and beyond.

Like most predators, bass exhibit an odd blend of curiosity, wariness, and aggressiveness. They are particularly cautious in shallow water. Sometimes you hook one striper on a tidal flat and it spooks all the rest of them. Other times you hook one and several of its friends follow it throughout the fight as if trying to figure out what it is doing. At times a striper follows a fly all the way to your rod tip and does not take it, and other days bass grab your fly as soon as it lands on the water.

Besides being a quarry of great size, strength, and cunning, the striper offers fishermen both the longest season and the greatest range of the four species. The reason is simple: Striped bass tolerate a wide range of water temperatures. They can survive in water as low as 38 degrees, which makes them the only fish of the four that can truly winter over in the estuaries and coastal waters of New England. On the high end, they can endure water nearing 80 degrees. As with most game fish, the oldest and largest individuals are more adapted to the cooler end of the temperature range, and the young ones prefer the warmer.

Stripers are attracted to heavy surf, rips, and frequently, rocky points of land. They also like coastal rivers, inlets, and salt ponds, tolerating a wide range of salinity and water conditions from clear to downright muddy. And everywhere they love bottom structure, especially a dropoff or edge. The smaller fish gravitate to the shallow inshore waters, and the larger ones frequent the deeper holes and reefs, each group seeking the most comfortable temperature range. Remember, though, that these are only trends and not fixed rules; many a trophy bass has been caught tight to the beach over a sand bottom.

In strategy, stripers are guerrilla warfare experts, much preferring a good ambush over an open field attack; hence their love for lurking around structure. They are primarily sight feeders. Therefore, the first step in engaging the prey is to make visual contact. In order to do that, a striper must be able to see the baitfish—or your fly—as something separate and distinct from the background. Our eyes distinguish figure from background through a process of comparison known as visual contrast.

This striper was feeding on sand eels when it was caught and released by Kevin Pelletier. *Photograph by Phil Farnsworth.*

Objects are discerned through the contrast of light against dark, one hue or one shape against another, or something in motion against its surroundings. A bass is able to see its prey through these same juxtapositions of visual elements. Thus a fly that contrasts with the background is usually more effective than a fly that blends in. And often it is motion that initially catches the striper's eye.

When water clarity is poor or light level low, however, vision is greatly reduced, and a bass switches to other senses to detect the presence of prey. Stripers now use their ability to hear and feel vibrations. That is why flies that push water, pop, or throw a wake are essential parts of your arsenal.

Stripers also have an excellent sense of smell. Some anglers take advantage of it by using a chum slick or by treating their flies with one of the fish-attracting scents available in tackle stores. Because of this keen sense of smell, be careful not to put unwanted odors on the fly. Flies that are freshly constructed may still reek of head cement, epoxy, or other unnatural scents. Let them air out before you use them. Also be careful not to transfer odors from your hands to the fly. For instance, an angler who pumps gas into a car or boat and then handles the fishing gear is off to a bad start.

As far as weather is concerned, fair, high-pressure days with nice puffy clouds are beautiful, but they are rarely right for striper fishing. Choose a day that is overcast and, better yet, a little unsettled. Gray skies, a light rain, wind, and changing barometric pressure are all good signs. The fishing just before a cold front passes through can be red hot, but it depends quite a bit on the time of year. In the spring, a cold front will give you a few hours of great fishing until the front passes through. Then the fishing will drop off considerably. Water temperatures are already low at this time of year, and any hint that they might drop further seems to send the bass to the bottom. In the fall, however, that same cold front could rip things wide open by forcing the warm waters to cool and thereby starting the fall migration southward.

When it comes time to dine, stripers show an extensive palate. They are opportunistic and able to consume a wide variety of things both large and small. In upper estuaries, small schoolies will feed on things that you normally associate with trout: nymphs, larvae, and small minnows. In the open salt, stripers can make a meal of anything from tiny amphipods to clams, crabs, lobster, and squid. Still, along the coast you can expect to find striped bass spending a good deal of time following and feeding on schooling baitfish, especially in the fall. Important ones are menhaden and other members of the herring family, mackerel, silversides, and sand eels.

The Right Retrieve for Stripers

The size, shape, and color of any fly play a role in its success, but so does the way you retrieve it. It may be easy to forget that fact, but sooner or later something happens to drive the point home. Usually it goes like this: You find yourself standing next to someone who is hitting fish after fish while you cannot buy a bite. And worse yet, the two of you are using pretty much the same fly. It could be that the other angler has a better spot, but just as likely he or she is retrieving the fly in a more effective way.

When this type of thing occurs, glance over and watch what the other angler is doing. Try to figure out what is different about the manner in which the fly is being worked. Pay special attention to both the speed of the retrieve and whether it is continuous or stop-and-go. Once you figure it out, give it a try.

Still, the good news is that though experimentation should never be overlooked, day in and day out certain retrieve styles seem to work well for stripers. When using a streamer or slider in shallow water, I prefer a slow, steady retrieve over the stop-and-go style produced by stripping the fly back. When you strip a fly back, it pauses and sinks for a brief time between strips. This series of hops may appear unnatural to stripers following the fly. This does not mean that you should not try the strip method, for it can be effective at times, but it is probably not the most productive approach across the season.

You can achieve a slow, steady retrieve by using the hand-over-hand method. After the cast, place the rod high up under your casting arm so that the reel and most if not all of the cork grip protrude from the backside of your armpit. Hold the rod snugly against your body by applying pressure with your casting arm. Next, let the rod angle downward so that the tip is pointed toward the water. Reach up with either hand and grasp the fly line at the first stripping guide, then pull down slowly while reaching up with your other hand to repeat the motion. The retrieved line should be falling into a stripping basket unless conditions allow for it to be dropped to the ground. The result should be a slow, continuous retrieval of line.

Strike any fish by simply pulling firmly on the fly line rather than lifting the rod tip. After the striper feels the hook, it will hold for a split second, during which time you must get the rod down from under your arm, all the while maintaining some tension on the line. As the fish turns and runs, lift the rod tip, still keeping a bit of tension on the fly line that is coming up out of the stripping basket. As soon as all the line is out of the stripping basket, fight the fish from the reel.

Another advantage of this retrieve is that you are essentially hand-lining the fly. Thus even a light take is easy to feel. In many cases, the strike of a striper is a real *thud*. But at night a striper can overtake a fly, inhale it, and continue to swim forward toward you, in which case the strike is soft, not unlike a trout picking up a nymph. If you are retrieving the fly continously, you have constant contact with the fly and can feel even the smallest change in resistance.

The third advantage of the hand-over-hand method is that it allows you to produce a very fast retrieve when needed. This is not as important for stripers, but it can be essential for bluefish. Because you have both hands free to take in line, it is easy to quicken the pace to a level unattainable by stripping the fly in.

It is a different story with poppers, however. Stripers seem to prefer a popper that has an erratic stop-and-go motion. Here the traditional strip retrieve has the clear edge. Furthermore, it allows you to control the amount of force going into the actual *pop*. I also find the conventional strip retrieve to be effective when fishing a streamer very deep with a fast-sinking line. I think the jigging motion of the fly helps a bass find it.

Catching stripers on a popper is something that requires a degree of patience and skill, regardless of the retrieve you use. Frequently they will follow the popper for a considerable distance without striking. You can tell they are there by the wakes, swirls, and bulges they create as they contemplate blasting this noisy intruder. It is tough not to get nervous, but keep your head. You may have to experiment with the speed of the retrieve to suit a given fish's mood. It is during the pause in the retrieve that a reluctant striper will often hit. And be aware that stripers have a habit of following a popper right to the rod tip before making up their minds. Many a time I have had them blast a popper as I was picking it up for the backcast. So stay alert.

Even after you entice a striper into hitting your popper, there is no guarantee that you will hook it. In fact, if you do not use the correct method, your hookup rate can be very low. It is a mistake to strike immediately after a striper hits the popper. And it can be a hard thing for an angler to correct, because the violence of the strike is so startling that it is tempting to instantly yank back. The correct technique is much the same as salmon fishermen use when working a dry fly: Wait until the fish goes down with the fly before doing anything. Once the striper heads down with the popper, drive the hook home with a solid pull, keeping the rod very low to the water. Your percentage of hooked bass will go way up.

Overall, striped bass are taken on a wide variety of streamers, sliders, and poppers, in a wide range of sizes from a sparse sand eel fly to a big, bulky bunker pattern. Standard hook sizes for these flies run from #1 to #3/0. Note that though the bigger flies do tend to catch bigger bass, small flies catch them too. Steve Lewis, a friend of mine, caught a 40-inch striper on a tiny #6 shad fly. And as a rule, when stripers get selective, the best idea is to go to a smaller fly, unless the bait is obviously very large.

The two flies in most common use in New England waters are the Clouser Deep Minnow and Lefty's Deceiver. Typically they ride #1/0 or #2/0 hooks and measure about 3½ inches in length. Popular colors for streamers include blue over white, green over white, chartreuse, and yellow. Black flies are best at night. For sliders I recommend silver, chartreuse, or black. In the popper department, color is not a burning issue, but if pressed I would pick chartreuse.

The Striper Season

As with all marine life, water temperature is an important determinant of striped bass activity and behavior. Water temperature preference ranges for game fish are not absolute, however, and they vary with changes in geographic location. Wise anglers develop logs for their local waters. Regardless of your location, the season is controlled by water temperatures and generally broken down into three main periods: the spring migration, the summer residency, and the fall migration. Each of these components does not have a distinct beginning and end. It is better thought of as a sliding continuum. Still, there are important differences in the type of fishing you are apt to find and the best technique to employ during each period.

Spring

As a general rule, 45-degree water seems to be a minimum for successful striper fishing. Bass at this temperature are barely active and often lie deep near the bottom. South Carolina anglers catch some in the estuaries by February, and slowly the action creeps north with the retreating weather. Striper fishermen are hooking up in New Jersey by late March in places like the Mullica River. Hudson River bass anglers are not far behind.

In southern New England, striper fishing usually begins by mid-April, as day length begins to equal that of night. If the winter has been severe, consistent action is delayed into the first weeks of May. Conversely, after a very mild winter, fish may be caught in the last week of March and the first week of April. These first bass are either stripers that have wintered over locally or migrants from the Hudson River.

Fish that have wintered over in a river are generally dark in color, especially along the back. Stripers that have migrated into an area from the open sea are usually much lighter. Another sign that a fish comes from a large school that has been recently traveling in the open ocean is the presence of sea lice. These small, brown creatures are about the size of a pencil lead and adhere to the flanks of the fish, often rear of the dorsal fin.

As you would expect, the farther north you are in New England, the later the season begins. In Connecticut, a few stripers usually come to the fly by the second week in April, although in abnormally warm years the action starts at least a week earlier. Rhode Island picks up at about the same time as Connecticut to a week or so later, depending on water temperatures. By the third week in April, schoolie stripers start showing around Martha's Vineyard, and within a week, they will also show on the southern Cape Cod beaches.

The season begins even later in Maine and New Hampshire because of their location along the Gulf of Maine, which is a colder body of water. New Hampshire striper fishing begins around the end of May. Southern Maine can match that same timetable, but as you travel farther north, anglers look to the middle of June for the first stripers to whack a fly.

Whatever geographic location you are fishing, you can safely assume that the first bass of the year are schoolies and that river mouths and estuaries supply the most action. One reason for this orientation to the river mouths is the season runs of herring in many locations. They could be Atlantic herring or, more likely in southern New England, the alewife followed by the blueback herring. You also can expect to find other baitfish, such as silversides and mummichogs, in these waters. Sand eels seem to come a bit later.

My favorite fly at this time of year would be a weighted streamer, such as a Clouser Minnow, in chartreuse. But you could add weight to almost any pattern you care to mention. The best delivery system is a sinking line. The fish are deep and will not readily climb up to strike a fly far overhead. Since the stripers' metabolism also is in low gear, a very slow retrieve or even simply letting the fly hang at the end of the swing is advisable.

Poppers are not productive during the early weeks of the season. Wait to use them until water temperatures have climbed a bit. Sliders are also not a first choice in the cold water of spring simply because they ride too close to the surface. But if you find stripers in shallow water—and you often do in the spring, as these waters warm first— sliders should produce.

The best time of day to wet a line in early spring is midafternoon. The water is the warmest then, and the fish are the most active. This is exactly the same strategy that pays off for the early-season trout fisherman. Roughly after the first month of fishing, dusk and dawn start being better choices, especially if there is a moving tide at those times of day. Night fishing, however, is generally not yet productive, although occasionally there may be some action.

Summer

In the Northeast, larger bass begin arriving from both the Chesapeake and the Hudson as water temperatures climb into the 50s. This happens about a month after the first stripers of the year show up. Here again, remember that local variations exist. In Connecticut, late May is the target date, and in Maine, you can plan on the beginning of July. These bigger fish do not tolerate warm water as well as the juveniles and schoolies, so as the season progresses, they will remain in deeper waters and leave the shallow bays and upper estuaries to the younger crowd. In most locations, adult stripers seek water in the 55- to 68-degree range; younger bass are often found in 65- to 75-degree areas. This separation by water temperature keeps the big guys away from the smaller crowd, thereby reducing cannibalism. The maximum water temperature for stripers is between 77 and 80 degrees.

By late spring and early summer, striper fishing is on a roll. June is a super time to be on the water from Montauk, Long Island, to Maine. Often the striper fishing rivals the best that the fall has to offer. Many of the important baitfish are around in good numbers, including sand eels and silversides. Adult menhaden, a popular target for stripers, have moved inshore too. Your fly box should now contain all three types of flies: streamers, sliders, and poppers. And you should have things ready to mimic the prevalent local baitfish.

Dawn and dusk are still great times to fish, but for shore-based anglers in many locations, action is waning in the middle of the day. Boaters, on the other hand, can still find stripers feeding during the day out over productive reefs. Still, with climbing water temperatures, stripers are most active after dark. Therefore, veteran surf anglers shift their attention to night fishing. The first hour after sun usually holds little action. Rather, you should wait until the sun has been down for two or three hours before wetting a fly. The exact time you head out should also be related to the time of tide. In Long Island Sound, I fish nights exclusively after the first weeks of June and will do so until sometime in the fall.

Fall

Like the spring migration, the fall migration is linked to water temperature and length of day. As days shorten and the water cools, an inner
clock tells stripers to head south. It also shifts them into a ravenous
feeding frenzy, as they pile on weight for their long winter rest. These
few weeks usually offer the best fishing of the year. Many years, the
migration starts in Maine around mid-September. Note that this is
about the time that the hours of daylight equal the hours of night. Once
the migration from Maine is under way, it begins a cascading effect
along the coast from north to south. Maine's fishing will taper off by
month's end. In early October, the action picks up along Cape Cod and
farther south into Rhode Island and Connecticut. It produces a few
weeks of intense fishing, then starts to taper off. November can still be
good in Rhode Island and Long Island Sound until water temperature
reaches 45 degrees and there are only ten hours of light each day.

Day length is not the only factor controlling water temperature;
weather patterns also play a large role. And since the weather can vary
greatly from year to year, fall fishing will be somewhat unpredictable. A
strong northeast blow in the fall will push the colder offshore waters
into the coast, rapidly lowering water temperature. Often these storms
are two- or three-day affairs, and the fishing during and after can be
great. If a storm also brings early snows, they usually melt quickly and
produce cold runoff, which also contributes to lower water temperatures near shore.

Night fishing in the fall often produces the biggest stripers, yet day
fishing can be excellent too. And for many anglers, after months of dark
fishing, day excursions are a welcome change. In late October or early
November in Long Island Sound, for example, stripers feed greedily in
broad daylight and may move in large schools accompanied by flocks of
gulls. Two other less common birds are also good indicators of late-
season action, and you should fish wherever you find them. The common loon is one. The other is the mighty gannet, a big bird that is
primarily white with black-tipped wings spanning 6 feet. The gannet
follows only the largest schools of bait. If you see this giant diving
through the sky from ten stories, rocketing into a school of bait, you
will have witnessed one of the most spectacular sights along the northern coast.

While New Englanders are putting their gear away, other anglers down the coast are still sharpening hooks. From the eastern tip of Long Island to Cape May, November continues to see stripers. Montauk is a super spot; expect things to hold up as late as Thanksgiving. But be aware that many times the fish are deep during this late season, and from shore the fly-rod opportunities may be slim. In warm years, the action could extend right up to the Christmas holidays. Still farther south in the Chesapeake, anglers see their best battles in the waning light of December and January.

BLUEFISH

Bluefish. They can jump. They can run like demons. They can rip your flies and leaders apart. And they never, never seem to give up. These traits and the fact that in recent years bluefish have been the most consistent quarry for the fly rodder have earned them a place of respect in the hearts of coastal anglers.

Like the striped bass, the bluefish is a highly migratory species. Blues travel all along the Atlantic coast in schools made up of individual fish of similar ages and sizes. Unlike bass, however, they do not spawn in estuaries. Most spawning takes place in two large areas, the South Atlantic and the Mid-Atlantic bights. The young-of-the-year are pushed back into shore by prevailing currents and wind. Once near shore, they use the rich waters of the coastal estuaries as nursery areas.

Bluefish populations have shown cycles of boom and bust. The most startling swing in New England waters happened in 1764, when bluefish vanished seemingly overnight. They were almost nonexistent for twenty years, and it took nearly fifty years for them to regain their former abundance. There have been similar cycles since, but none so severe. More recently, 1986, 1987, and especially 1988 were poor recruitment years; 1981, 1984, and 1989 were good years. Still, for the last three or four years, bluefish have been showing signs of declining. Given the heavy fishing pressure applied to blues and their cyclic nature, we might be in for a sudden downswing in the population. At the very least, we should all be pushing for better management of this valuable sport fish.

Bluefish are the most aggressive of all our game fish. In today's vernacular, their personality might be best described as "in yo face." Certainly, they are known for putting on the most vivid displays of coastal consumption in the form of awe-inspiring blitzes. With their legendary razor-sharp teeth, blues can rip baitfish to shreds, releasing the oil from their small bodies to form slicks that may cover acres of water at a time. So devastating is their attack that it is possible to smell the carnage at a considerable distance.

Blues grow rapidly and live to about eleven or twelve years of age. They reach a maximum recorded size in excess of 30 pounds and 3 feet long. In New England waters, young-of-the-year blues are known as snappers. Bluefish from 3 to 6 pounds are very common and supply many a fly rodder with his or her introduction to salt water. At this size they are called "harbor blues" because of their preference for bays and coves. Some anglers also call them "cocktail blues" because of their perfect size for the grill. They feed ravenously in large schools, and once you get within casting range, it is usually easy to hook them at will.

On a fly rod, blues of 8 to 10 pounds are great sport. If you get into a school of these middleweights, you are going to be plenty busy. Blues in the lower to middle teens are harder to come by, but not rare. Expect to hear them referred to as choppers, gators, slammers, or even gorillas. A fish of this size puts up a ferocious battle, taxing you right to the very end. Once you have been through it, you will never forget their raw stamina. Catching blues bigger than 16 pounds on a fly is rare, but it is not impossible, particularly offshore and in the late fall.

The bluefish has a powerful and streamlined body and a large head. Its teeth are dangerous and deserve respect. You will find a single row in both bottom and top jaws, with the former being the larger and stronger of the two. Never, under any circumstances, try to remove a fly from a bluefish's mouth without the utmost care, and always use pliers. If a large blue chomps down on your finger, it could cut you to the bone, and a blue stressed after a fight is likely to clamp down and refuse to let go. I even know an angler who was badly bitten by the severed head of a bluefish he had filleted. Enough said.

In coloration, adults are bluish green along the back and silvery to white on the sides. Young-of-the-year blues lack the blue-green and are instead very silvery and bright all over. So markedly different is their appearance that in the distant past, some believed they were two unrelated fish.

Bluefish are opportunistic feeders and will make a meal of many things. Still, like striped bass, bluefish seem to key in heavily on a diet of other fish, of which more than seventy different species have been recorded. They seem to prefer schooling baitfish, and menhaden are likely their favorite target. Whereas striped bass swallow their food

Large bluefish such as this come very close to shore at night and will put up a tremendous battle. *Photograph by Phil Farnsworth.*

whole and preferably head-on, bluefish are more apt to hit a baitfish from the rear and chop it up. Frequently they might simply bite off a piece of their quarry including its tail, leaving the baitfish helpless. In some cases, the blue will then eat the rest, but when in a hurry, blues can leave the remainder behind. This behavior coupled with their perceived greed has gained them a reputation as a violent and even destructive predator.

When you are concentrating on blues, look to rips, reefs, and inlets. Many blues are caught in the surf too, but they seem more at home in open water. Perhaps this reflects the fact that blues are not as ambush-oriented as striped bass and appear instead to prefer an open chase. I catch many more bluefish over sand bottoms than I do over rock, and blues also seem to be less tolerant than bass of murky or roiled water.

Like stripers, blues are mainly sight feeders, so the same concerns about a fly's visibility underwater apply. Furthermore, bluefish seem to be very attracted to neon colors, particularly hot orange. They are also very sensitive to smell and sound. As a result, chum lines and poppers are two of the most popular ways along the coast to find the blues. Note, too, that with blues, poppers are successful after dark, unlike with stripers, which shun things that go bump in the night.

The Right Retrieve for Bluefish

Blues love to chase a fast fly. In fact, it is difficult to retrieve a fly too quickly for a blue. This holds true for poppers, sliders, and streamers. The hand-over-hand retrieve used on striped bass is also an excellent method to produce a very fast-moving fly, although poppers are difficult to *pop* this way, and instead produce a kind of high-speed gurgle.

One June I got a chance to fish a school of small blues every single day for a week. These fish would race back and forth every morning in full view along a stretch of shallow beach. They were chasing silversides, and most days the blues hung around for several hours. The water in this location is extremely clear, the bottom an uninterrupted expanse of light-colored sand. This coupled with fair, sunny days made conditions perfect for sight fishing. With a pair of polarized sunglasses, I could see the whole blitz as if it were taking place in an aquarium.

Rather than chase these blues up and down the beach, I would wade out and position myself in their path. Before long, I would see them coming, and it was a simple matter to cast a streamer out to intercept them. Once the blues were within several yards, I would start a retrieve using the hand-over-hand method. One or more blues would instantly leave formation and track the fly. These fish were so dependable that I felt I could do some experimenting with retrieve speed. On a slow pace, the blues would look at the fly but quickly turn off and return to the pack. A moderate speed produced more interest and a few hookups, particularly if more than one fish was following the fly. A fast retrieve, on the other hand, resulted in blues falling all over themselves to be the first to grab the hook. Clearly, retrieve speed made a remarkable difference.

The effectiveness of this high-speed retrieve seems to be built on two related phenomena. First, bluefish are accustomed to seeing baitfish hightail it away, so a fast fly looks natural. You could also say that something that swims casually away from a bluefish looks fake. This is especially true when the bluefish run up close to the fly. Now they can see the fly very well, and any baitfish worth eating would certainly have seen them. Second, I believe that bluefish attack a fast-moving object in an almost knee-jerk reaction. You could say that the fly dares them to catch it.

Now that I have said why bluefish like fast food, let me tell you that just as with any other technique in fishing, there are exceptions to the rule. At night, bluefish take a slow-moving fly. Why? Because at night they expect to be able to catch bait unaware, and therefore a slow-moving fly looks completely natural. Bluefish will also hit a slow-moving fly in cooler water temperatures when their own metabolism is also slowed. Also, in discolored water, a slower retrieve gives fish a chance to find the fly.

As you might expect, when a bluefish hits a fly moving at a good clip, the fish tends to hook itself. The only consistent problem occurs with poppers. Unlike when fishing for stripers, you do not want to wait before trying to drive the hook home. Hit a bluefish immediately. In some cases, a bluefish will give you a short run and then drop the fly. A bluefish can clamp down with such force on the body of a popper that it is impossible to set the hook properly. So be ready to lose a small percentage of these fish. The only thing you can do is to hit these fish as hard as the tippet allows and see what happens.

Snapper blues and harbor blues will also take a whack at your popper, but the problem here is different. The mouth of a smaller blue sometimes does not have enough room to take in a fly deep enough for you to set the hook. If you are presenting to these smaller fish, use a scaled-down popper. A #6 smallmouth bass model might turn the trick nicely. Do not be afraid of experimenting.

Bluefish are by nature's design a different type of fighter than striped bass. With their forked tails and more streamlined bodies, pound for pound blues have a bit less power but can swim faster and pull longer. Any bluefish over 10 pounds is quite a fly-rod adversary and can be expected to take you into the backing. Even after you have the fish in the boat or on the beach, a blue will continue to twist and turn, all the while snapping its jaws. It is an impressive show of raw energy and will. Blues in the mid-teens can be a hair-raising experience. If hooked in shallow water, they often run to deeper water with great speed, tearing line off the reel. It would not be uncommon in this circumstance for a fish to go into the backing more than once.

In addition to their great endurance and speed, bluefish are the only fish of the four that can truly jump. It is a kind of tail walk, combined with a good deal of head shaking and flared gills. This adds an exciting dimension to the fight. The first jump usually occurs at the end of the initial run, but not always. Still, after a few long-range leaps, many a blue will save one or two jumps for the very end when you least expect it. So be prepared.

Although you may have seen fly rodders bow their rods to jumping tarpon, no such maneuver is necessary with a blue. In fact, doing so may help the bluefish cut through the leader. When you bow, you create slack in the line, which could allow the leader to drape into the blue's open mouthful of teeth, and presto, the fish will be off. Instead, keep a tight line at all times during the fight.

The Bluefish Season

Bluefish are found from Florida to Maine, but overall they are more of a warmwater species than striped bass. The extent of their northern range is largely determined by the margins of acceptable water temperature. Before the mid-1970s, bluefish entered New England waters as far as Cape Cod. Since that time, warmer seas have allowed them to enter the Gulf of Maine in great numbers. As with other marine fish, the oldest and largest of the species travel the farthest north. Therefore, trophy bluefish are most often found in the cooler waters. And by nature's grand design, the largest of the menhaden, a baitfish that blues prefer, also travel to these northern waters.

Spring

Bluefish start moving up the coast from their winter grounds as surface water temperatures reach and exceed 53 degrees. In March, blues are busy along the Florida coast, and by April, they are on a roll in North Carolina and up the coast to Maryland. The first bluefish to enter New England waters round Montauk and enter Long Island Sound sometime in early May. These are fair-size fish, although few in number. They will seek shallow bays, power plant releases, and other areas where the water temperature is even a few degrees warmer than the surroundings.

Another early group seems to head from Montauk toward the islands. Martha's Vineyard usually gets some action around the second week of the month. These early arrivals provide very little fly-rod action, however. Generally they are not very aggressive and feed more by smell than sight. These fish also are just moving through, and as soon as water temperatures lift even a small amount, they will travel farther north.

Right on the tails of these big blues are large schools of fish in the 3- to 6-pound range. These blues are a different story. They come to the fly with abandon. In southern New England, look for these fish to supply red-hot action in the first weeks of June wherever you find them. These fish are also seeking the limits of their water temperature tolerance. But they require a warmer environment than their bigger cousins and therefore will not travel as far up the coast. Once again, these differences in preferred temperature help separate the bigger blues from the smaller and thereby reduce cannibalism.

Early-season bluefish hit all types of flies, including poppers. Still, streamers and sliders moving at a moderate to slow pace seem to take more of the first arrivals. This changes quickly with rising water temperatures, and by June in southern New England, a moderate to high-speed retrieve is in order. Regardless of the fly and its retrieve, hot fluorescent colors appear to have a special attraction for bluefish. Chartreuse and especially neon orange flies are killers. I use them regularly.

Shock tippets are required bluefishing equipment. Not only can a hooked blue cut through a mono tippet, sometimes it gets help from its friends too. Seeing the fly dangling from the mouth of its cousin, a competing bluefish will attempt to steal it away from the other fish and in so doing cut your line. If you do not believe this theory, next time you have hooked a bluefish in clear water, watch to see how many of its companions follow it in to the beach. You are apt to see up to five fish accompanying yours. If a second angler throws a fly nearby, the unhooked members will charge it at flank speed. Certainly they are keyed up enough to rip the fly from the mouth of the first fish if the chance arises.

Heavy monofilament is still used as a shock tippet by some anglers, but most coastal fly rodders have switched to solid leader wire. Commercial leaders with wire shock tippets are now available, and they do the job. For those who prefer to do it themselves, start by purchasing a package of leader wire in about 60-pound test. I use a product that is commonly available, tests at 58 pounds, and has a diameter of .016. Cut off an 8-inch piece, and haywire-twist it to the eye of the fly. Next, form a loop in the far end such that the distance from loop to loop is 3 to 3½ inches. Haywire-twist the second loop, break off the excess, and you are done.

At this time of year, the best part of the day to be on the water is often midmorning to midafternoon. This is especially true if the tide is pulling hard during these hours. With each passing day of the season, however, daytime fishing, though remaining good, is being replaced by dawn as the best time to wet a line. Night fishing for bluefish is not a good idea now; it comes into its own later in the year.

Toward the end of spring and the beginning of summer, it is possible to come across bluefish daisy-chaining on the surface. Most likely this is a prespawn ritual that allows fish to group before heading offshore. In the Northeast, I see this event at least once a year, and it usually takes place on a calm, bright day. What you see are the dark dorsal and tail fins of several blues sticking through the surface. These fish mill around slowly in a loosely formed circle.

Usually these daisy chainers are fair-size blues and very skittish. Any noise is apt to put them down. Even the shadow of a fly line cast across them may cause them to sink out of sight. The fish rarely go far, however, so if they go down, it pays to wait. If you are quiet and persistent, you may get a fish or two. Try a streamer fly when the fish are on top, as it does not disturb the water much. If that does not work, switch to a popper or slider. And if the fish go down, work the area anyway. Often you will get one to come back up.

Summer

As summer arrives, bluefish have established more or less permanent feeding grounds for the warmer months. This means dependable action in the local hot spots, with dusk and dawn being the prime times of day. With water temperatures in the mid 60s and above in many parts of the coast, anglers see the smaller blues filling the bays and harbors, while the big guys feed in deeper locations. There can be exceptions to this territorial division, but as a general rule it holds true.

Bluefish blitzes become more numerous as water temperatures rise. Generally these feeding frenzies are easy to spot, with a great deal of surface commotion and large numbers of accompanying gulls. If you are inside casting range, the fishing is usually easy and red hot. Using a fly that approximates the size of the bait is a good idea, but the longer the blitz goes on, the more the big flies are the best producers regardless of the size of the forage.

Although it is good to be close to the action, you do not want to be wading in the middle of the melee. Bluefish on rare occasions, and I want to stress that it is indeed rare, have bitten swimmers who wandered inside a blitz. How do you find yourself wading through a blitz? What often takes place is that a blitz comes to you. Let me give you a typical situation: You are wading a shallow beach and see a bluefish blitz nearby. Suddenly the school turns and heads toward you. Without further warning, you find yourself standing in the middle of the bait and surrounded by blues. This has happened to me several times.

In at least half the cases, the school continues to move and is gone in the wink of an eye. Other times they do not move, and when that happens, I back up toward shore, stepping away from the location. How dangerous is this situation? I have never been attacked, and furthermore, I have never heard of anyone wearing waders who was bitten. Likely the waders mask any attractive odor or color, another good reason not to wade wet. Still, common sense tells me to move.

Night fishing can be very productive, especially in locations with heavy concentrations of bait and current flow. Estuary mouths and points of land are typically good bets. Unlike stripers, blues will hit noisy surface poppers in the dark, and an all-black model is the answer. Nevertheless, I use streamers and sliders more often and find them excellent night flies. Here again, black is the ticket, except on nights with a very bright moon. In that situation, a white fly can be better, particularly in clear, shallow water.

Fall

In most years, the fall migration south produces the finest bluefishing of the season. The action begins in Maine sometime in September. Falling water temperatures linked to shortening days are the powerful stimulant. And as with striped bass, northeast storms can really heat up the action. You can expect good fishing as the water temperature dips below 59 degrees, and on down to about 53 degrees.

Big flies and poppers are the best medicine for larger fish. They are especially important wherever bluefish are targeting adult menhaden. Frequently, this is the case as the larger bluefish are following the southerly migration of menhaden. The two move down the coast in locked step, often very tight to the shoreline. Shore-based fly rodders can get some incredible action at this time. But it does not happen every year. If there is a series of storms or a severe bout of cold weather early on, both bluefish and menhaden may take the quicker offshore route.

Early October is the beginning of the prime bluefish season in southern New England, and the action builds all month. In warm years, water temperatures can allow for good bluefishing until around the first week of November in Long Island Sound. The smaller fish have mostly moved on, and these late-season travelers are big blues in the 10- to 18-pound class. These are superb fly-rod fish, although they are sluggish in comparison with their warm-water performance. Once the water temperature dips to 50 or below, bluefish to a fly are rare.

Farther south, the season extends for several months. New York and

New Jersey see plenty of action well into November and possibly even December as blues continue down the Atlantic coast to their wintering grounds. Just after Thanksgiving, the beaches of North Carolina light up as jumbo blues put on the season's final curtain call.

Flies for Bluefish

Like striped bass, bluefish are caught on a wide variety of flies in a wide variety of sizes. This should not be surprising, since they often feed in the same waters over the same bait. Blues, however, are not quite as fussy as bass over fly size and color. When they do get picky, first try something larger. They generally prefer a bright-colored fly over a dull one, and a fly that makes a bit of commotion over something that slips silently along. Standard hook sizes for blues range from #1/0 to #3/0.

The most popular fly in the Northeast for bluefish is apt to be a #2/0 hot orange popper rather than a streamer. Maybe this is because blues like them better, or perhaps it is because anglers love to see a blue wallop one. Maybe both. At any rate, they work. The second most commonly used bluefish fly is probably a Lefty's Deceiver. For streamers and sliders, hot orange and the tried and true blue over white are the best bets.

BONITO AND LITTLE TUNNY

Atlantic bonito and little tunny have an intense and growing following among saltwater fly rodders in southern New England. These two semi-tropical fish are the newest and therefore the least known of our fly-rod quarries. When I say "newest" quarry, however, do not for a moment think that these fish are just now showing in New England waters. Written records show that bonito were occasionally netted in the Gulf of Maine going as far back as 1876. Today they are appearing on a much more regular basis in our waters, likely because of recent coastal warming trends. And this has produced heightened angler awareness.

Much like bass and blues, bonito and little tunny migrate along the Atlantic coast roughly from New England all the way to South America. They usually travel in large schools, commonly offshore. The Atlantic bonito *(Sarda sarada)* is a bit more tolerant of cooler water and has been recorded as far north as the southern end of the Gulf of Saint Lawrence. The little tunny *(Euthynnus alletteratus)* makes it as far north as Massachusetts and is probably the most numerous tuna in the western Atlantic. Many anglers refer to the little tunny as false albacore or even albacore, which leads to quite a bit of confusion. This fish should never be thought of as the true albacore tuna *(Thunnus alalunga),* which is a much larger fish and found on our supermarket shelves. Already trouble exists. For example, in Florida and Bermuda, the little tunny is widely known as the bonito.

On average, neither reaches the sizes attained by striped bass or bluefish. Still, I think they are undoubtedly the winners in any pound-for-pound tug-of-war. Both are capable of extremely long, lightning-fast runs that seem to burn backing right off your reel. Some sources say that little tunny and bonito are capable of swimming speeds reaching 40 miles per hour. I believe it. In addition, these ocean rockets seem very restless, rarely ever out of high gear. On a couple of occasions, I have seen them cruise slowly along, but never have I seen them fully at rest as you might a big striper.

Both fish are members of the Scombridae family, sometimes referred to as the mackerels. The entire clan shares some common trademarks. The feature that most clearly identifies members of this family is a row of finlets running from behind the dorsal and anal fins to the tail. These small, triangular fins give the back end of the fish a serrated look. The caudal peduncle is extremely thin and bony and joins a pronounced sickle-shaped tail.

The Scombridae family is made up of oceanic fish capable of remarkable speed. There appear to be two slightly different body shapes. One is more elongated, such as the king mackerel, the Atlantic mackerel, the wahoo, and the Spanish mackerel, which is occasionally entering New England waters too and will take a fly. The other has greater bulk through the midsection and appears more powerful. Those legendary big game fish the tunas fall into this category. Both the bonito and the little tunny have this unforgettable form, often described as football-like.

Given the similarity in shape and behavior, it may be difficult at first for an angler to tell these two fish apart. The bonito is the smaller and more colorful of the two. Its back is an iridescent blue-green, although in places like Long Island Sound, where the water has less salinity than the open ocean, the back is decidedly more green than blue. The bonito has a number of long, thin stripes on the side, starting behind the pectoral fin and running upward toward the dorsal area on a slight incline. These stripes are mainly but not entirely above the midline of the fish, and the belly is white and free of markings. At times, bonito will also

Page Rogers holds a nice bonito. Note the stripes and the shape of the dorsal fin.

have several wider, triangular-shaped bands. These, too, start behind the pectoral fin and run vertically from the dorsal area downward, pointing toward the belly. Upon death, all of these colors and markings fade rapidly.

The little tunny has different coloration and markings. It lacks the stripes found on the bonito, although high on the back is a series of wormlike lines similar to the markings on the common Atlantic mackerel or vaguely like those on a brook trout. The flanks and belly are silver white and without markings below the midline, except for four or five distinctive round spots directly behind and below the pectoral fin. Anglers can use these spots as an instant way to distinguish these two fish. On occasion, however, a little tunny may lack these spots.

The forward end of the dorsal fin on the little tunny stands up in a sharp peak and then immediately dips down low to the body before traveling rearward; the bonito's dorsal fin is triangular in overall shape. The shape of the dorsal fin, together with the presence of stripes, is a quick way to separate the bonito from the little tunny. Another feature that helps discriminate between the two is the shape and appearance of their mouths. The bonito has a longer, more pointed mouth, extending back beyond the eye. Furthermore, the bonito clearly exhibits a row of

The little tunny has a few wavy lines on the upper back and often a group of spots under the pectoral fin. The dorsal fin is tall and steeply angled.

fine teeth with which to grasp the bait. These teeth are not big enough to require that anglers use shock tippets, but a little care in handling is still recommended. The tunny's mouth does not extend back beyond the eye. Nevertheless, it is large enough to accommodate a fair-size victim. No teeth are immediately discernible.

Along the New England coast, bonito average between 5 and 7 pounds. They run in schools composed of all similar-size fish. It is possible to catch bonito of 10 pounds or better, but this size is far from common, and a bonito of more than 13 pounds on a fly is headed for the record books. Little tunny also are a schooling fish but regularly exceed 8 pounds, and a fish in the low teens is large but no record. It would take a fish in the high teens to cause you to break out the champagne.

Both fish feed on schooling baitfish. Sand eels, silversides, tinker mackerel, anchovies, and immature herring are favorite targets. They also eat shrimp and squid. This preference for small baits often puts fly rodders at an advantage over surf casters, who are usually throwing larger lures in a size more geared to bluefish.

All members of the Scombridae family show some preference for deeper offshore waters over shallow bays and beaches, and bonito and little tunny are no exception. Therefore, boats are the best ticket to consistently catching these fine gamesters. Nevertheless, both fish will venture within casting range of shoreline anglers in many locations. Offshore islands such as Martha's Vineyard and Nantucket are prime examples. The coast of Rhode Island is another. In these places, many are caught each year by anglers casting from jetties or working a beach. Sometimes these fish will feed extremely close to shore, swimming within a rod's length of the water's edge. They rarely stay there for any period of time, however, and commonly are gone in a flash. More often these fish lie disappointingly just out of casting range, prompting some fly rodders to use a variety of small craft such as canoes and sea kayaks to close the gap.

But just when you think these great game fish are nearly impossible to catch on a fly from shore, you come across situations where they are practically right at your feet. Furthermore, these fish may sometimes stay in the same general area for days, weeks, or even months. For this to happen, a place must be home to a very large amount of bait, and it should at least be adjacent to deep water. Rips and currents are helpful but not absolutely necessary.

When little tunny or bonito do hit a shoreline regularly, they tend to attack it in a fairly fixed sequence—there is an observable pattern to the way they feed. They seem to select a route based on the contours of the bottom structure. From the beach, it might look something like this: First they erupt all over the surface at spot A. Seconds later they explode at spot B, 30 yards down the beach, and then appear at spot C, farther on. Next, the water goes quiet for thirty minutes or longer, and then all of sudden they are back at spot A and the whole thing happens again.

The first impulse is to chase these fish from spot to spot. Do not attempt it! It rarely works well and takes a lot out of you. The trick is to be patient. Position yourself in one of the prime spots. Do not wait for the fish to show before you start casting, because a high percentage of the fish caught are hooked just before any surface activity takes place. So begin blind-casting, and use a cast only long enough to reach the better-looking water. In the sequence described above, choose point B, because when they erupt at point A, you are forewarned that they are coming.

Much has been said about the eyesight of bonito and little tunny. These two fish tend to attack their quarry at very high rates of speed, and their keen sense of vision helps them lock on to their intended targets at long range. Aiding their ability to see is that both fish consistently prefer gin-clear water. Many anglers will tell you that with their excellent vision, these fish can never be caught without long, fine leaders and that they will shy away from wire shock tippets. Nevertheless, I hooked a bonito with a fly sporting a wire tippet. Some would say that every school of fish holds a village idiot. I prefer to think that this particular fish simply demonstrated that although bonito have good eyesight, it is not as good as some people would have you believe. This is backed up by the fact that some bonito are caught each year on large plugs equipped with strong wire intended for bluefish. In one case, a bonito was caught on a rubber worm with a slip sinker rigged as commonly done to fool largemouth bass in fresh water.

Part of the reason some anglers swear these fish can see a tippet from far off is that bonito and little tunny can be hard to hook. Even when you are casting directly into a feeding frenzy, there is no guarantee of success. Since under these conditions a striper or bluefish is quite willing to sock a feathered hook, many anglers surmise that bonito and little tunny must be superselective. I believe, however, that this is not solely a result of visual selectivity and is to some fair degree a problem of placing the fly correctly in the fish's path. Where the water is deep, both bonito and little tunny trap bait near the surface, rocket up through their victims, and immediately head back down. This much is not unusual. Stripers and bluefish do pretty much the same thing. Neither of those fish, however, does it with anywhere near the same velocity as bonito and little tunny.

Furthermore, in this high-speed "up and down" attack, bonito and little tunny are the least capable of the four species of doing any maneuvering. The sickle-shaped tail common to the mackerel family gives them great speed and endurance, but at the cost of maneuverability. Once committed to a direction, they stay locked on to it, traveling in a straight line. Tuna fishermen have long understood this particular aspect of their quarry, and for that reason they choose lures that track straight rather than using artificials that zigzag. The wide tail of a striper, on the other hand, may be a poor tool for long high-speed chases, but it gives the striper the ability to instantly turn right or left with its intended prey.

Even if your fly is traveling across a school of bonito or little tunny feeding near the surface, for a fish to take it, it still must be in almost exactly the right spot where one of these fish ascends. Once in high gear, the fish cannot swerve off and change directions easily to catch a fly moving away from it on a different heading. This can be extremely frustrating for anglers: You see the fish breaking the surface, your fly is out there in the middle of the action, and still you do not get a hookup.

The Right Retrieve for Bonito and Little Tunny

Someplace along the line, a myth was born. It goes like this: High-speed retrieves are mandatory for bonito or little tunny. Folks, it is just not so. In fact, a fast fly can even reduce your chances by pulling the fly too quickly through the strike zone. Sure, these fish can catch anything, but when bait is abundant, why race off after food when other meals nearby are easier to get?

Many times a moderate retrieve or even a fly simply hanging in the flow is the answer. This is particularly effective when the angler can get upcurrent from the action and swing the streamer back wet-fly style. By letting the fly hang in the strike zone or using a very slow retrieve, the fly remains an easier target for the fish. And the longer it remains in the right area, the more likely it will eventually be intercepted. Since the bonito and little tunny tend to work heading with the prevailing current, a fly facing into that current is lying in the best possible path. One fall an unfortunate fly rodder who had been casting for hours from his anchored boat without a strike made the mistake of putting his rod down with the fly hanging overboard. As he reached for his coffee, a little tunny struck the fly and pulled his rod and reel into the briny deep!

In addition, I have seen bonito hit both flies and spinning plugs the instant they landed on the water. They can do it very softly, making it difficult to strike them before they drop the artificial. Little tunny tend to hit much harder. I once hooked from the beach a little tunny that hit a Clouser Minnow as it was sinking. This fish actually hooked itself, because it was off and running before I could start the retrieve. The fly dropping through the water column must have looked like an injured baitfish falling to the bottom and a very easy meal.

When baitfish are in tightly packed schools, they are operating on the safety-in-numbers philosophy. If the school formation is disrupted by an attack of predators, members that have become separated will be disoriented. These baitfish swim slowly, waiting for the school to reorganize. For this reason, a fly falling under the school or slowly moving at the edges can look very natural to a marauding game fish. When baitfish are not concentrated or the tide is slack, however, bonito and little tunny may patrol slowly just beneath the surface seeking a meal. Then a fly zipped past their noses is the right retrieve to provoke a strike. A slow-moving fly in this case will be viewed as unnatural in the same way that bluefish frequently refuse a fly that does not hightail it away from their approach.

A sinking fly or a fly used in conjunction with a sinking line also seems to increase the odds of a hookup. In open waters, some fly rodders use the fastest-sinking lines available. A sinking line works well because there are always many more fish below the few that show on the surface. Therefore, more fish get a chance to see a fly that is deeper in the water. Also, a fly hanging down in the water column is seen by marauding fish both on their way up to the surface and on their way back down, so a sinking fly offers them two opportunities to strike it.

Do not think for a minute that I am saying floating and intermediate lines do not work. They do! Nevertheless, I firmly believe those lines are best suited to situations where the fish are chasing bait laterally down a shallow beach and not feeding in an "up and down" style. In those cases, bonito and little tunny may run just under the surface, and a floating or, better yet, an intermediate line serves the fly in the right zone.

If I had to pick one time of day to cast for bonito and little tunny, it would definitely be the hours just after sunrise until about ten o'clock in the morning. This is especially true when these hours also hold a good moving tide. Like bluefish, these gamesters will continue feeding right through the hottest summer days. And as you might expect, they tend to be more active when the tide is moving and slack off as the tide wanes. Unlike stripers and bluefish, however, they are not nocturnal feeders, and action tapers off completely with the setting of the sun.

Little tunny hit a fly with considerable force, and this frequently results in a solid hookup without much work on the part of the angler. Bonito, on the other hand, may take with a solid strike but can also be expected to strike softly at times. In part, this difference between the little tunny and the bonito is likely the result of differences in their mouths. The little tunny overtakes its prey and uses its relatively large mouth to swallow its food whole. Naturally, a fly attacked in this manner is easy to drive home. The bonito has a narrower, pointed mouth and uses its teeth to momentarily grasp its victim. As a result, a bonito may grasp a fly by only the tail and not take the hook deeply into its mouth. When that happens, it is hard to get the hook properly set. Thus a fair number of bonito pull free during the fight. This happens especially as you are about to land them, so it is good to have a landing net handy. Other solutions are to use long-shank hooks or dress your flies so that they do not trail far behind the hook bend.

The little tunny is the easier fish to hook on a fly for other reasons

Bonito have a row of sharp teeth top and bottom, but you do not need to use a wire shock tippet.

as well. More than the bonito, it prefers to feed where there is very fast current. Rips and inlets are ideal places to find little tunny. In these fast currents, it hits its prey quickly and hard, and therefore has less time to study any fraud. The little tunny is also more predictable as to the times and places it feeds and even the route it will take when it feeds. This gives anglers a better chance to get the fly in the right spot.

Streamers in general get the nod for these two speedsters. The Lefty's Deceiver is right up there, but I prefer a Clouser for this work. Standard hook sizes go from #1/0 down to #2, although little tunny are frequently caught on hooks as large as #3/0. The best colors are blue over white, blue over green, yellow, and chartreuse, and a bit of flash in the fly is good, too. Big flies, greater than 4 inches, are fine for little tunny but not as productive for bonito. When fishing for bonito, I go down to 3 inches or a bit less, depending on the baitfish in the area. For one thing, it is easier to hook a bonito solidly if the fly is small enough to fit entirely in its mouth. Otherwise, the fish may grab the fly sideways or just pinch it from the rear.

When these two guys get selective, which seems to be often, go to a smaller fly, especially a small epoxy-type fly. Epoxy creations really come into their own in these situations.

Do bonito and little tunny ever hit sliders and poppers? The answer is yes, but few anglers try them. Sliders work for both species. And little tunny will definitely hit a conventional #2/0 popper. If you want a bonito on a popper, you will need a much smaller one, closer to #2 or even #4.

The Season for Bonito and Little Tunny

The season for Atlantic bonito and little tunny in the Northeast is relatively short. Neither fish is a full-time resident of our waters, and like bluefish, they migrate up from warmer southern locations to feed until fall.

Atlantic bonito are the first to show in the Northeast, and their arrival depends on water temperature. They usually enter southern New England in early August, with water temperatures in the middle 60s. In a warmer than normal year, they could appear around the second week of July. Little tunny arrive in mid-August to early September. Little tunny action generally heats up by the middle of September and will trail off by mid-October as water temperatures head toward the 60-degree mark.

Bonito, on the other hand, can tolerate water temperatures as low as 55 degrees, so they are still around into the first weeks of November if conditions allow. Again, prevailing weather trends play a large role in the fishing.

With the bonito, the initial action is offshore. Gradually the fish move in closer to land, where there is sufficient bait. These early bonito are known to be extremely fussy feeders, refusing many artificial lures and flies.

This is generally compounded by the fact that most anglers, upon seeing these guys break the surface, assume that they are bluefish. It is a natural mistake, given that bluefish are the predominant game fish in our waters and are well known for their blitzes. But bonito will rarely if ever respond to the larger, noisier things thrown by anglers at blues. This especially holds for large poppers. So you are apt to see boaters racing over to the scene of the action and casting away furiously, only to end up empty handed and wearing puzzled looks.

Telling these two fish apart is easy only if they leap clear of the water during the melee. The bonito has a distinctive football shape; the blue is more noticeably elongated and frequently larger. There is also a subtle difference in the way they disturb the surface as they feed. The bonito, with its narrow mouth and high speed, tends to slam the bait, sending up spurts of white water about as wide as your hand and twice as high. Blues create considerably more noise and produce a more erratic-looking surface disturbance. The best clue is the rate at which the location of the action keeps moving. Bonito can be on top in one area for a few seconds, and then show hundreds of yards away in little more than the wink of an eye. Blues move slower and stay on top in a given location longer.

Because bonito and little tunny move so rapidly, it can be frustrating to try to position a boat over the action. It is common for anglers to hightail it over to the surface activity, only to find the fish already down or gone. For that reason, some veteran captains prefer to watch the general direction of the school and position themselves ahead in the hope that the action will come to them. Another method is to anchor in a rip where bonito have been busy and simply blind-cast. Both ideas work. And a sinking line is often the key to success.

After the bonito have been in place for several weeks, the little tunny start to arrive. Their feeding habits, including time of day and surface activity, are similar to the bonito's, and at times both will work in the same general area. Here again, a sinking fly or fly line is frequently more productive. The little tunny is a larger fish and more apt to leap clear of the water as it pursues baitfish. Its big football shape is often enough to let anglers know that they are not dealing with the smaller bonito. By the end of September, both of these fish get increasingly active and predictable.

From the shore, some of the best opportunities for a hookup come from inlets or breachways that connect salt ponds to the sea. An ebbing tide, especially around dawn, often finds them outside the mouth of a jetty feeding in the rip line formed by the exiting water. Unfortunately, this frequently puts them out of fly-rod range. A dawn incoming tide is better, as the bonito and little tunny will ride inside the inlet to feed, making them much more accessible to fly-rod anglers. They will feed there until about the time that the tide stops moving inward, then they tend to drop back outside the mouth.

Both of these fish are capable of long, lightning-fast runs of over 100 yards. Clear the fly line that is in the stripping basket or lying on the deck in rapid order. Once up on the reel, make no attempt to stop the initial run. The best approach is to hold the rod up and let the fish tire against the drag. At the end of the first run, either fish will likely hold momentarily, but just as fast they could well turn and run directly toward you. When this happens, the line goes slack for a second, and you might be fooled into believing that the fish has gotten off. The best course of action is to reel as fast as possible. If the fish is still on, and likely it is, the line will again tighten. You can expect this reverse run more than once during the fight, especially with the little tunny. So be prepared.

Bonito can really take off, although they cannot go as far and fast as the little tunny. With an 8-weight rod and a reel holding 200 yards of backing, you usually will not find it necessary to chase the fish either on foot or with the boat. Still when there are obstructions in the water, it is best to move quickly to a position where you can avoid letting the fish hang up on one. Expect bonito to change direction rapidly and often during the fight. And always be ready for the fish to turn and run directly at you. At times you may hook a bonito that runs very little and instead elects to battle it out while in close. It is a mystery why some do this, but you will still get quite a war.

The little tunny is noticeably faster and more powerful than the Atlantic bonito. I once hooked one within 20 feet of shore where a powerful rip came close to the beach. It blistered off with the current at an astounding rate. After a long battle, using a 10-weight rod, I ended up beaching that fish close to a quarter mile down the shore. It weighed only about 9 pounds. If you hook one over 13 or 14 pounds, it could empty an entire reel spool, and a quick captain at the helm or a wide open beach free of obstructions is required to land that fish. Little tunny change direction less than a bonito and instead usually take off on a longer sustained run. They generally move either toward deeper water or in the direction of the current. At the end of a run, like a bonito, a little tunny will turn and run at you. So be ready to reel rapidly.

When you hook a little tunny from a boat over deep water, it may elect to suddenly dive deep rather than run. This can be a real problem, for the fish will usually head under the boat, pulling the rod sharply down toward the water. The rod is apt to snap if it touches the gunwale with the weight of the fish on it. Immediately hold the rod outside of the boat as far you can. Be ready to walk aft, toward the bow, or even around the transom or bow to the opposite side of the boat as the situation dictates, all the while keeping the rod clear of the sides of the boat. Steer the fly line clear of the prop and your anchor line if you have one out. If you are in rough seas, take care not to fall. And be sure to warn other anglers in the boat that you are moving in their direction so that they can get out of your path.

If you are trying to land either of these two great game fish in deep water, expect them to hang directly below you and doggedly turn in tight circles. At this juncture, you must pump the fish to the surface. To pump a fish, slowly lower the rod while reeling in line, then stop reeling and slowly lift the rod, forcing the fish upward. The rod should not be lifted very high during this procedure—an angle just above parallel with the water is enough. This entire process should be repeated in a slow, steady, continuous way, keeping a good deal of pressure on the fish at all times. It is the best way to gain ground at this moment in the fight.

Fall

As you near mid-September, the little tunny fishing tends to heat up, as these fish fatten up for the long haul back down the coast. This action will continue until mid-October in most years, but these fish can disappear overnight at that point of the season, especially after the water temperature dips to 60 degrees or lower. This is particularly the case when a series of northeast storms hits the coast back-to-back. In the fall, just as with striped bass and bluefish, little tunny and even more so bonito get much more aggressive and seem to throw caution to the wind. So anglers often can have some fantastic action. Bonito also are fattening up, but they are better able to tolerate the effects of the cooling water. Therefore, the best of the bonito fishing often starts as the little tunny are almost done, lasting into November when conditions allow.

13

Fighting Your Quarry: From Start to Finish

The sun is setting over the hills, and a hatch of mayflies rides the quiet waters. In the head of the pool, among the rocks, a fly fisherman lifts his rod high to hook a trout that dimpled on a tiny dry. With a splash, a 12-inch brown turns and takes off downstream. And to the evening stillness is added the gentle whir of a fly reel as the angler attempts to preserve a fragile tippet.

Miles away on the coast, a line of burning red rims the horizon as the sun sinks over the darkened waves. Knee-deep on a tidal flat, a fly fisherman lays out a line. Suddenly, in a huge swirl, a 12-pound striper stops the fly, doubling the rod over. And the evening stillness is filled with the sound of a wildly spinning fly reel as the fish heads to sea, taking the angler ever deeper into the backing.

Two fly fishermen now both work their tackle to the limit, but the battles are very different. One is a test of finesse—a slow-motion struggle where a light-handed touch does the honors. The other is clearly more physical; here forearm, shoulder, and back muscles join in the foray. This difference is a real and important one. And many recent converts to the salt fail to realize how hard they can pressure a big fish with a fly rod.

With an 8-, 9-, or 10-weight rod and a tippet of 10 pounds or better, an experienced coastal fly rodder is not afraid to work a fish hard. In fact, it is really what is required. Given too much of a chance, a fair-size saltwater game fish puts up a protracted war. Some battles have waged for well over half an hour simply because the angler was reluctant to apply the necessary pressure to land the fish. That same fight could have been finished in a third of the time by a veteran of the salt.

A protracted fight should be avoided for several reasons. The longer the fish is on the line, the greater the chance that something will go wrong with the equipment. Hooks pull out, knots fail, and leaders are cut or snagged. And as time goes on, you get tired and are apt to make more mistakes—mistakes that may cost you a fish. But most critical is that in an extended fight, fish become exhausted to the point where reviving them can be very difficult or even impossible.

PREPARATION

Fighting a powerful fish begins long before you actually have one on the line. Sharpening a hook, correctly tying strong knots (chapter 11), and setting the drag constitute the essential preparation to successfully hook, fight, and land any saltwater game fish. They must all be done before the battle begins.

Sharpening Hooks

The tough mouth of a saltwater game fish demands that a hook be extremely sharp. To reach that level of sharpness, many hooks need sharpening right out of the box, and absolutely all hooks need resharpening periodically. To check the sharpness of a hook, drag the point across your thumbnail. If the point immediately catches and begins to dig in, the hook is sharp. If the point simply slides across your nail, the hook requires attention.

The best method for sharpening a hook is a matter of opinion; even experienced anglers do not all agree. One thing is clear: The type of hook you wish to sharpen determines to some degree the best tool for the job. Hooks with conical points, or needle points, are round in cross section and only sharp at their extreme tip. This type of hook cannot, in my experience, be properly honed with a traditional flat file or the newer double round files. The Tiemco 800 series, the Daiichi 2546, the Partridge saltwater models, and some new Mustad hooks have conical points. With this type of hook, I recommend you use an electric sharpening tool specially designed to work on conical points, such as the Hook-Hone-R II.

Another type of hook is the cut or knife point hook. A good

example is the common Mustad 34007. On this type of hook, the metal from the tip to the barb is somewhat triangular in cross section and has sharpened edges as well as a fine point. To sharpen this type of hook, most anglers use a short flat file specially made for the task, such as the Luhr Jensen. You might also use a double round file, such as the Shur Sharp or the Donnmar Big Game sharpener. Never use a common bench grinder to sharpen a hook; it creates too much heat and can change the temper of the metal.

The double round file is faster and easier to use in the field. You simply pass it over the outside of the hook point, stroking in one direction only, toward the tip. It sharpens the hook by establishing two new cutting edges, in effect, diamond shaping the point. A flat file can be used to diamond shape as well, but most anglers use it to redefine the hook's existing cutting edges. This method of sharpening is called triangulating the hook and it works quite well. Here is how to do it.

Start by filing the bottom edge of the hook point. File toward the existing point, and always use the file in one direction only. Never use a back-and-forth motion as you would with a hacksaw. After each stroke of the file, lift it clear of the hook and return it to the place where you began the stroke. Then make the next pass.

Next, file each of the two sides, being sure to follow the existing angles. The number of passes of the file needed is determined by the roughness of the file, how dull the hook is, and the hook's composition—for example, cadmium is harder and takes longer to sharpen than stainless steel. In most cases, three or four passes over an edge will get it sharp. After you do the two sides, make one final pass over the bottom edge of the point. Now see if the hook passes the thumbnail test. If not, repeat the procedure.

Setting the Drag

Though many fly fishermen spend time preparing their hooks, few give equal time to their reel's drag. Setting your drag correctly is just as important as sharpening your hooks, and it is easy to do. The basic idea is to adjust your drag according to the breaking strength of the tippet and the conditions in which you will fish. You set the drag by measuring the force it takes to pull line directly off the reel. To accomplish this, you will need the rod, a loaded reel, and a small hand scale such as a Chatillon.

Mount the reel, but do not string the line through the guides. The drag adjustment knob or lever should be backed off at this point. Pull

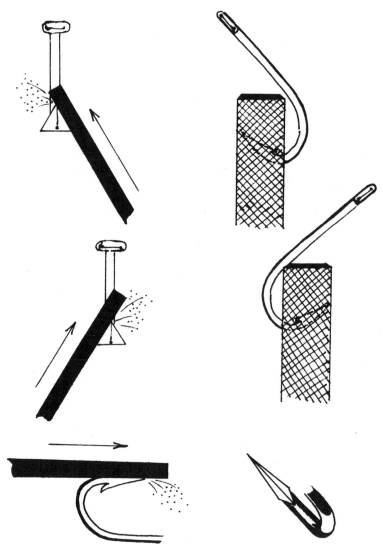

Hooks with cut points can be sharpened with a flat file.

the leader off the reel until you reach a spot at which to attach the scale. A loop knot or a braided butt connector are two good places. If necessary, tie a loop knot in the end of the tippet. Slip the hook end of the scale through the loop. With the rod grip in one hand, use the scale to pull the line off the reel while watching to see how much pressure is recorded.

When fishing an open sand beach with few if any submerged obstacles, I set the drag to about 10 percent of the breaking strength of the tippet. With a 9- or 10-weight outfit, I use a 12-pound tippet. So my drag is set near a pound of resistance. When fishing a location where a fish could quickly cut me off on some rocks or wrap the line around a snag, I set the drag higher, going to 15 or 20 percent of the breaking test of the tippet. So with my 12-pound tippet, I would now set the drag to about 2 or 2½ pounds. In very tight quarters, such as when fishing around docks and piers, I might even go to 3 pounds of drag.

When you are fighting a fish, the bend in the rod coupled with the friction of the guides adds dramatically to the total drag pressure. The exact amount depends on how high you are holding the rod and how hard you are pulling back. This is why the drag is not set with the rod rigged up in the first place. By setting it directly off the reel, you can be absolutely sure of your starting point.

Now you should get a feel for the actual force being generated at the end of the line when the rod is bowed as it would be during an actual fight. This greatly helps you learn how to better fight a fish to the limits of your tackle. Acquire the help of a friend. Set the reel drag to 1 pound of resistance, and then string up the rod. Pull off 80 feet of line, and connect the leader to the scale. Have your friend hold the scale to the ground as you walk far enough to bring the line tight. Point the rod directly back at the scale, holding it roughly horizontal to the ground. Without adding any resistance to the fly line with your hand, slowly and smoothly lift the rod, bringing it to vertical. Ask your friend to read off the pressure being registered by the scale during this operation.

Note how the pressure built as the rod bent. The drag pressure probably doubled from what you initially set on the reel. Now increase the drag, but not by readjusting the drag knob. Hook the index finger of your rod hand around the fly line, and pull it toward the rod blank as you bend the rod. This is a valuable technique when fighting a large fish, as it allows you to greatly increase the amount of drag force, and you can release it instantly if needed. Get accustomed to it. A warning is in order, however. *Never hook your finger around the line while a fish is running at high speed.* When in motion, the fly line, and especially the backing, can inflict a nasty burn.

If you have a rim-control reel, you can apply pressure to the rim as an alternative to using your finger on the line. Either way, you can quickly reach 3 or 4 pounds of resistance with a 9- or 10-weight rod. At this point, you have quite a bend in the rod, and perhaps you are wondering just how much more pressure a 10-weight rod can take before it breaks. There is no need to worry; smoothly applying 3 or 4 pounds of pull, without any sudden jerks, should not break a healthy 10-weight rod. Such a rod is capable of lifting over 10 pounds, and perhaps close to 15. Under no circumstances, however, do I recommend that you try to find out your rod's limits.

Now think about this. Knowing what you have just seen, can you break a 15-pound tippet by slowly bending back on the rod? Even using a 10-weight, it is nearly impossible to exert that much force. The blank, in all likelihood, will snap first, assuming your knots are strong and your leader is not scraped or nicked. Even with a 12-pound tippet, you would have to bend the rod dangerously deep into the corks in order to break the line. By the way, if you snag bottom at some point in your career, point the rod straight at the fly and step backward, holding the fly line tight. Keep the rod out of it.

Repeat these drag exercises several times until you can bend the rod and closely guess the actual pull at the leader end of the line without being told. For example, call out to your friend holding the scale when you think you have reached 3 pounds of pull. He can confirm this or correct you. Remember, the more line you have in the water and the more current, the greater the drag resistance becomes.

FEELING THE STRIKE

Saltwater game fish are, for the most part, very aggressive. And it makes good sense for them to be that way. Most of what they eat is capable of escaping quickly if given half a chance, so they tend to nail their food hard. As a result, feeling the strike is usually not a problem as long as the line is fairly tight. At times, however, the take can be soft, and you absolutely must make a habit of staying in touch with the fly.

Your best indication that the line is tight is whether you can feel the fly during the retrieve. The resistance of the fly moving through the water causes a slight sensation of weight on the end of the line. If you can sense that weight with your hand as you retrieve the fly, you will also feel any strike. When there is slack in the line, either you lose touch with the fly completely or your contact is intermittent. In those situations, you can easily miss even a strong strike.

You can aid your contact with the fly in several ways. Keep the rod tip pointed down at the water and aimed directly at the fly during the retrieve; in some cases, you might even want to put the rod tip underwater. When you cast across a current, be sure to follow the fly's progress downcurrent with the rod tip, and avoid letting the current put a large bow in the line. When large waves are lifting the fly as it comes back to you, vary the speed of the retrieve. Speed it up when you start to lose touch with the fly, and slow the retrieve once you are back in control. And use a heavier, more resistant fly or a sinking fly line if necessary in order to stay in contact with your offering.

SETTING THE HOOK

After you feel the fish take the fly, setting the hook becomes the first in a long chain of events that with luck will bring the fish to hand. Frequently, large fish help hook themselves by clamping down on the fly with a great deal of force and then turning sharply away. If the line is relatively tight and the hook keen, the impact of that event aids in driving the steel home. Still, there is much to learn about this part of the game.

There are two aspects to this task of driving the hook home: when to set the hook and how hard to do it. If you react before the fish has the fly fully in its mouth, you simply pull it away. Everybody does this at one time or another, and it is a terrible feeling. If you wait too long, on the other hand, you risk the fish discovering the fraud and dropping the fly. Or you may react right on schedule but fail to set the hook with adequate force.

You should set the hook immediately upon feeling the fish take, whether it does so with a jolt or a small tap. Note that I said *feel* rather than *see* the fish take. When fishing near or on the surface where you can see the fish coming for the fly, it is easy to react too quickly. Wait until you feel increased weight on the line before striking. This is true even with poppers, when a striped bass explodes on the fly.

When using the conventional strip retrieve, you set the hook by instantly trapping the fly line firmly against the rod blank with the index finger of the rod hand. At the same moment, twist at the waist, pulling the fly rod horizontal to the water and rearward away from the fish. Do so with a strong, fluid motion so that the rod bends deeply. Note that the rod tip should not be lifted up in the air as is so commonly done in fresh water, for two good reasons. Raising the rod tip gently is fine when driving home a #14 hook into the soft mouth of a trout, but it does not generate enough force to sink a #2/0 into the jaws of a blue. And if the fish or you miss, the raised rod tip pulls the popper up into the air and far from the fish. A low rod tip drives the popper ahead across the water but leaves it at a distance where the fish can find it for a second attempt.

If you are using the hand-over-hand style of retrieve, as soon as you feel the fish, simply grasp the line tightly and give two quick pulls. This immediately draws the fly line tight to the weight of the fish and sinks the hook deeply. In essence, you are setting the hook with the line and not with the rod. Some anglers also twist at the waist during this maneuver, pulling the rod tip back away from the fish. With this type of retrieve, however, there is no need to twist at the waist or do anything to move the rod tip from its present position pointing down at the water. It works extremely well.

Once the fish is on, it usually holds for a split second, surprised by the circumstances, and then turns and runs. The immediate problem is to get the excess fly line, which at the moment is sitting in the stripping basket or lying on the deck, out through the guides without giving the fish slack. This is a critical moment. If the fish struck at the farthest reaches of the cast, there is not much loose line lying around to worry about. But if the fish latched on to the fly just about when you were ready to pick up for another cast, there could be 80 feet or more of line to contend with. Striped bass love to test your skills this way by striking right at your feet. It certainly makes things interesting.

Do not watch the fish! Instead, keep your eyes on the excess fly line as it lifts from the deck or the stripping basket. It is imperative that you do everything you can to get this line out through the guides smoothly. Some anglers form a circle around this loose fly line with the thumb and first finger of the free hand. This stops some potential tangles from forming in the line. I do something slightly different, loosely closing my entire hand around the line. This helps me keep a little tension on the line as it heads to the first stripping guide. Only after you have every-thing on the reel should you look up.

Anglers converting to fly from spin-tackle or plug-casting gear are going to be surprised at the coordination it takes to handle this event. With a spinning or revolving spool reel, all line that is retrieved is stored directly on the reel, so when the fish hits, the angler immediately has the fish under the control of the drag. Fly gear is different.

Occasionally a knot forms in the loose fly line, but generally it will pass through the guides after a rough ride up the rod. Do not be too concerned, even though the sight of this weird ball of fly line zipping off after the fish looks fatal. Your chances of landing the fish are still very good. If, however, the knot jams in the guides, immediately push the rod toward the fish to gain some slack, and roll the rod over with a twist of the wrist so that the guides are facing up. This often frees the knot, particularly one hung up in a snake guide. If that does not work and the tippet is still holding, try pulling back on the fly line to loosen the jam, and then release the line again in the hope that this time it will exit the rod.

Once in great while, the fly line coming up out of the stripping basket jumps around the rod's butt extension, the reel foot or handle, or possibly the frame of the first stripping guide. In a boat, it can grab just about any piece of hardware that is not flush with the deck. I have even seen a fly line wrap around loose articles of clothing or something dangling on a lanyard, like a pair of clippers. When this occurs, use the same strategy as with knots in the fly line itself. Push the rod forward at the fish to gain enough slack to free the line. Act quickly, or you and your fish will likely part company.

Once you have the fish up on the reel, apply pressure by raising the rod tip upward. If you are using a direct-drive reel, the handle will be spinning wildly. This is another point where both freshwater fly rodders and light-tackle surf casters have to be careful. Trout anglers often are fearful of losing so much line to the fish, and as a consequence, they are tempted to make a grab for the reel handle. The result is apt to be a bruised set of knuckles and a broken tippet. Surf casters, on the other hand, are well aware of the distance a saltwater fish can run. Because spinning reels are antireverse in design, however, surf casters are also used to holding the reel handle throughout the fight, something they cannot do with a direct-drive fly reel.

FIGHTING A BIG FISH FROM THE BEACH

A bass or bluefish over 10 pounds can wage an exciting battle. If hooked on a shallow beach, expect it to make an all-out attempt to reach the sanctuary of deeper water. Often this comes in the form of a single, awe-inspiring run that takes you well into the backing. The biggest and strongest fish might even go upward of 100 yards. This is especially true in locations where a fish can take advantage of a strong current to aid its escape. With an Atlantic bonito or a little tunny, the first run could conceivably go well over 100 yards.

With a tough customer on the line, you have to take action. Push the butt end of the rod into your stomach just below the sternum. If your reel is a direct-drive model, be careful to allow the reel handle

It is important to learn how to fight a fish to the limits of your tackle. Here an angler leans into a striper. *Photograph by Phil Farnsworth.*

room to turn freely. Once in this position, I like to use my free hand to push my stripping basket behind me out of the way; this makes it much easier to move around as well as to land the fish. Now smoothly apply pressure to the fish by bending the rod.

Conventional wisdom in fresh water regarding the best way to wage the war has anglers holding their rod tips up high. True, in this position, you are able to protect a fine tippet, but unfortunately it also makes it harder to really pressure the fish. Dropping the rod nearly horizontal to the water and pulling to the side is far more effective at turning a big fish.

One disadvantage of this technique is that it holds more of the fly line in the water. On a sandy beach, that is not a problem. But over a rocky bottom or wherever submerged objects could snag or cut the line, there is the possibility of trouble. I keep the rod tip higher in locations of barnacles and mussel shells. These things are so sharp that they can actually cut right through the 40-pound butt section of your leader! Still, the closer the fish gets and therefore the less line that is out, the more I keep the rod low to one side as I finish the battle.

A second disadvantage of holding the rod over on its side is that the fly line tends to load unevenly on the spool as you retrieve. If it gets too lopsided, the reel could jam. Note that the shape of your fly reel plays a small role in this too. A tall, narrow fly reel loads faster and more evenly than a short, wide one. Glance down every now and then to see how the spool is doing. If you see a problem, use the index finger of your rod hand to guide the fly line as it heads toward the spool. Occasionally alternating sides with the rod helps too.

At the end of the first run, a striper or blue will hold momentarily in an attempt to gain back its strength. Do not let it rest! As soon as it stops, smoothly apply increased pressure to get it back to work. I press the fly line to the rod blank with the index finger of my rod hand and lean back a bit on the rod to increase the weight on the fish. If you have a rim-control reel, you could apply pressure there instead. Regardless of which method you pick, here is where your practice with understanding drag pressures comes into play.

A little tunny or a bonito is apt to do something different at the end of its first run. Expect these guys to turn and race straight at you. So be prepared to reel like crazy if the line suddenly goes slack. If you are standing on the beach, consider backing up as you reel to speed up the process, but be careful not to trip over anything in the excitement.

PUMPING

There is an excellent old adage that states that if you are fighting a fish correctly, you are either gaining line or losing it. In other words, the fish should not be allowed to rest; it should be either running out against the drag or coming to you under pressure. There is a lot of truth to this, but even the most experienced anglers at times find themselves in a standoff. They place as much pressure as they dare, but still the fish refuses to budge.

When this happens, you should resort to an extremely valuable technique called *pumping*. It forces a fish back into action and gets it moving toward the beach or boat. The procedure has frequently been described as "reel down, lift up." Essentially, it is a series of short, steady pulls with the rod. Here is how it works.

The idea is to generate maximum pressure on the fish, so start with the rod butt firmly braced against your stomach to give you better leverage. Clamp down on the fly line, pressing it to the rod blank with the index finger of your rod hand. Then lean back on the rod, bending it as much as reasonably possible given the breaking strength of the leader. To give you some idea, you should be placing 5 or more pounds of pressure at the tippet. This amount of force usually makes even the largest fish move slightly toward you. Do not attempt to simply reset the drag adjustment on your reel.

Now ease off your index finger and lower the rod toward the fish, simultaneously reeling in the line you gained. This is what is meant by "reeling down." The key here is to never lower the rod tip faster than you can reel, or you will create slack. Immediately after the rod has been lowered, pinch down on the fly line again and lift up on the rod. Once again this moves the fish a bit closer to you. Never jerk the rod; lift it up in a smooth, continuous fashion. Keep repeating this "reel down, lift up" process without pause.

If at any time the fish starts a run, stop pumping. Let the fish continue against the drag as you normally would. As soon as the fish stops, however, resume pumping.

The distance the rod travels during the pump has an effect on how quickly you win the war. Some folks use a long pump, reeling the rod tip down to the water and then slowly lifting the rod nearly behind the head. Though this does work, short quicker pumps actually work the much fish harder. Try moving the rod tip only a few feet or less.

Pumping can be just as effective, and some would argue more so, if performed with the rod moving across a horizontal plane at your side (unless you are fishing from a boat and the fish is directly below you). In all other ways, it is identical to the vertical method. You may even witness an angler switching back and forth, pumping a fish in both the vertical and horizontal planes.

Pumping is a valuable technique when fighting a big fish from the beach. A big bluefish, if near the top, is apt to jump as the line constraints it. Do not bow to a leaping blue as anglers are so often seen doing to a tarpon. Simply keep the heat on. If you bow the rod, for one thing, the leader may drape inside the blue's mouth, where it will be cut through in a flash. A truly big striper often tries to hold fast, resisting for a few moments all attempts to move it. If it does, pump it.

A powerful fish may move down the beach roughly parallel to the shore. Often you can turn that fish back toward you in short order by laying the rod over horizontally and using side pressure. If the water is full of rocks and sharp obstacles, however, you run the risk of getting cut off. Occasionally you may have to follow the fish down the shoreline. This is particularly the case in a strong rip where you otherwise would be forced to pull the fish back to you through a current. Also, by getting closer to the fish, it is possible to apply greater pressure than you can at a distance, given the stretch in a fly line. If you do decide to move down the shoreline with your quarry, be sure to keep tension on the line at all times and proceed with care. If you are on the beach, it should be no problem, but if you are in the water, wading fast is tricky. During the excitement of battle, it is easy to fall while chasing a fish through the surf.

Once the fish turns and comes back, the battle swings your way. You have now broken its best run. Reel quickly and keep the tension on. As the fish is swimming at you, it is also resting to a small degree, so expect a sudden return to action. The second run of a blue or bass never equals the initial burst, however, and all subsequent runs are shorter still. If the fish attempts to hold again, resume pumping.

LANDING A FISH

Now the problem becomes one of landing your prize. If you are fishing a steep sloping beach with strong surf, you can use the waves to help propel the fish toward you. Each time a wave lifts up under your fish, apply a little extra pressure with the rod. The fish, weakened by the fight, is unable to resist the forward motion of the wave and is carried shoreward by it. This technique is practically essential to get the fish from the last wave onto the beach itself.

As the weakened fish nears the water's edge, clamp down on the fly line again with the index finger of your rod hand, and take a step or two backward timed with the waves. Take care not to trip. Keep the rod to one side of you with the rod tip very low to the ground. This should draw the fish up onto the beach. Unfortunately, if the surf is heavy, the backwash may quickly suck your fish back into the waves. Be prepared to move fast. The best way to handle a bluefish, an Atlantic bonito, or a little tunny is to lift it by the caudal peduncle. This method does not work very well for bass. With a small striper, try to lip it, grasping the lower lip with your thumb and forefinger. With a large one, try gripping the lip while slipping your other hand under the belly.

If the waves do draw your fish back into the surf before you can reach it, do not panic. The last thing you want to do now is suddenly apply a lot of pressure. Because both the force of the surf and the weight of the fish are momentarily moving away from you, any yank is going to pull the hook free or bust the tippet. Simply maintain some tension on the line. In a second, another wave will advance, once again lifting your fish forward toward you. Now is the time to reapply pressure.

To land a fish while wading, you can simply bring the fish to you or back up to place it on the beach. With a large fish, I prefer beaching it if convenient. To do this, start moving slowly in toward shore as the fish nears, all the while maintaining pressure. There is an old saying salmon anglers use: "Walk them and they come, reel them and they run." The idea is that if you use slow, steady pressure on the fish by walking backward, the fish will follow with little protest. But if you pull hard on that same fish, it will fight you every inch of the way.

Here again, be careful not to trip while heading to the beach. Generally the fish will weave back and forth in tight circles as it is led in to shore. Eventually it will sense the rising bottom as its body brushes against it. At this moment, expect a bluefish to jump repeatedly in a last-ditch effort to escape. A striper will not jump but is likely to attempt to surge back out. As the water depth drops to less than 2 feet, most fish roll on their sides and are easy to handle.

If you do not want to beach the fish and prefer to land it where you are, reel it as close as possible. Be ready for the fish to suddenly put up a flurry of action as it senses your presence. A bass will thrash on the surface, and a blue might jump. Some fish even swim a circle around you. If the fish is still strong enough to attempt a run at this point, it likely will go only a very short distance, and you can stop and turn it very easily.

With the requisite 9-foot rod, it is a little difficult to get the fish

An angler prepares to land a fish on a steep beach. Because of the powerful backwash, this can be a difficult proposition. The berm behind the angler marks the level of high tide and is a typical sight on many ocean beaches. *Photograph by Phil Farnsworth.*

close to you. The best method is to push the rod behind you at a full arm's length. That should bring the leader within reach. Now grasp the leader and pull the fish toward you. *Be careful at this point that you do not sharply bend the rod tip. It is possible to snap it.* Next, get the rod down under your casting arm. Easy Lok makes a rod holder that slips onto your wader belt. It holds a fly rod with a butt extension. Again, be sure there is no pressure on the rod tip. If you have to, release a little line from the reel to take the weight off the tip.

You now have both hands free to unhook the fish. It is critical at this point that you establish which species is on the end of the line. In daylight that is easy to do, but on a dark night it is a far different matter. The black and white stripes on the side of a striper are usually visible, if your eyes are fully adjusted to the dark. But even if you have been catching stripers all night and stripers only, never assume that the next fish is a striper until you see it.

You can also use a light at night to help with both the identification and unhooking of the fish, but since a light tends to spook other fish and causes you to lose your night vision momentarily, do not turn it on unless absolutely necessary. I prefer a small waterproof flashlight that can be held between the teeth. I wear it around my neck on a lanyard. It leaves me free use of both hands. A headlamp like the ones used by miners also does the trick, although it is a little uncomfortable to wear for extended periods. Most anglers who use them just hook them around the neck and let them hang rather than wearing them on the head.

I generally handle a striped bass by grasping its lower lip with my thumb and index finger. By lifting slightly on the tippet, you will get the fish's head up, and most will open their mouths at this point too. Do not lift much of the fish's body out of the water. The harder you pull upward, the more the striper will thrash about. Expect the fish to jump about as soon as you touch it; it may take three or more attempts with a frisky fish to get a grip on its lower jaw. Usually the smaller the bass is, the harder it is to handle, and the larger it is, the more it lies still after being caught. Rolling any of them belly up will immediately quiet them right down. Hook removal is an easy task from there.

An alternative method some coastal fly rodders use on stripers is to hold the leader in one hand and slide the other hand down the tippet to grasp the eye of the hook. From there you have the option of either tackling the hook bend with pliers or making a grab for the lower lip. This approach can be done only when the fly is showing outside the mouth, which it is in most cases. Care must be taken when you have a wire shock tippet in front of the fly. These wire tippets can have razor-sharp burrs wherever you have cut the wire with pliers.

UNHOOKING A FISH

There is a new release tool that looks like a J-shaped piece of heavy-duty wire attached to a short handle. Many anglers simply call it a "dehooker." It works extremely well if the hook is not deep in the mouth, and it allows you to release the fish without even touching it. It works with all species.

To use this tool, place your rod under your arm and grasp the leader with one hand. Next, slip the U-shaped portion of the J around the lower end of the leader. Then slide the tool down to the hook bend. (Flies with bulky bodies, such as poppers, require you to place the tool in the hook bend.) Lift the fish by the tool's handle while simultaneously pulling down on the leader with your other hand. The fish will fall off the hook point into the water.

Anglers used to catching fish with spinning lures holding two or three treble hooks are going to be very pleasantly surprised by how easy it is to handle and unhook a fish caught on a fly. Not only are there fewer hooks to look out for, you do not have free hooks dangling outside the fish's mouth. The risk of hooking yourself in the process of releasing the fish is very low.

With a bluefish, hold it by the caudal peduncle, and immediately roll the fish on its back. You should have pliers or a release tool handy at this juncture. I keep them in the front pocket of my chest pack. If you like, you can attach them to a vest or chest pack with a long lanyard. Should they slip from your grasp, you can easily retrieve them. If the fly is visible, use the pliers or release tool to remove the hook. Never use bare hands to remove the fly from a bluefish; you risk being bitten by their sharp teeth. If the fly is hidden inside the mouth, it could prove difficult to remove, simply because some blues will refuse to open their mouths until they are practically dead. Pulling on the leader is of little help and may make things worse. If all else fails, snip the leader. If you plan to eat the fish, you can get the fly back later.

Atlantic bonito and little tunny fight so hard that they are usually very docile once you get a grip on them. Still, like the bluefish, I highly recommend that you roll them on their backs. The Atlantic bonito has sharp exposed teeth. Here some kind of tool is needed, although the bonito is not as dangerous to handle as a blue. In most cases, a bonito will have the fly hanging on the outside of the mouth. No problems there. The little tunny can be unhooked without a pliers, but take care as parts of the mouth are rough, and hiding under the gum is a fine row of teeth.

FIGHTING A LARGE FISH
FROM A BOAT IN DEEP WATER

Fish hooked from a boat over deep water fight differently than when hooked in the shallows. They generally do not run as far, preferring to go down rather than to run horizontally away from the boat. Bonito and little tunny are exceptions in this regard. Both can easily run out to the 100-yard mark. As soon as you realize that you have hooked a strong fish, calmly (if possible) let the captain know. It may be necessary to maneuver the boat at some point in the battle to land this fish, and an alerted crew will react faster. So communicate with the people around you.

Many fish dive under the boat, causing anglers a good deal of trouble. If you are standing back from the gunwale, move to it so that most of the rod will be outside the boat. If the gunwale reaches up above your knees, you can brace yourself against it. Never allow the rod to touch the gunwale during the fight—the rod will snap. Be prepared to walk quickly around the stern or bow if necessary to follow the fish to the opposite side of the boat. But be especially careful not to allow the line to catch on the motor or any anchor line in use.

As soon as the fish stops pulling, begin pumping. The technique is ideally suited to this situation. Each time you pump the rod, you lift the fish toward the surface. Be careful when you lower the rod tip that the blank does not touch or rest on the gunwale. And remember, short, quick pumps are better than long ones in terms of tiring the fish out.

In a long battle with a fish that stubbornly hangs deep below the boat, a shorter rod is a better tool. It gives the angler increased leverage and lifting power. Many anglers effectively shorten the rod during the fight by sliding one hand up the blank midway between the grip and the first stripping guide. A fair amount of additional lifting power can be gained in this manner, but there is a risk too. By gripping the rod up high, you have changed how the weight is distributed over the rod blank. This can cause the rod to snap suddenly under a strain it was not designed to take. Travel rods can be especially prone to this problem because of their design. Three-piece rods have a ferrule immediately above the first stripping guide, and four-piece rods have one immediately below.

FIGHTING A FISH IN A RIP

Perhaps no place is an angler put more to the test when fighting a big fish than in a swift rip, especially when the angler is fishing from the shore rather than from a boat. In these waters, not only does the fish get to use its power and stamina against the angler, it also has the current to aid it in making an escape. Most fish will automatically turn and run downcurrent. Needless to say, you can expect a very long run.

If the fish gets far below you, you may develop a large bow in the line. The force of the current pushing against this bow greatly increases the weight on the tippet. If possible, try to move downcurrent so that you can get more directly across from or, better yet, below the fish. This will take some or all of the bow out of the line, and it will also help you force the fish to turn into the current, where it will tire more rapidly.

Once the fish starts to tire, try hard to get it out of the main current and into slower water. This is especially important in situations where you cannot move downcurrent and therefore must bring the fish back up the rip to land it. Dropping the rod horizontal to the water will help you pressure the fish to one side. This is an excellent way to move a fish across the current. And generally, once a tired fish starts across the rip, it will come readily rather than fight the flow. If the rip is loaded with rocks, however, lowering the rod also brings the line in more contact with the sharp bottom. So there are risks involved.

Occasionally a truly large fish will head upcurrent after being hooked. This happens particularly in locations where the water ahead of the rip is substantially deeper than the water in the tail. Likely the fish entered the rip from the deeper end and feels it is the safest exit. It is relatively easy to tire a fish that employs this tactic. Still, be prepared for the fish to suddenly reverse directions as it weakens.

PREPARING FOR THE NEXT CAST

After landing your fish, or for that matter even if it gets off, it pays to take a moment to check your gear before casting again. Quickly run your hand down the leader and see if it has been badly abraded during the fight. Replace it if necessary. Check that the fly is still riding correctly on the hook shank and has not become twisted or fouled under the hook bend. Then make sure that the hook is still sharp and ready to go. Finally, if the fly line is loaded unevenly on the reel, peel some off and level up the spool.

14

Fishing at Night

As the shadows lengthen and darkness descends, the coast becomes a different world. Hungry striped bass and bluefish begin to prowl, working their way back into the surf and shallows. And for the coastal fly fisherman, fishing at night is the stuff of angling dreams.

Under the stars some of the very finest fishing takes place. Striped bass and bluefish, the two most popular game fish on the coast, feed heavily after dark. And not only can you catch more of them at night, your chances of hitting a big fish are better too. In southern New England, the action begins in June and lasts all the way into November. As an added bonus, you get to feel the beauty and solitude of the coastal night, which lends a special sense of adventure to the game. And the good fishing spots, often crowded during the day, are now empty. At night you can have the best places all to yourself.

Still, the idea of fly rodding after dark is foreign and even intimidating for many anglers. To be consistently successful on the coast, however, you must change your way of thinking. Night fishing in the salt is an integral and even critical part of the season, especially for fly rodders working from the beach. To miss it is to miss a great deal of the best angling. So by all means be prepared to give it a try.

Although night begins with the setting of the sun, night fishing does not. In fact, the first hour of true darkness is frequently a poor time to be on the water. During this time, both baitfish and predators are adjusting to the changing light level and moving into new positions for the night. The best night fishing begins at least an hour and a half, if not longer, after darkness has settled. This fact is very important. I have had people new to the salt tell me they had tried night fishing and never caught anything. But it turned out that they had merely fished through sunset and stayed for a short time into darkness. That is not night fishing! The experienced saltwater fly rodder often does not pull on his or her waders until most of the world lies fast asleep.

WHY NIGHT FISHING IS SO EFFECTIVE

Night fishing along the coast is effective for many reasons. Striped bass and bluefish feed at night because it is easier to ambush baitfish in the darkness than chase them in the light. During the day, when baitfish are schooled together, they are highly alert to the presence of predators and quick to react with evasive maneuvers. But the school is largely held together through a visual bond, and as the light wanes, it is forced to break up. Once that happens, a striper or blue can glide up in the darkness and nail the bait with ease.

The availability of other food is greater at night too. Some tasty morsels come out only in darkness. Marine worms, which remain buried in the sand during the day, come up at night and roam in search of food. Crabs often roam more freely under the stars as well. And eels, one of the delicacies most preferred by striped bass and bluefish, are largely nocturnal too.

Stripers and blues are more at ease entering very shallow water to feed when they can do it under the cover of darkness. Not only do they feel less exposed, but the recreational noise of the day is lacking. In addition, the warm inshore waters of the summer months will cool down as the night progresses, dropping water temperatures to a more comfortable level for larger fish.

On the angler's side of things, though night fishing does limit your ability to see, it actually helps you in numerous other ways. Since these two important game fish are more apt to come close to shore under the cover of darkness, more fish are likely to be in fly-rod range. And once you have found fish, they tend to move around less at night, giving you plenty of chances to drop the fly in their path. The fish also are less selective, so the problems of matching the fly in color and size to the bait in the area are reduced. Furthermore, the fish are much less wary at night, and a careful angler can get within 20 feet or less. This means that short casts of less than 50 or even 30 feet are common at night. Not only does this help anglers cover fish, but the shorter lines make it easier to feel the strike and set the hook. And often the breezes quit with the last light, giving fly fishermen a break from the steady winds of the day.

TRICKS OF THE TRADE

Preparation and concentration are the secret weapons of successful anglers. And at no time are these two tools more important to success than at night. The most essential part of preparation is becoming totally familiar with the area you intend to fish. You should know the best way to approach the shoreline, where the fish hold, what stage of the tide is most favorable, and how to move around safely.

Get in the habit of thoroughly checking your equipment before you head out. Make sure you have the right flies and that all the hooks in your box are honed. Assemble spare tippets and leaders, check flash-lights and spare batteries, find your pliers, set the drags, and reexamine the tide tables. Be sure your waders, foul-weather gear, and stripping basket also make it to the car. A last-minute check on the weather

This striper was caught at night where a sand beach turns to cobble. Note how the angler supports the fish prior to release.

report is always a good idea. And of course, for safety reasons, you should always night-fish with a friend.

Once on the beach, stay focused on the tasks at hand. Move slowly, and learn to use the landmarks that are still visible to guide you along the beach. Often the silhouette of a large rock or the glow of a street-lamp on a nearby beach road can help you establish your position. I have gone so far as to count off steps between a prominent stationary object on the shore and a good fishing spot. By pacing off the distance, I can make a short cast and drop my fly right in the prime waters even on the darkest nights.

As you fish, all of your senses should be on high alert. Since your night vision can never equal your daytime vision, you have to pay more attention to small clues. A big swirl that would be easy to see at noon appears as just a small disturbance at midnight. But you can still pick it up if you are attentive. With your vision reduced, hearing has to take up some of the slack. Listen carefully for the sounds of feeding fish. Big fish may roll or splash as they feed. Bass make a distinctive popping noise as they suck in bait. If you think you have heard a fish, make several casts in the direction of the sound, covering the water in a fanlike pattern. Though it is difficult to estimate distances in the dark, if the sounds seem to be out of casting range, consider moving slowly and carefully in that direction. At night, about 90 percent of the time the right retrieve is a slow retrieve. Stop periodically and cast ahead to intercept any fish that may be closer than you anticipated.

Along with your sense of hearing, you will also need to sharpen up your sense of touch. And in many ways your fingers become your eyes. Though striped bass and bluefish frequently hit a fly like a bomb during the day, at night they occasionally take very softly. Striped bass can follow a fly, suck it in, and all the while continue swimming toward the angler. Until the fish stops or turns, you feel only the smallest change in resistance at the end of the line. I have caught many a bluefish weighing in the teens that simply closed its mouth on the fly without as much as the slightest yank.

Always make it a habit to check the fly every few casts. Be certain that its wing or tail has not fouled around the hook. Also check to see that you have not picked up any seaweed. This is an important procedure for night fishing. If you fail to do so you run the risk of spending long periods of time fishing with a fly that is not working properly. Should a fly foul repeatedly, change it. If you are picking up seaweed on nearly every cast, consider moving to another location. While you are checking the fly, also check that the hook is still sharp. Occasionally during a backcast, the fly will hit a rock, dulling the point of the hook.

FISH AT THE WATER'S EDGE

At night, the fish can be right at the water's edge. And many novice coastal fly fishermen, in their eagerness to wade out, have walked right through the best fishing. After dark, always assume that the fish are in the first wave right at your feet until proven otherwise. One way to test this area before wading through is to make a cast almost parallel to the shoreline and retrieve the fly along the water's edge. Repeat the cast, varying the angle until you are casting straight out. Then start the process over again until you are reasonably certain no fish are close by.

Swirls and pops near the water's edge are sure signs of fish feeding in close, but there is another equally good clue. The presence of baitfish on the beach right above the water line is solid evidence. As you walk down the beach, run your flashlight briefly along the water's edge. Baitfish with their shiny sides will stand out boldly in the beam. These unfortunate creatures were driven out of the surf by marauding blues and bass. If the bait is dead, the action may have taken place hours ago, but a few casts in the area are nevertheless in order. If the bait is alive,

These baitfish were pushed onto the beach by game fish feeding right at the water's edge. When you find this situation, the action could be very close by.

the action took place a few minutes before and is likely still going on nearby. Immediately begin searching the area with a series of casts.

Here is another tip. During the warmer months, at night you share the beach with raccoons, skunks, and red foxes. Naturally, these animals are not simply out for a stroll; they are patrolling for food. If there is any bait lying on the sand at the water's edge, they will find it. As you approach, these midnight diners tend to head back quickly over the dunes. Many times, however, you can catch a glimpse of them or perhaps see their eyes reflected in your flashlight beam. If you see them coming up from the water's edge, you should head down and take a look around.

Fish do not appear to have any ears, but never for a moment think they cannot hear. Their sensitivity to sound is very acute. Therefore, when you wade in shallow water, move slowly so that you will not scare off any fish in the area. Normal conversation is not a problem. It is the vibration through the water that you want to keep to a minimum. For the same reason, I also recommend that you tread lightly as you walk along the water's edge in search of fish.

FISH UP CLOSE

Even after wading out from shore, the problem of fish right at your feet does not go away. Striped bass and bluefish may be so near that you will have to back up in order to present the fly. Never is the problem brought home more quickly than when a big fish suddenly swirls within 5 feet of you. The first time it happens to most anglers, it really makes them jump. But they rarely ever forget the lesson.

At night, it is good to bring the fly almost all the way back to the rod tip, because some fish hit very late in the retrieve. Since you cannot see the fly line, your sense of touch must come into play here. When your stripping hand feels the larger diameter of the weight-forward part of the taper, the last 30 feet of fly line have entered the rod. The exact length of the head varies, depending on which style of line you are using. Subtracting the length of the line inside the rod, you now have about 20 feet of fly line outside of the rod tip, plus the leader. Before picking up for the next cast, retrieve another 10 feet of line. This brings the end of the fly line within about 10 feet of the rod. You can do this by counting the number of strips you make. If each one takes in a foot of line, for example, then ten does the job. With so little line left outside the rod tip, it will require a few more false casts than usual to get enough line back out for a cast, but it is well worth the effort.

Expect some striped bass and bluefish to strike during the last couple of strips of line. In this case, I do not suggest that you set the hook by continuing to retrieve; if the leader gets inside the guides, it may jam as the fish runs out. Instead, when you feel a strike in the closing moments of the retrieve, grasp the fly line tightly, and twist hard at the waist, moving the rod tip low to the water and to the rear away from the fish. This is also the way to deal with fish that take the fly as you are in the process of picking up for a backcast.

At night, wading anglers may find that fish are not only very close in front of them, but are behind them as well. This commonly occurs when working a shallow beach during an incoming tide. When you first wade out, the water near shore is too shallow to hold fish, so you naturally progress out to deeper water. But as time goes by, the water behind you grows deeper, and gradually some fish are going to swim between you and the shoreline to feed in this area. If you are concentrating all of your casting in front of you, you are going to miss these fish. So as soon as the water between you and shore reaches 2 feet deep, turn and fire a few casts back there occasionally. It pays off.

USING LIGHTS

A flashlight is mandatory equipment for night fishing, but you must also learn to use it wisely. A sudden burst of light over dark water often scares fish away. To avoid this problem, you can do two things. First, pick a flashlight with a beam that can be focused tightly. The Mag-Lite is a coastal favorite because of this and its rugged nature. Second, when you need to use it to change flies or fix a problem with the line, step back away from the waters you are fishing. Keep the flashlight on a lanyard around your neck so that both hands are free to work. Turn the light on and let it hang on the lanyard so that the beam is directed into your stripping basket. Now you can use the inside of the basket as a work area. It will hold the line as you untangle it or hold a fly box as you select a different pattern. A white or cream-colored basket is a real help because it maximizes the light where it counts.

An alternative to stepping back from the water when you use your light is to turn your back to the fish. In this position, your body will shield much of the beam. I often use this method when unhooking a fish. Never turn your back, however, where the surf is strong enough to knock you down.

Flashlights universally produce a white beam, but at night a red light is easier on your eyes. Furthermore, red will not cause you to momentarily lose your night vision the way a white light does. You can convert your flashlight to red by cutting a colored gel for the lens. This often decreases the output of the flashlight considerably, however. It should be fine for working on tackle problems and unhooking fish, but you may want more light for things like finding your way over rocky ground. So if you convert your flashlight beam to red, you should also carry a conventional white light too.

Your flashlight can also serve to help you communicate with your friends. At night when you and your partners have spread out a bit to fish a beach, it can be hard to stay in touch with each other. A predetermined set of flashlight signals is a great way to do it. For example, three short flashes might alert your friends that you have found fish. A long single flash confirms that the message was received. Two long flashes could tell the others you have yet to get a strike. Swinging a circle at arm's length might be a signal that you want to move on. Make your own system, and use it often. You will be surprised at how much it helps coordinate things.

CASTING
Casting at night is not really difficult, but it does take some getting used to. Perhaps the most immediate problem for many anglers is not being able to time the cast visually—you cannot watch the fly line as it travels forward or rearward as a signal for when to start the next part of the casting stroke. Instead, you have to rely on feeling the rod load and unload. For that reason, a fast-action rod, one that does most of its bending in the upper third, is not a good night tool, especially for someone learning the game. Its inherent stiffness stops the rod from loading deeply and thereby reduces your ability to feel the cast. With a slower, more progressive action rod, one that bends more fully into the midsection, you can better sense the rod as it loads. A fast-action rod can be made into a better night-casting tool simply by using a fly line one or two weights larger than recommended.

All this may go against the grain of those who feel that fast-action rods, because of their distance capabilities, are the only proper rod design for the salt. But distance is rarely a factor at night. In fact, the opposite is closer to the truth. You need a rod able to handle short to moderate distances well. One of the first rods I used in the salt was a Winston glass 10-weight. Compared with today's high modulus graphite rods, this rod blank would seem more like a boiled noodle. But it cast smoothly and powerfully for many years.

Concentrate at first on developing a cast of a fixed length as a way of getting accustomed to working in the dark. Fifty feet should be fine. Pull that much line off the reel, and make a 5-inch-long black mark directly on the fly line at that point using a permanent laundry-type marking pen. When you first arrive at the water at night, pull fly line off the reel, laying it in the stripping basket, until you reach the mark. If you cannot see it, turn on your light. Then turn off the light and start working out line until you feel the thinner running part of the forward taper in your hand. At this point, the weight-forward part of the line is outside the rod and ready to cast. A single or double haul combined with a false cast or two should shoot the remaining line out of the basket.

Practice casting using this set length of line until you can handle it smoothly and instinctively. Eventually you will need to vary the length of the cast to meet fishing conditions, but this is easily done once you feel more at home with casting in the dark. If you are working with a shooting head, the procedure is much the same. Most heads are 30 or 40 feet long. Work the head out until you feel the thin running line in your hand. With the head just outside the rod tip, you should be able to shoot an additional 20 feet of line with a false cast or two.

STAYING IN TOUCH WITH THE FLY

Staying in complete contact with the fly is always essential, but at night it requires even more concentration on the part of the angler. For one thing, slack or a belly in the line can be seen in the light, whereas detection at night is not so simple. When you retrieve a fly, the hand on the fly line feels a subtle weight or resistance at the end of the line caused by dragging the fly forward through the water. That weight changes with the size and design of each fly. Feeling this weight is essential to your ability to feel the strike and set the hook. At night, when fish are apt to strike more softly than they do in the day, you absolutely must maintain good contact with the fly.

To increase your feel for the fly, remember to keep the rod tip low to the water. This is always the first step in improving your control. Next, be sure to keep the rod tip pointed directly at the fly. These two things are critical to your success. Make them habits. If you still seem to be having trouble feeling the fly, try speeding up the retrieve just a hair. Sometimes this helps keep a tighter line between you and the fly.

Remember that even a little bit of wave action between you and the fly is enough to create slack in the fly line. Each wave is lifting the fly up and simultaneously pushing it toward you. A heavier fly will help

Mark Lewchik holds a striper caught along the edge of the cordgrass at night. *Photograph by Phil Farnsworth.*

because it remains deeper in the water and is easier to feel through the fly line. In some shallow situations, the waves are spaced very far apart. Here it is possible to speed up the retrieve momentarily as a wave passes under the fly line. This removes some of the slack and may mean the difference between catching fish and just getting short strikes.

When you are working a current or rip at night, be careful to follow the fly with the rod tip as the fly moves downcurrent. If you do not, you are going to miss fish. It may take a couple of casts to get used to how fast the fly is traveling in a particular situation. After the cast is made across the flow, lower the rod tip and begin to swing the rod so that it follows in the direction of the fly. Your night vision is usually sufficient for you to see the first few feet of fly line outside the rod tip. The behavior of this line helps inform you how fast the remaining fly line is moving and allows you to track the downcurrent movement of that fly line with the rod tip.

If the strikes you get are coming directly across the current or even upcurrent from your present position, it may be tough to hook a high percentage of these fish at night. In that situation, consider moving farther upcurrent if at all possible. The more the fish are downcurrent of you, the easier it is to get a solid hookup.

FIGHTING AND LANDING A FISH

Fighting a fish at night requires many of the same skills used during the day. You must get the fish onto the reel. You must apply pressure. There are some additional considerations at night, however.

If the fish feels very strong and is difficult to control, alert any anglers fishing close to you so that they can move to avoid crossing your line. You do not have to yell it out; a simple announcement is sufficient.

A reel with a click in the line-out position helps you determine how fast you are losing line during the fish's run and how far the fish has gone. If there are known obstructions such as pilings or large rocks in the area, you can gauge how close you are to getting in trouble. By applying additional pressure at the right moment, you can save yourself from losing a good fish. If you are wading, be ready for the fish to possibly circle you as you prepare to land it.

THE BEST TIMES FOR NIGHT FISHING

For night fishing, just as for daytime fishing, you want the best stage of the tide for the specific piece of shoreline you have in mind. Naturally, you want that stage to occur during the hours of darkness.

A particular tide will take place in the night for a period of several days, each night getting later until it finally occurs near dawn. So if, for example, you wished to fish a high tide after dark, you would look on a tide chart for days when that stage of the tide happened after sunset. Let's say that you found a date when the high tide crests at 10:30 P.M. Three days later, that same high tide would crest after midnight. Three more days would find the crest of the tide near 3 A.M. In another couple of days, the high tide might be happening through dawn.

In the spring or fall, it seems less important to pick times when the best stage of the tide occurs very late at night. So a tide that happens long before midnight or in the hours just before dawn is a good choice. In the dog days of summer, however, the fishing is noticeably better during the hours close to midnight or shortly thereafter. The warmer the water gets during the day, the more fish seem to feed in the deepest parts of the night, because at that time the water temperatures are considerably lower.

As a general rule, the darker the night, the better the fishing. Cloud-covered nights or periods during the darker phases of the moon are preferred times to fish. This may come as a surprise to those anglers who have always heard that the best fishing was around the full moon.

A full moon can produce good fishing out over deeper water, such as an offshore reef where the light does not penetrate the entire water column. But in the shallows along the shoreline, a bright moon seems to spoil things. The only exception I have encountered is a bright moon late in the fall when the water is already cool.

Perhaps the ideal situation is a sliver of a moon and a little starlight to go along with it. This makes for dark conditions but gives anglers just enough light to help them move around and fish a little more easily.

A cloudy night during the new moon period makes for a very dark night. The action could be good, but it is definitely harder on the fisherman. Dark nights also may bring on a phenomenon known as fire in the water, which reduces your chances of hooking fish.

Some nights the ocean itself seems to glow with thousands of tiny lights, as if every star in the sky were now somehow joined by a sister star in the sea. It is a beautiful sight, especially when seen in the wake of a boat. Anglers call it "fire in the water." But as beautiful as it is, no fly rodder really wants to see it.

These tiny lights in the water are caused by the bioluminescence of small invertebrates, including combjellies and the dinoflagellate *Noctiluca*. Like the fireflies of our summer meadow nights, these creatures are capable of emitting a soft, pale green light. This fire is more likely on dark nights and weaker under a bright moon. It is also more apt to take place during the warmest months of the summer. The more you disturb the water by wading or with the motion of your fly line and fly coming through the water, the more these tiny lights twinkle.

If there is only a sporadic and limited amount of fire, the fishing is not greatly affected. But if there is a lot of fire in the water, fishing is usually poor. The long trail of cold light activated by your fly coming through the water appears to ward off the fish.

If you elect to stay and try your luck anyway, here are some suggestions. Consider going to the lightest line and smallest, sparsest fly you have. The smaller and slimmer the fly and the diameter of the fly line, the less you disturb the water. Also, keep the retrieve as slow as possible.

There is one instance when fire in the water might result in excellent fishing. Squid are capable of emitting quick flashes of light as they feed. And wherever squid are, you can reasonably expect stripers and blues to be lurking nearby. The twinkling light produced by creatures like combjellies is small, never bigger than a cherry tomato, and either stationary on the bottom or drifting slowly with the tide. The flashing light from a squid is larger, more the size of your hand, and often moves rapidly like some underwater shooting star. I am on the lookout for this phenomenon in the spring and late fall, particularly near inlets, harbors, and salt ponds.

Moonrise and Moonset

Like the sun, the moon rises and sets each day. Yet the times of moonrise and moonset are not fixed to the times of sunrise or sunset. We have all seen the moon high overhead in the middle of the day, at one time or another. So on some days, the moon has risen long before the sun sinks in the west, although often we may not be able to see it well until darkness arrives.

When the moon rises in the middle of the day, you can expect that it will set early in the night, long before dawn. If the moon is bright, the darkest part of that particular night will be hours after the moon sets. For example, when the moon rises in early afternoon, it will often set below the horizon around midnight. The hours after midnight will be darker, and that may bring on an increase in the fishing action. The reverse situation is possible too. On some nights, the moon does not appear in the sky until very late in the evening, making the hours before moonrise the darkest and therefore the most promising.

Some coastal veterans firmly believe that like the brief improvement in the fishing we experience as the sun sets, there is a similar brief increase in action as the moon sets in the night, and that just as there is a short window of fishing action associated with dawn, there is usually a moment of good fishing as the moon rises in the night.

The exact times of moonrise and moonset can be found in the back of the *Eldridge Tide and Pilot Book*. Like the tides, the times of moonrise and moonset for a specific day change each year. Furthermore, there is no dependable link between the phase of the moon and the times of moonrise and moonset. So you will need a new chart each season in order to follow this heavenly event.

15

Saltwater Fly Casting

Without a doubt, one of the single largest hurdles facing any angler new to the salt is learning how to effectively cast a fly rod in the surf. Most of these anglers anticipate that dealing with the wind will be 90 percent of their trouble. Granted, coping with the wind is an important component of the challenge; however, the biggest problem is something far more basic. It involves breaking old casting habits and learning new ones better suited to efficiently handling larger fly rods and longer casts.

All too often a newcomer to the salt simply tries to use sheer physical force in place of the right casting technique. As a result, I have seen anglers attempting to use a 10-weight rod totally exhaust themselves in less than an hour's time.

Saltwater fly fishermen cast differently than freshwater fly rodders out of necessity. A trout fanatic may wield a rod weighing only 2½ ounces to throw a cast of 35 feet or less. A coastal angler wields a rod twice as heavy to throw a line twice as far. Obviously, a casting technique that makes solid sense for one of these situations might be totally wrong for the other. I learned this the hard way by trial and error many years ago.

Today, anglers wishing to throw a better line can turn to a number of well-illustrated books devoted to the subject. Still, regardless of what any of these books may espouse, please do not believe for a moment that there is only one correct way of wielding a fly rod. This is especially true in the area of distance casting, where the differences between casting styles often become pronounced. Ultimately each angler must match his or her own special mix of coordination and physical strength to the task. Never forget it, and never feel bad about doing it. The techniques in this chapter are those that have worked well for me.

In the following discussion, I am going to assume that you already have some experience casting a fly rod and that you understand such terms as backcast, forward cast, false casting, double haul, shooting line, and so on. If that is not the case, you should get a book on fly casting or arrange for some basic lessons before attempting saltwater fly casting.

CASTING HABITS YOU SHOULD LEAVE
ON THE STREAM

Trout anglers develop casting techniques that are effective for delivering short, delicate, and highly accurate casts with light rods. One of the most notable features of this style of fly casting is the tendency to limit upper body movement almost entirely to the wrist and forearm. In order to accomplish that, the elbow of the casting arm remains close to the side and somewhat stationary during both the forward and backward strokes.

Saltwater fly casters use a far greater range of upper body movement. For one thing, the casting elbow is allowed to move outward from the caster's side, up, and even to the rear during the cast stroke. This permits a greater range of travel for the rod during the cast stroke and thereby develops considerably more power. Equally important, it spreads the work load over the upper torso and brings larger muscle groups into play.

Coastal fly rodders also use a different casting stance. This too helps them incorporate more upper body movement into the cast. Freshwater casters often stand with their shoulders at 90 degrees to the direction of the cast, with their feet close together. Again, this is a technique designed for making short, highly accurate casts. In the salt, you are better off positioning your shoulders at more of an angle to the direction of the cast. In addition, your feet should be spread noticeably farther apart. In this position, you can rotate your torso at the waist to help drive the rod through both the forward and backward strokes. It also permits you to extend the casting arm farther to the rear during the

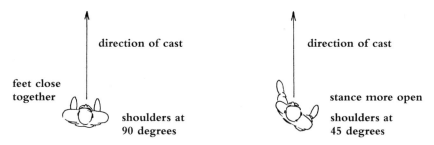

Your stance affects your ability to throw a long line. Freshwater casters stand with feet together and shoulders square to the direction of the cast. Saltwater fly rodders position themselves more on an angle, with the foot under the casting arm dropped back. (This illustration depicts the stance for a right-hander. Lefties must reverse the foot positions.)

backcast, another plus. And it provides a more stable platform from which to work a heavier rod and a longer line.

When trout fishermen want to throw a much longer line, they resort to false casting. This technique gradually loads the rod deeper and deeper while keeping aloft longer and longer lengths of line. Clearly, false casting works; however, it is a highly inefficient method of gaining distance. First off, it is unnecessary. If you know how to load a rod quickly and deeply, which will be explained shortly, you can cast an extremely long way with little or no false casting whatsoever. Furthermore, with a saltwater-size outfit, repeated false casting is tiring. And to make matters worse, each false cast is yet another opportunity for the ever-present wind to play havoc with your cast. So in the salt, repeated false casting is uncalled for and simply not practical.

For freshwater fly rodders to learn saltwater fly casting, they not only need to break a few casting habits, but they also must learn to use one new piece of equipment: the stripping basket. In fresh water, when anglers want to shoot more line into the cast, they peel off additional fly line from the reel and drop it on the water in preparation. Ultimately this seemingly simple step greatly reduces their total distance potential, because the surface tension of the water slows down the amount of line they can shoot. A stripping basket offers no such resistance and thereby maximizes your ability to shoot line into the cast.

LEARNING THE BASIC SALTWATER CAST

Now that you are aware of the basic differences between freshwater and saltwater casting, you can begin learning to make the necessary changes in your technique. So get your rod ready. For this task, I recommend an 8-, 9-, or 10-weight rod and a full-length fly line over a shooting head. Do not start with a fast-sinking line, however. These lines have unique casting characteristics and will be covered later in the chapter. An intermediate fly line in a weight-forward taper would be ideal. Be sure that the fly line is clean and ready to zip through the guides. Also get a stripping basket and several different brightly colored waterproof marking pens.

To the end of the line, attach a short, stiff leader of about 7 feet tapered to 12-pound test. (A basic leader design is shown in chapter 11.) For a practice fly, I suggest a #1/0 Lefty's Deceiver. Snip off the hook bend with a pair of pliers, for both safety and convenience.

Your initial goal in learning the basic saltwater cast is to make a 60-foot cast without any false casting whatsoever. In other words, you will use one backcast and one forward cast only. You first need to be able to load the rod quickly and deeply. To accomplish this, work on shooting 10 or more feet of fly line into your backcast. You also will employ the muscles of your upper torso in the casting stroke to help you drive the rod forcefully and efficiently. Do not worry; it is easier than you think. In fact, with perseverance and practice, I know you can better that 60-foot mark. If your double haul is rusty or weak, however, you may want to spend some time refining it first.

Find someplace where you have at least 125 feet of open space. Practicing over water is superior to practicing on a lawn, as grass provides less friction on the fly line than water does. Hence, on the lawn you do not load the rod as well as you do over water, nor do you get as good a feel for the rod in general. If all you have at your disposal is a lawn, however, it will suffice. Rig up your rod and be sure to fully engage the ferrules. Drive both tip-over-butt and spigot ferrules together firmly, then twist them a quarter turn. During the cast, an improperly seated ferrule usually emits a click that you can sense in your casting hand. If you continue to cast, you could easily crack the ferrule.

Pull some line off the reel and string up the rod. If the line comes off the reel in tight coils, stretch it before attempting to cast. I recommend that you get in the habit of always stretching your lines before going afield. You can place the rod under your casting arm and stretch short lengths between your hands if you wish, although I prefer another method. Hook the leader to a stationary object, such as a parked car, or ask a friend to grasp it firmly. Back away until the fly line comes tight, then pull slowly on the line, stretching it. You can remove the coils from an entire fly line at once with this simple procedure.

Strip off about 75 feet of line from the reel, and pull it all out the rod tip. Measure along the line 30 feet from the tip, and make a 3-inch-long band using one of the colored markers. Measure off another 10 feet, and make a mark at 40 feet. With most weight-forward lines, this is about where the tapered part of the fly line ends and the level running section begins. This is an important spot, so make a larger, more visible mark here using a different color. Continue on, making smaller marks at 45, 50, 55, and finally 60 feet. These marks will help you judge your performance.

Strap on the stripping basket so that it is approximately at navel height or slightly lower, and directly in front of you. The inside of the stripping basket should be clean and dry. Reel up the fly line until the 60-foot mark reaches the rod's tip-top. Then strip the fly line into the basket until the 40-foot mark reaches the rod tip. You should now have 40 feet of fly line lying outside the rod in a straight line and enough additional fly line in the stripping basket to produce a total cast of 60 feet plus the leader.

How you grip the rod is an important factor in both your control of the cast and your overall comfort. I like the first joint of the thumb to be directly on top of the cork handle. This allows you to use your thumb, the strongest finger, to help drive the rod during the forward cast. Do not squeeze the grip harder than is necessary to support the rod's weight. Many casters new to larger rods seem to feel they must

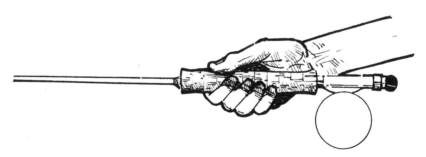

The most popular grip is with the thumb on top. Note that the thumb does not lie perfectly flat on the cork. Instead, it angles downward, with the first joint supplying most of the pressure.

practically crush the cork handle, but too firm a grip quickly tires the muscles of the forearm.

Using the face of a clock to help visualize the casting stroke is an old idea. In this system, the caster is imagined to be standing sideways inside the face of a clock. The caster's head is at 12:00, feet at 6:00, and belt buckle aimed at the 3:00. The rod, as it travels through the casting stroke, is thought of as the clock's hour hand.

We will first concentrate on making a good backcast. This simplifies things for a moment and gives an excellent opportunity to focus on an important ingredient in distance casting—how to shoot line on the backcast. Once you master this, the rest is made considerably easier.

Angle yourself to the direction of the cast, and take up the proper stance. Your casting shoulder should be pointed somewhat in the direction of the backcast. Grasp the fly line up near the first stripping guide on the rod with your other hand, which I will refer to as your "line-control hand." Bend the elbow of this arm, and place the fly line between the thumb and forefinger. Now angle the rod tip down toward the ground or water. The rod tip should be at about 3:30.

The next series of moves should be performed as a smooth, seamless flow. To describe them, however, I must handle them as if they were somewhat separate events.

Start the backcast by pulling upward with the forearm of the rod hand to produce a smooth but powerful lifting of the rod. Simultaneously, begin turning at the waist, moving the casting shoulder rearward in the direction of the backcast. Notice how your stance permits this turning at the waist to become part of the casting stroke.

Only when the last of the fly line is about to leave the surface of the water does the wrist finally come into play. Usually this occurs roughly as the rod reaches 10:30 or 11:00. The action of the wrist is a very brief but forceful upward snap that imparts speed to the line but momentarily stops the reel's rearward motion. This is also the moment when the first half of the double haul takes place. This snap of the wrist and its accompanying haul accelerates the airborne fly line to the rear. As soon as the snap ends, immediately ease your grip on the fly line. If you have timed it right, additional line is quickly pulled up from the stripping basket and out through the guides, lengthening the backcast as the rod passes through the 12:00 mark.

After stopping the rod, freshwater casters tend to hold it fairly stationary in anticipation of the forward cast. In the salt, however, after the snap, both the rod and the casting arm should be allowed to again move rearward. Do it slowly enough so that you never lose a feel for the weight of the line on the rod tip. This change makes for a longer casting stroke, produces a longer backcast, and leaves the casting arm in a position that gives you greater leverage with which to drive the forward cast. To get this extension, as the rod passes 12:00, let the casting elbow swing out from your side and upward at the same time. As the elbow rises, simultaneously begin straightening out your casting arm to the rear, forcing the rod farther and farther back.

Please note that you are not allowing the rod tip to fall to the horizontal position. That would lower your backcast too far. At the end of the backcast, you are in a position not unlike an athlete about to throw a baseball, football, or javelin. The arm is extended 180 degrees away from the final target, with the elbow slightly bent and just below shoulder height. Meanwhile, the forearm is near vertical, with the hand just above shoulder height and the rod at about 2:00.

This rearward extension of the casting arm is hardly a new development in distance casting. In a French fly-fishing book written by Charles Ritz in 1948, there is a photograph of a caster standing on a

At the end of the backcast, the casting arm should be extended rearward. Note that the elbow is bent and held just below shoulder height much in the same way that someone might throw a football. At this point, the body weight should be greater on the foot under the casting arm.

low bridge. The caption tells us that he is about to deliver a 36-meter (118-foot) cast with a cane rod. Caught immediately before the start of the forward stroke, the caster's arm is fully extended to the rear.

Let your backcast unfurl to its fullest extent and then fall to the ground. Now put the rod down and study the marks on the fly line. You started with 40 feet of line outside the rod tip. How much line is outside the rod tip now? Did you shoot 5 feet into the backcast? If so, it is a start, but you need more practice. If you got 10 feet, great. Shoot another 10 feet on the forward cast and you are home free. If you got more than 10 feet, you are a natural. I would not be surprised to see you reach 80 feet or better when you add the forward cast.

Repeat this exercise until you are comfortable with it. When you can consistently pick up 40 feet of line and make a nicely formed backcast reaching at least 50 feet in length, you are ready to add the forward cast. Be sure to keep the backcast high, and start your forward cast only when the backcast is nearing its complete rearward extension. Peek over your shoulder to watch the line if you want. Initiate the forward cast by turning at the waist, using your upper body to drive the rod forward. With 50 or more feet of line in the air, the rod loads deeply as you begin the forward stroke. Remember this feeling well. It means that you are working the rod correctly and is a sure sign of success.

Do not forget the second haul on the forward power snap. If all goes well, it should not be hard to reach 60 feet. Once you master it, aim for 70 or 75 feet, whatever your ability allows. Next, try starting with 30 feet of line out and see if you can still reach 60 feet without false casting. This requires you to further hone your new skills. Once you are comfortable with this casting style, from time to time allow yourself one false cast. For example, try starting with 20 feet of fly line out and see if you can reach 60 or greater feet with the aid of one false cast.

Many casters lean slightly forward at the waist before the start of the backcast. As they begin to pick up line from the water, they straighten up, adding extra momentum to the stroke. You can also lean your upper body slightly rearward as the backcast unfurls. This puts you in a position to really drive the rod forward. To use this technique well, you must shift your body weight from one foot to the other. On the pickup, your weight is mainly on the leading foot, the one opposite your casting arm. Then it smoothly transfers to the rear foot during the backcast. On the forward stroke, the weight shifts back.

Another thing you may notice is that some saltwater anglers have a

On the forward cast, the angler helps drive the rod by twisting slightly at the waist and shifting his or her weight to the leading foot.

habit of rolling the casting wrist during the power snap. It happens on both the forward and backward casts. To visualize it, imagine for a moment that you are standing directly in front of someone casting. Picture the relationship of the fly reel to your position. As the rod lifts for the backcast, you see the fly reel on edge. As the power snap is made, however, the caster also rotates his or her wrist outward so that the reel points 90 degrees to the direction of the cast. Therefore, as the backcast unfurls, you would be looking at the side plate of the fly reel. As the forward snap is made, the wrist is rotated clockwise, swinging the fly reel back toward the caster, and once again you see the reel on edge. It is a tricky maneuver and far from mandatory. Furthermore, if not done well, it can invite trouble. Try it only after you have mastered the basic cast. If it helps you, fine, use it.

CASTING A FAST-SINKING LINE

Although saltwater fly fishermen use fast-sinking fly lines, trout fishermen rarely do. Consequently, converts from fresh water are often unprepared to deal with them. The single biggest difficulty comes when you want to pick up the line to make a backcast. Because fast-sinking lines lie underwater rather than near or on the top, they offer considerable resistance. Anglers used to easily lifting 40 or more feet of intermediate or floating line off the surface are going to find these sinking lines to be quite a surprise. The simplest remedy is to reduce the amount of line in the water by retrieving the fly closer to you before attempting a back-cast. This solution usually forces you to make two or more false casts, however, in order to get the belly portion of the fly line back outside the rod tip.

You can use a roll cast to help free a sinking line from the water. To see how this works, cast out about 35 feet of sinking fly line and let it settle a bit. Now begin a conventional roll cast by slowly raising the rod to the 1:00 position. Notice that in the process, you have removed some of the line from under the water simply by raising the rod. At the same time, you are also pulling the remaining line nearer to you.

Begin the forward portion of the roll cast by making a strong downward snap of the wrist, driving the line forward and over itself in a rolling loop. As the loop travels forward, it lifts the submerged fly line to the surface. Immediately after the loop stops unrolling, lift up the line for a backcast. If you have a lot of submerged line, you may need to make more than one roll cast before getting under way.

With their smaller diameters and greater densities, sinking lines develop considerably more line speed during the cast. As a result of this increased speed, sinking fly lines cast into the wind better than other types of lines. But this line speed also changes the timing of a cast, and you must adjust to it. Expect the backcast to take less time to unroll than with a similar length of floating or intermediate line. Failure to do so will result in reduced distance and a jerky cast.

This greater line speed sometimes produces real problems when you attempt to shoot line into either the forward or backward cast. The momentum of the line in the air can yank additional line from the stripping basket violently, causing it to form a knot. If this happens repeatedly, reduce the force with which you are driving the cast. You may want to put less effort into your double haul, too. Both things lower line speed and make line control easier. Also, cast a bit more sidearm with sinking lines to avoid being hit by one. If you are unfortunate enough to be struck during a cast, you will know why I mentioned this. Because of the line's momentum, it packs a fair wallop.

CASTING WITH A SHOOTING HEAD

Shooting heads are popular with some anglers on the coast. Heads are economical, and even a relatively inexperienced caster can immediately gain some distance by using them. Nevertheless, for reasons discussed in chapter 10, I do not think they are the best answer for the fishing needs of coastal anglers. Still, many are in use and many anglers enjoy them. In the salt, shooting heads are often 40 feet instead of the conventional 30 feet. This additional 10 feet of line makes for a slightly heavier head. The additional weight is a real help in loading a large rod and casting a heavy fly. Whether you are using a 30- or 40-foot head, a shooting head should be one line size bigger than the line size for which the rod is rated.

Like sinking fly lines, shooting heads develop greater line speed—the timing of the cast is faster than with a full intermediate or floating line. Unlike all other lines, when using a shooting head, you never attempt to lengthen the cast by false casting. Only the head and 3 to 5 feet of running line should be outside the rod during the backcast. Holding any more line than that in the air detracts from rather than aids your casting performance.

Now retrieve the line until the head is about 3 feet away from the rod tip. Using the basic casting method described earlier, make a backcast, but be careful not to haul so much that you pull the head inside the rod. It should remain outside during the cast. As the rod drifts back, you can shoot a few feet of running line into the backcast, but only a few feet. Generally, the more experienced you become, the more you are able to handle a bit more running line outside the rod tip. Haul on the forward cast, again only enough to bring the head close to but not inside the rod tip. Then shoot as much line as possible on the forward cast.

By not allowing the head to enter the rod tip, you maximize the performance of the shooting head and avoid having the connection point between the running line and the head come in contact with the guides. Not only would this connection be a little bumpy traveling back and forth over the guides during the cast, but also the guides would tend to make the connection wear faster than normal.

Extremely fast-sinking shooting heads made from lead wire can be purchased or made from a section of lead trolling wire. These heads are very effective at reaching fish that are lying deep; however, they are also very hard to use, even for seasoned veterans of the coast. In fact, it is fair to say that they are the most difficult of all lines to cast. Use them with great care! Getting hit by one is probably like being whacked with a frying pan; it could knock you off your feet.

CASTING IN THE WIND

Learning to saltwater fly-fish is in some part learning to cast in the wind. Fortunately, winds during the warmer months when most coastal anglers are active are the weakest of the year. Still, you should expect at least 10- to 15-knot breezes every day of the season. That is normal on the seaboard. Winds of 15 to 20 knots make casting difficult, although not impossible, especially for the coastal veteran. And every season there are days when the winds race over 20 knots. They send nearly all fly rodders looking for cover. (Note that I said *nearly* all.)

The direction of the wind is more important than its strength in determining your ability to fly-cast. Onshore winds—winds in your face—are far more limiting than winds at your back. A wind coming into your casting shoulder is dangerous; a wind into your other shoulder is not. To some degree, an angler can choose locations where, for a particular day, the winds are favorable for casting. Everybody does it. Yet there are some very good reasons why you must learn how to cast in less than ideal conditions.

For an angler working from the ground, an onshore wind frequently produces the best fishing conditions. This wind drives the baitfish in toward the beach, and with them come the game fish. It is especially promising for larger trophy fish too. Also, you might well find yourself in the middle of some red-hot fishing, when the wind swings around or the boat turns such that the winds are working against your cast. Your ability to adapt is then critical to your angling success.

Wind into Your Casting Arm

A wind directly or even angling into your casting arm is real trouble. It immediately raises the possibility of your getting struck by the hook or the line. If it is a heavy sinking fly line, it can hurt just as much as the hook. A wind into your casting side will push the backcast directly in line with you. The forward cast then must come right over you from behind. If you are ambidextrous, you could simply switch casting hands, but most anglers are not. Another remedy is to learn how to make a back-handed cast. Here is how to do it.

Retrieve the fly normally, but before you attempt to pick up the line for a backcast, reposition yourself so that the wind is now hitting you in the back. Extend your casting arm out from your side, and roll your wrist so that the fly reel is facing upward. Lower the rod tip and point it directly at the fly line in the water. By twisting at the waist and lifting your casting arm, make a more or less conventional casting stroke across your upper body. The rod should load easily because of the weight of the fly line in the water.

It should feel at this point as if you are making a forward cast 180 degrees away from your intended target. Now reverse the motion. As the line starts to straighten out, roll your casting wrist so that the reel is again skyward. Turn your head back to the water as you twist at the waist, making a sweeping forward cast across your body. As the line straightens out over the water, keep the rod tip high. Dropping it tends to reduce distance greatly. After the line lands, reposition yourself to fully face the water you are fishing.

Once you get accustomed to this technique, you can deliver a cast in either direction quickly. In some situations, that ability can be a real help. Let's say you were standing on a casting platform in the bow of a boat, casting to the port side, when someone suddenly yells, "There are fish breaking behind you!" You could stop and slowly turn completely around, or you could fire a back-handed cast to starboard and then turn.

This back-handed style also has some advantages when working nearer to the transom of a boat. If you are a right-handed caster and wish to cast off the starboard side, your backcast must cross the boat widthwise. This raises the possibility of hitting the superstructure or even someone else aboard. If you move down the gunwale to the transom and back-hand cast, the fly line travels over the water on both casting strokes, thereby avoiding any contact with the boat or its occupants.

Wind in the Face

A wind blowing directly in your face is the fear of every fly fisherman. Here the problem is not so much the possibility of being struck by the hook as simply failing to get any distance at all. One bright side to this situation is that an onshore wind drives the fish closer to the water's edge and frequently produces the finest fishing on the coast.

With a wind in the face, some anglers cast sidearm. This keeps the line low to the water, taking advantage of the slower-moving air just above the surface. But as good a technique as sidearm casting is, it does not handle all head-wind situations. Onshore winds create waves too. A low sidearm cast is often out of the question for anglers on exposed beaches, because the fly line will not be high enough to cross over the surf. In that situation, you can turn and cast at a 45-degree angle, so that each cast goes across the wind rather than directly into it. This frequently produces adequate distance to reach the fish.

Wind at Your Back

If you have wind at your back, but it is not very strong—10 to 15 knots—simply cast as you would normally. Although your backcast will

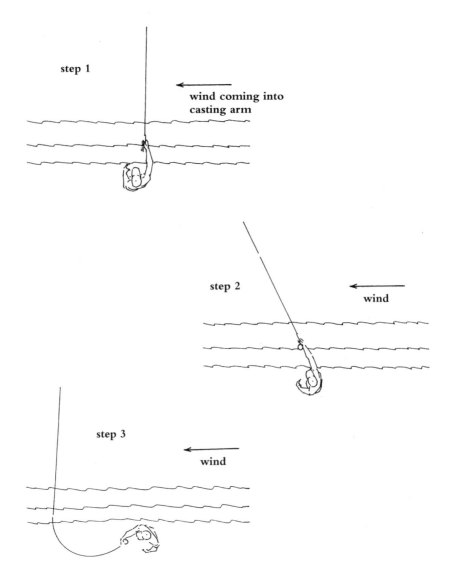

step 1

wind coming into
casting arm

step 2

wind

step 3

wind

When the wind is coming directly into your casting arm *(step 1),* a back-handed cast is very effective. *Step 2:* Reposition your stance so that the wind is striking your back. With the line lying on the water ready for a backcast, roll your wrist so that the fly reel faces up. Your casting arm should be extended out from your side and roughly parallel to the water. *Step 3:* Twist at the waist and make a casting stroke high and across the chest.

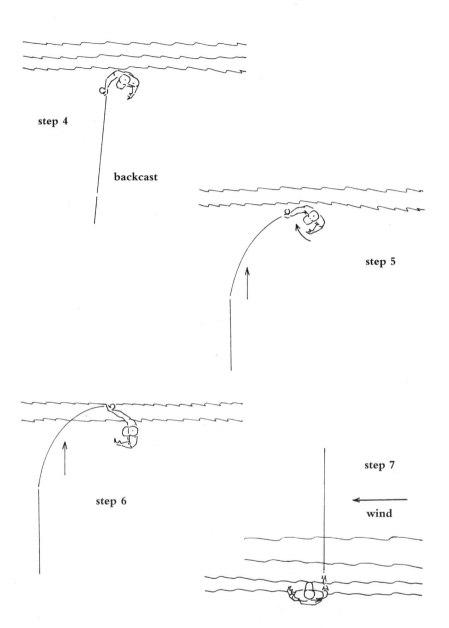

step 4

backcast

step 5

step 7

step 6

wind

Step 4: As the backcast straightens out, roll the wrist so that the reel is upward again in preparation for the forward stroke. *Step 5:* Reverse the body motion, twisting at the waist back toward the intended target. *Step 6:* Simultaneously make a casting stroke across the chest. Do not drop the rod tip quickly, as this would shorten the cast. *Step 7:* After the cast lands on the water, reposition yourself to face the water.

not unroll properly, the direction of the wind will give additional forward momentum to the forward cast. Hence, one thing cancels out the other.

As the wind gets stronger, however, you may need to change plans. A strong wind at your back will stall even your best backcast. One way anglers casting from the beach can combat the situation is to make a sidearm backcast to take advantage of the reduced wind speeds lower to the ground. As the backcast straightens out behind you, raise the rod tip a bit, and make a somewhat more overhead forward cast to take advantage of the wind.

Wind-resistant fly lines, such as the thicker floating variety, and wind-resistant flies like poppers may cast farther than anything else in a tail wind. During the forward cast, their width catches the wind and sails with it, maximizing the range you can cover. Under most circumstances, sinking lines and slim flies are easier to handle in a wind than are any other lines.

USING A STRIPPING BASKET

Stripping baskets are essential in the salt. Not only do they store the line in preparation for the cast, they help the angler keep the fly line out of harm's way. Currents, waves, seaweed, barnacle-covered rocks, and other such things are constantly threatening to pull, knot, snag, or even cut your fly line. Even when working from a clean, sandy beach where it seems you are safe from these problems, your own feet might betray you, catching line and ruining an otherwise perfect cast.

Many newcomers to the salt are uncomfortable the first time they try to use a stripping basket. The novice often hits his or her hand on the basket during the retrieve. To remedy this, start by being sure that the basket is correctly positioned. It should be at about navel height or slightly lower. This position allows plenty of room for your hands. The only time you should raise the basket higher is if you are forced to wade very deeply. Next, train your hands to work inside the space between the stripping basket and the rod. The best idea is to simply watch your hands until you develop a rhythm. With time, it becomes second nature. As you practice, you will find that there is a maximum range of motion that each hand can go through. A longer pull simply causes the hand to strike the basket.

Another common problem is that the line tangles inside the basket.

Loops of fly line in the bottom of the basket become interwound, and when you try to shoot line into the cast, the fly line comes up in a knot. This can occur because of water in the basket, wind, angler movement, high line speed during the cast, or the condition of the fly line.

There are several things you can do to prevent this. If the fly line comes off the reel with noticeable coils, stretch it before you begin casting. These coils are more noticeable the longer you leave a fly line on the reel. Colder weather can also cause some fly line to coil more.

If you walk or wade with large amounts of fly line in the basket, your movement shifts the line back and forth and can cause it to tangle. Make it a habit to reel up the fly line before you move, especially if you plan on a long walk down the beach. And as a general practice, do not have more line in the basket than you plan on casting. The excess just provides more opportunity for knots to form.

Wind can push your fly line around, too. You can reduce this problem by using a deeper basket. Most anglers use dishpan stripping baskets that are about 5 inches tall. They work quite well, but deeper, 7-inch-tall dishpans provide more protection and are better in very windy conditions.

Sometimes the high speed at which the fly line jumps up out of the basket when you shoot line into the cast causes tangles. This is especially the case with sinking lines, because they develop the most speed. Lowering the force with which you cast reduces the frequency of knots. You can also form a ring around the line with the thumb and forefinger of the noncasting hand. Make this ring just above the basket to deflect knots as the line heads toward the stripping guide.

Waves and spray create puddles of water in your stripping basket, but never allow the water to accumulate. As it sloshes around, the water moves the fly line with it, creating tangles. Some anglers feel that the solution to this problem is to drill holes in the bottom of the stripping basket to allow water to drain out. Do not do this. As you wade deeper, water will enter through those holes, increasing your problems. Instead, occasionally dump any accumulated water out. To do so, grab the stripping basket along its forward edge, and tip it up to your chest. The water will pour out the sides and harmlessly down the front of your waders.

The more experienced you get, the more you will want to try fishing in heavier surf. These larger waves can completely fill a stripping basket in a single surge. If I see an exceptionally large wave headed my way, I will tip the basket to my chest in anticipation. Not only does this prevent the basket from being filled, it helps deflect the wave away from me.

Do not let any loose fly line hang outside the basket. Even a small loop can gradually pull the remaining line with it. So if you see line draped over the edge, place it back in the basket. This problem often crops up immediately after you make a cast. As fly line is shot into the forward cast, it jumps from the stripping basket, occasionally leaving a piece hanging over the side. Get in the habit of checking for loose line immediately after the cast and before you begin the retrieve. If a piece is over the side, place it back in the basket.

PHYSICAL CONDITIONING

A famous fly fisherman once said something to the effect that saltwater fly fishing was like sex after lunch—only good for people with hard stomachs. It is a funny line, but it also contains a grain of truth. Saltwater fly fishing is more physically demanding than its freshwater counterpart. Wielding a big fly rod in the surf takes real effort. And if you are out of shape, expect your back and shoulders to give you the bad news. So you should consider getting into shape before taking on the salt.

A regular walking program plus light weight training for the upper body make for an excellent combination. The former prepares you for a day of hard fishing or just walking down a long beach in your waders. And improving the muscle tone in your arms not only helps you control a big fly rod, but also protects you from shoulder and lower back injuries that can be brought on from hours of continual casting. A little weight training can also reduce your chances of getting tendinitis in the forearm, better known as tennis elbow. This is an inflammation brought on by repetitive motion, in this case, casting. It is a painful and even chronic condition, and many coastal fly rodders suffer from it.

These anglers often had fly-fished for years in fresh water without a problem, but graduating to bigger saltwater fly rods and the demands of longer casts made a difference. Things that seem to dispose individuals to the injury include inadequate physical conditioning, using a rod too big for one's physical stature, and continually trying to overpower the cast to make up for some perceived lack of distance. Very stiff, fast-action rods are likely part of the problem too. A grip with too small of a diameter probably contributes as well, because it forces anglers to close the hand tighter around the handle, elongating the tendon.

16

New England Planner

As a saltwater fly rodder, you should learn your local waters well. Search out and fish your own special shores, both because it makes practical sense and also because home waters are so frequently the source of the finest angling memories. Avoid the hysteria that has so often led freshwater anglers to jam together in well-known spots. It just makes no sense to fish like that. In part it is simply a matter of angling etiquette; we should never deliberately crowd one another. Presently the most discouraging example of poor etiquette in the salt is the cowboy mentality that overtakes some boaters as they race each other to reach surface-feeding fish. The word *blitz* often better describes the anglers in these situations than it does the fish. By far the most important thing to remember is this: Without some degree of solitude, fishing rapidly loses its ability to renew the soul.

The following pages detail a few well-known coastal fishing spots in my home area of New England, with the accent mainly on places to fish from shore. From the protected shoreline of Connecticut north and east to the rocky beaches of Maine, there are thousands of miles of shoreline to explore. Points of land, inlets, and estuaries all beckon to the fly rodder.

To newcomers to the sport, the following guidance will provide a chance to see some productive water. As good as these places are, however, do not expect them to produce fish every day. Saltwater fish, unlike those in a trout stream, are constantly on the move. You must fish a place often and learn its secrets of tide, wind, and time of year.

The spots listed here give just a taste of what the coast has to offer. It is still largely a fly-rod frontier, and I am sure you can find additional places every bit as good as these. The listings are arranged by state and give a little insight into the nature of the fishing to be found in each one, including the species caught and the length of the season, as well as specific locales. The rest is up to you. Good fishing!

CONNECTICUT

The Connecticut coast and Long Island Sound offer fine fly rodding in relatively shallow, protected waters. And there is good evidence that saltwater fly fishing likely got its start in the New World along this shore. The most prominent feature of this shoreline is its rivers. Three major rivers—the Housatonic, the Connecticut and the Thames—enter the sound, and each holds good to excellent fishing for striped bass and bluefish. The lower ends of these rivers and their adjoining coastline offer some of the best fishing in the state.

Long Island Sound in general holds good numbers of small to medium-size game fish, but big fish are caught here too. In 1992, New Haven Harbor provided one lucky angler with a striped bass of over 75 pounds, the third-largest striper on record. This fish was not taken on a fly, but it does show that big fish swim in the sound. Because of its large rivers, and its southernmost location in the region, Connecticut's fishing season is the longest in New England, running a full eight months. In most years, it begins the first or second week of April with striped bass and extends all the way through until the end of November. Bluefish arrive in May, but good bluefishing generally is not under way until later in June. Bonito show up in small numbers as early as mid-July and as late as mid-August. Little tunny show in mid-August to as late as Labor Day.

The western end of the sound has more tidal flats and less surf than the eastern end. It also has less tidal current, although its tidal range is higher. There are many harbors here that hold good numbers of menhaden during the summer months. These large baitfish in turn attract big blues and bass to feed in the same area. Sand eels and silversides are also common baitfish. Starting near the New York line, you have good fishing in Greenwich and Cos Cob harbors on the Mianus River. Farther east at Norwalk, there is good fishing in Sheffield and Cockenoe harbors, and the entire general area known as the Norwalk Islands. This area has given up world-record striped bass on a fly in years past.

Though the state of Connecticut provides adequate public boat-launching facilities, fly rodders who wish to fish from shore will find getting to the water more difficult. The Connecticut coastline is largely private, and therefore it is hard for anglers to gain access. State parks and town beaches are often the best bets. State parks are open to both residents and nonresidents. Generally there is a modest daily cost, although after dark, fishermen may be allowed to enter for free. Town beaches, on the other hand, are sometimes restricted to residents only, although some towns allow nonresidents to enter for a fee. It is always best to check on the situation before arriving.

Sherwood Island State Park and Fairfield's Penfield Reef are two fine access points for anglers who want to fish from shore. Sherwood Island is located near the town of Westport. There is a daily parking fee of about $5 during the week and higher on weekends. Anglers arriving before 8 A.M. or after 6 P.M. can park for free. During the day, when swimmers and bathers are using the park, fishing is allowed on both the jetties at either end of the island and a rocky area near the concession. After dark, things open up, and fly rodders can move around.

Penfield Reef is on Reef Road in Fairfield, just minutes from the center of town. This is not a state park, but there is a public right-of-way to the beach. Though you do not have to pay any fees here, parking has been a problem. It is best to consult a local tackle shop on the present conditions. The reef extends nearly a mile out from shore. It is totally exposed at low tide and is easy to wade starting about two and a half hours after high tide. You can fish either side of the reef, which is a help in coping with any wind. The tip is usually a good spot, but many fish are caught along the reef's entire length. Be sure to return to shore as the tide floods back over. Fall offers the best fly rodding.

The lower end of the Connecticut River from Essex down to the mouth is a superb fly-fishing area. Unfortunately, again access from the ground is severely limited. The state of Connecticut, however, does offer two boat ramps, one under the I-95 bridge on the west side of the river, and the other on Smith Neck Road off Route 156 in Old Lyme. Small craft of 14 to 16 feet are fine inside the river, and you will occasionally see anglers using canoes in the quieter stretches. Striper fishing is best from April to June and then again in the fall. Bluefishing picks up in late June and extends through October.

The waters along the river side of Great Island are good, as are the areas around the breakwater on the west side of the mouth. Upstream, the mouths of the Lieutenant River, Ragged Rock Creek, and Calf's Island are all worth exploring. Long Sand Shoal outside the mouth also fishes well, as does Cornfield Point to the immediate west and Hatchett Reef to the southeast.

Rocky Neck State Park in East Lyme offers a jetty from which to fish. Late in the fall after the swimmers disappear, you can also work the beach itself. Another state park for fishermen is Harkness Memorial in Waterford. It is a good place in the spring and later in the fall. Both striped bass and bluefish prowl this beach. Goshen Pond empties into Long Island Sound on the western edge of the state's property. The mouth can be good on a dropping tide. To the east, the beach is rocky. It gives up quite a few fish in the fall. In years past, you could drive in at any hour of the day or night, but night access has been curtailed. On the other side of the Thames River is Bluff Point State Park near Groton. It is a very long walk all the way out to the end, but good fishing happens closer to the parking lot. It is best in late fall.

RHODE ISLAND

Rhode Island has a less protected and more rugged coastline than that of Connecticut. The wind and the surf are stronger. For those reasons, it is more difficult to fly-rod these beaches, but they do have excellent potential for all species and for larger-size fish. The south coast of Rhode Island from Point Judith westward to Watch Hill holds the most promise and is a growing mecca for saltwater fly rodders. The season here begins around mid-April and lasts into November. Expect to find striped bass, bluefish, bonito, and little tunny swimming in these waters. Spring and summer provide good angling, but late-fall fishing can be out of this world.

After the summer season, many beaches in this part of Rhode Island can be traveled with a four-wheel-drive vehicle. To do so, you need to obtain a permit from the rangers at Burlingame State Park, located just off Route 1 near Charlestown. Some landowners recently complained of noise, overcrowding, and conservation concerns brought on by allowing four-wheel-drive vehicles on the beach. The same thing has already happened in other states along the seaboard, most notably Massachusetts. If you do use a beach buggy, be sure to obey all rules and regulations and in general tread lightly wherever you travel.

The Watch Hill area, including Napatree Point and Watch Hill Point at the lighthouse, are famous for good fishing. Napatree Point is a long, narrow barrier beach composed mainly of sand, with a more rocky terminal end. It is about 1½ miles in total length, and a hike all the way out in waders is not a picnic, but that keeps the crowds to a minimum. The sandy beach facing south is long, steep, and crescent-shaped. Often it has moderate to heavy surf that can be frustrating to a fly rodder. Lower stages of the tide are the best time to fish here for two reasons: The waves will be at a minimum and there is a dropoff about 100 feet out from the high-tide line. Many big fish travel the beach along this edge. At low tide, you can get close enough to this area to reach it with a fly.

The beach on the north side faces into Little Narragansett Bay. These are protected waters where waves are rarely a problem. This beach has a gradual slope, and you can wade out in many spots. Expect to find mainly smaller fish here, particularly schoolie bass. If you want a chance at the largest fish, work the rocky terminal end of the point. You can fish either tide, but be sure to find a flat rock to stand on. Caution is advised, because the rocks near the water are slippery and the surf can pound.

Watch Hill Point, sometimes called simply "the Hill," is one of the most beautiful places on the coast. Like Napatree Point, it holds the promise of bragging-size striped bass and bluefish for the shore anglers, especially for those willing to brave the cold days of late October and November. There is a parking lot at the lighthouse, but it is reserved for the disabled and senior citizens during most of the season; very late in the fall, however, anglers are sometimes permitted to park inside the gates. Normally you must park in town and walk out, but it is not a bad hike.

The east side is nearly impossible to fly-rod. The surf is very heavy, and the fish are frequently far outside of fly-casting range. The west side can be worked with a fly, especially around the rock jetty. The rip out in front of the lighthouse holds excellent fishing for boat-based fly fishermen, with good numbers of bonito and little tunny from September into mid-October and beyond. November is traditionally the time for the largest bass.

An extremely important feature of the fishing along the south shore of Rhode Island is a series of large salt ponds. These bodies of water, rich in baitfish, are essentially shallow lagoons that empty into the ocean through four narrow openings protected by rock jetties. These jetties are home to some of the finest fishing Rhode Island has to offer. They are, from west to east, Weekapaug Breachway, Quonochontaug Breachway, Charlestown Breachway, and the two jetties at Galilee.

Weekapaug Breachway lies at the western end of Misquamicut State Beach in Westerly. At the breachway itself, the state provides a free parking area just for anglers, although it can fill quickly when the action is hot. The parking lot sits tight against the jetty on the east side of the opening, which is the side preferred by most anglers.

Fly rodders working these jetty walls like an ebbing current for striped bass and bluefish. A flooding current, however, is better for anglers hoping to hook a bonito or little tunny. Note that in all three breachways, the time of current occurs well after the time of tide. Generally, the ebbing current begins two and a half hours after the scheduled high tide and the flooding current begins three and a half hours after the scheduled low tide.

Quonochontaug Breachway drains a large salt pond of over 700 acres. On the east side of the breachway the state owns 49 acres of land officially referred to as the Quonochontaug Fishing Area and Breachway. This public access point lies at the end of West Beach Road in Charlestown. The west side of the breachway is undeveloped land leased to the Rhode Island Mobile Sportsfishermen (RIMS), who travel it in four-wheel-drive vehicles.

The tip of the east jetty wall is popular, but you must be careful not to trespass on private property on your way out. The first few hours of the dropping tide are best. After the middle of the ebb, a rocky reef becomes exposed in front of the mouth, making it difficult to cover the water. Fly rodders can also work the edges of the channel all the way back to the salt pond. Private property should be respected here too. In this location, a flooding current after dark is a good choice for striped bass and bluefish. Where the channel opens up into the pond, there is a shallow area that you can wade during lower stages of the tide. Ask a local angler to guide you.

Charlestown Breachway is in Charlestown and drains two large salt ponds, Ninigret and Green Hill, with a combined area of over 2,000 acres. The west side of the breachway is adjacent to 2½ miles of undeveloped barrier beach accessible only by four-wheel-drive or on foot.

Charlestown Beach Road leads to the east side of the breachway. Here you will find a state-owned parking lot, but the parking is very expensive, expecially for out-of-state visitors.

The east side of the breachway is often crowded, making fly fishing difficult at best. Still, the action here can be intense. You can also work the quieter waters bordering the parking lot, where the channel heads back up into Ninigret Pond. The large beach in the front of the parking lot is very good, particularly in the fall. Striped bass and bluefish can be in the surf right at your feet. At times even bonito and little tunny are within range of a fly.

Between Point Judith and Watch Hill are several beaches that can be very good, particularly in the fall. Expect these places, especially the state beaches, to be crowded with bathers in the summer, however. East Matunuck State Beach and Matunuck Beach are two to check out. Matunuck Beach is likely the better of the two, and many anglers work the bowl on the east end of the beach, referred to locally as Matunuck Deep Hole. Between the Charlestown and Quonochontaug Breachways is a long barrier beach that is part of the Ninigret Conservation Area. Anglers call it the East Beach. Farther east are Quonochontaug Beach, Misquamicut State Beach, and the adjoining sandy stretches leading to Watch Hill.

MASSACHUSETTS

Massachusetts has a lot to offer the saltwater fly fisherman. Plenty of opportunities to wet a line exist at Cape Cod as well as the two famous offshore islands of Martha's Vineyard and Nantucket. The season starts in the first week of May with schoolie bass and runs until November. There are striped bass, bluefish, bonito, and little tunny. The tidal range is much greater in a good portion of these waters than found farther south in Rhode Island and Connecticut. On the islands of Martha's Vineyard and Nantucket, it is only 1 to 3 feet, but on the Cape you find upward of 10 feet of tidal change.

On Cape Cod you have two quite different bodies of water to fish: the bay side and the ocean side. The bay side of the Cape is protected and shallow, making it ideal for fly rodding. Here are a few locations to consider, although some of them require a four-wheel-drive vehicle or a boat. In Sandwich, try Town Beach near the mouth of the Cape Cod Canal. In the Barnstable area, try Sandy Neck, the mouth of Scorton Creek, and Barnstable Harbor. Farther North in Wellfleet, fish the waters of Wellfleet Harbor, Great Island out to Jeremy Point, and Billingsgate Shoal.

The ocean side of the Cape is steeper and home to strong surf. You will have to pick your days, tides, and locations with care. I suggest hiring a local guide for your first trip. Here are a few spots to consider. The waters of Chatham Roads on the west side of Monomoy Island are fairly shallow and sheltered. This is an attractive place to cast a fly. To the immediate north, try the protected waters of Pleasant Bay or the wilder water of Chatham Inlet. Farther north again, you can work Nauset Beach and Nauset Inlet. At Provincetown, try Herring Cove, Wood End, the mouth of Hatches Harbor, and Race Point.

To the south of Chatham, the shoreline from Harwich Port westward to Buzzards Bay has much to offer. There are several rivers, salt ponds, and bays to fish. Perhaps the best-known river in the area is the Bass River near Dennis. This entire stretch of coast is one of the first to see stripers in the spring. West again from Buzzards Bay toward the Rhode Island line are many additional places to work a fly. The Elizabeth Islands are famous for their fishing, especially around Cuttyhunk, the last island in the chain. Try the Westport River and the Weweantic River, particularly for bass in May.

Martha's Vineyard holds a special place in the hearts of saltwater fly rodders. Here the sight of someone fly fishing the beach is as common as someone using a spinning rod. Starting in the west, you have Lobsterville Beach on the north shore in Gay Head. This is a fairly shallow, sandy beach that is easy to fly-rod unless the wind blows from the north. Immediately adjacent is Menemsha Inlet, which drains Menemsha, Squibnocket, and Nashaquitsa ponds. The jetties guarding the inlet are favorite fishing spots for both local and visiting anglers. The jetty on the west side is favored, but both offer excellent potential. During the annual island-wide fishing derby in the fall, this place is a madhouse, and to my way of thinking should be avoided. Directly opposite Menemsha Inlet on the south side of the island are some rugged beaches with higher surf and in some cases rocky ground. This area is famous for striped bass. It is not easy to fly-fish, however, given the rocks and waves.

At the eastern end of Martha's Vineyard is Chappaquiddick Island. To reach it, you take a short ferry ride from Edgartown. Chappaquiddick Beach at the ferry launch is easy to fish and can be productive. To the southeast, Wasque Point is a very popular spot. If you have four-wheel-drive and a special permit, you can drive out Cape Poge from the marked trails found near Wasque. This gives you access to East Beach and all the fine fishing out to Cape Poge.

Nantucket may not offer the variety of fly fishing that Martha's Vineyard does, but it is still a fine place to fish, and fly rodding is really catching on here. A four-wheel-drive vehicle is practically a necessity here. There are newly created laws governing four-wheel use of the beach, so be sure to check and obey all current regulations. In the northwestern corner of the island are places with lighter surf and more manageable waters for the fly fisherman. Eel Point and Dionis Beach are two spots to try. Other places to wet a fly line are Jetties Beach and Miacomet Rip, Smith's Point Cove and Great Point Rip. Though Nantucket is thought of as a fall fishing place, note that in June, herring that have been spawning in the island ponds exit back to the salt and attract feeding game fish. The action can be very good.

In the northeastern corner of Massachusetts, right on the New Hampshire border close to Gloucester, is the mouth of the Merrimack River in the town of Newburyport. The Merrimack and a long barrier island known as Plum Island hold good waters for the fly rodder. This is a large area, complete with open beaches, protected sounds, marshes, and river mouths. Inside the mouth of the Merrimack River on the south side is an extensive area of shallow water called Joppa Flats. This is a good spot for striped bass on a fly. And by the way, in May the schoolies are joined by a good shad run too. On the opposite side diagonally across is a rocky fishing location known as the Badgers. It is harder to fly-rod but worth the effort. Expect blues in the river by the second week of July. Also try the flats near the old Coast Guard station.

Several rivers join behind Plum Island, forming Plum Island Sound, before exiting around the southern tip of the island into Ipswich Bay. The largest is the Parker River; others include the Rowley, Eagle, and Ipswich rivers. The sound's protected waters have a lot to offer the saltwater fly rodder. Channels, marshes, and flats abound.

NEW HAMPSHIRE

New Hampshire does not have an extensive coastline, but fine fly-rod potential exists. And it is largely untapped. Expect the season to start in late May with small stripers. This coincides roughly with the time the first mackerel move inshore and alewives enter the river systems. By mid-June, schoolie action can be excellent, and larger bass will start showing a few weeks later. Bluefish join the fun in July. The fishing holds up well right through the summer and on into September, and possibly the beginning of October.

A good portion of the fishing is focused on the swift Piscataqua River, which exits to the sea near Portsmouth. The river holds good runs of herring and shad, which in turn attract the stripers and blues. Boat anglers pay special attention to wherever bridge abutments break the river flow, such as upstream where the General Sullivan Bridge crosses the mouth of Little Bay. Here even large stripers are caught in only a few feet of water. Downstream at the mouth of the Piscataqua is Odiorne Point, a state park offering good shoreline access for fly rodders. On the Maine side of the river mouth, Sea Point Beach at Kittery Point has fine bluefishing.

Five miles outside the river mouth lie the Isles of Shoals, a beautiful set of seven islands that holds excellent angling potential. The northern sides of these rocky islands are good, but the southern shores are the most popular. White Island and White Island Ledge are the two of the most productive locations.

Along the 12-mile stretch of coastal Route 1A running south from Portsmouth to Hampton Beach, anglers will find plenty of easy access. Beaches and points run mile after mile, offering good fishing in uncrowded surroundings. As you near Hampton, it gets a bit harder to gain access because of private land. Still, Hampton Beach and Hampton Bay offer striper and bluefish opportunities as well. By the way, the Hampton River is a good early-season location for fly rodders seeking stripers.

The state of New Hampshire stocks two species of Pacific salmon: coho and chinook. The chinook are a recent idea, and it is not yet clear how well it will work. The coho stocking started many years ago, and each year some of these fine fish are caught on flies. The Lamprey River, a tributary of the Piscataqua, is a good place to try your luck. Some seasons the run is much better than other years. New Hampshire also has some sea-run brown trout. Like the salmon fishing, the run is hot and cold from year to year. The best fishing is from October to December at Berry Brook, which flows under Route 1A.

MAINE

In recent times, southern Maine has become famous for large striped bass and bluefish on a fly. Here big fish are the rule: Stripers of 20 pounds or more are not uncommon. And bluefish of 15 to 18 pounds are caught regularly by fly rodders. The bluefish boom is likely to fade, for their population along the Atlantic appears to be in steep decline. But expect great bass fishing to persist in Maine.

The season starts in late May to early June and runs out to the end of September, occasionally a week or two beyond Columbus Day. June is generally an excellent month to fish for striped bass. By the second week of the month, expect some fish to move up inside the rivers. And by the middle of July, bluefish will be cutting through the thick schools of menhaden. Do not expect to find bonito or little tunny this far north.

Tidal ranges are great in this portion of the coast and deserve your attention and respect. They are on average over 8 feet, and reach as great as 18 feet in Eastport to the far northeast. In most areas where fishermen work the coast, the range is about 9 feet.

As in so many other New England states, the river systems host the hottest action, and no place has more rivers entering the salt than Maine. In the southern part of the state, there is the York River, just a short haul above Kittery. Next in line is the Mousam River. At its mouth is Parsons Beach, one of the most popular fly-rod spots in Maine. You can fish the entire area, but the river mouth often holds the best action. The fishing is best at the bottom hours of the outgoing tide. There are quite a few baitfish here, including sand eels. Some of this beach is private, so stay below the high-tide line. Expect the best fish to be sitting in holes near the rip lines.

Traveling farther northward, you come to the mouth of the Saco River in Saco, just south of Old Orchard Beach. There are good opportunities here. Try the jetties at the mouth of the river. Then take a look at Ferry and Old Orchard beaches. In season, these two places are madhouses. So fish early and late. Northward again, you find the confluence of the Scarboro and Nonesuch rivers. Pine Point and Scarboro Beach are nearby and are good places to wet a line. Turning the corner to Cape Elizabeth, you find the mouth of the Spurwink River and its adjacent Higgins Beach. This is another excellent and attractive fishing location, well worth the visit. Try the last of the outgoing tide.

Above Portland, by the town of Bath, is the Kennebec River. The Kennebec, which originates in the 30-mile-long Moosehead Lake far inland, has its own population of spawning stripers, quite a success story. Popham Beach is a good bet in this area too.

17

Marine Conservation

Fishing is forever. Or so we like to think. Be it yesterday's memories or tomorrow's dreams, fishing lives inside us. Though our memories are safe and no one can take them from us, our hopes and plans for the future are on rockier ground. The quality of tomorrow's fishing, the overall health of the entire ocean, and even the visual aesthetics of the coast are all open to question. And the answer lies to a large degree in our hands.

I try never to measure anglers by the quality of their equipment, the distance they can throw a line, or the ability and speed with which they can tie a fly. Yet I am quick to measure them by a far more meaningful criterion: their commitment to the health and future of our natural resources. Every angler can make that commitment in his or her own fashion. Still, I encourage you to consider trying two proven ways. First, join one or more marine conservation groups and be an active member. If you already belong to a saltwater conservation group, I tip my hat. If you are looking for such an organization, you will find a few listed at the end of this chapter. Also, practitice hook-and-release, following the basic suggestions given here.

We all need to treat our marine resources with care. Handle fish gently, and get them back into the water as quickly as possible. *Photograph by Phil Farnsworth.*

HOOK-AND-RELEASE

Know the law. Know your state fishing regulations concerning the quantity, size, and season for the fish you seek. Release all fish that cannot be kept legally or are not needed for food.

Carry the right tools. Pliers or some other type of tool designed to remove hooks is an absolute must. I also suggest that you make measuring marks on your rod with waterproof tape. This way you are prepared to quickly measure the fish against the rod to see if it can be kept legally.

Pinch down your barbs. This simple step greatly aids in a speedy and relatively stressless release.

Use the rod. Fight the fish to the limits of your tackle so that you can land it as soon as possible. The longer the fish struggles, the harder it is to revive. And the larger the fish and the warmer the water, the more exhausted the fish is likely to be. Little tunny deserve special care. They fight so hard that they become totally exhausted.

If possible, avoid using nets, gaffs, and tailers. The rough fibers of most net bags scrape the skin of a fish, removing protective mucus from them. Gaffs do more serious damage to the fish and are illegal to use on striped bass in some states. Tailers, like nets, can also damage the skin of the fish, leaving it prone to infection.

Hold a fish properly. Keep your hands out of the fish's gills and away from its eyes. Learn the best methods for grasping various species (see "Landing a Fish" in chapter 13). Try rolling a fish onto its back. This is an excellent way to make the fish stop struggling, but be careful of your hand any time it is near a sharp dorsal fin. *Do not let a fish over 10 pounds hang from its lower lip. The weight tends to damage the jaw.*

Keep the fish in the water. Many times you can simply reach down and unhook a fish without ever lifting it out of the water or dragging it up onto the beach. The fish stays wet and in better shape.

Remove the hook carefully. A barbless hook should back out easily. A barbed hook may require a bit of work; avoid tearing surrounding flesh. If the hook is deep in the throat and hard to reach, consider cutting the line rather than holding the fish out of water for a long period.

Take any photos quickly. Have your camera handy and ready to go. If you want to lift the fish up for the camera, use both hands and support its belly.

Do not weigh the fish. Sticking the hook end of a hand scale into a fish's gill plate is asking for trouble. Instead, learn to approximate the weight by the fish's length. If you must have a more exact weight, measure the fish in both girth and length using a plastic tape measure. Then plug the figures into this time-honored formula:

$$\text{length (inches)} \times \text{girth}^2 \text{ (inches)} \div 800 \approx \text{weight (pounds)}$$

Release with care. Hold the fish upright in the water until you feel it gaining its strength. Remember that the longer the fish has been held captive, the less able it is to swim off immediately. And never simply drop an exhausted fish back into a strong rip. Revive it fully, and if possible, release it in slower portions of the current.

Take special care with stripers caught in fresh water. Research shows that hook-and-release mortality for striped bass is much higher in places of low salinity, such as the upper reaches of coastal rivers.

Cadmium hooks can be a problem. Research with striped bass has shown that when cadmium-plated hooks are left in a fish, they significantly reduce the chances of survival as compared with bronze, nickel-plated, or stainless steel hooks. Most likely, cadmium, a heavy metal, is poisonous to the fish. Fish in the test were able to expel bronze hooks faster than all other types. Stainless steel, though not breaking off or rusting, did not have the kind of adverse results seen with cadmium hooks. Nickel-plated hooks rusted quickly; a fair number broke off. These findings likely hold true for all saltwater species we seek.

CONSERVATION AGENCIES

You can make a real difference in the future of our coastal fisheries by joining an organization dedicated to their conservation. The following are a few organizations that are informative and effective. But there are many others.

American Littoral Society, Sandy Hook, Highlands, NJ 07732, telephone (908) 291-0055. The Littoral Society has a newsletter, organizes outings all along the coast, and has an active and successful fish-tagging program. There are regional offices in Florida, Massachusetts, New York, Pennsylvania, and Washington.

Coastal Conservation Association. This nonprofit organization was founded in Texas in 1977 to protect the redfish. Since then it has spread up and around the coast, effectively addressing management issues, from billfish to striped bass. Along the Atlantic there are offices of the New England Coastal Conservation Association in Maine (11 School Street, Boothbay Harbor, ME 04538), Massachusetts (P.O. Box 869, East Sandwich, MA 02537), and Connecticut (P.O. Box 14, Old Saybrook, CT 06475); the Atlantic Coastal Conservation Association in Virginia (P.O. Box 61871, Virginia Beach, VA 23462), North Carolina (1994 Eastwood Road, Suite 2, Wilmington, NC 28403), South Carolina (P.O. Box 1823, Mount Pleasant, SC 29465), and Georgia (P.O. Box 15034, Savannah, GA 31416); and the Florida Coastal Conservation Association in Florida (905 East Park Avenue, Tallahassee, FL 32301).

Stripers Unlimited, 880 Washington St., P.O. Box 3045, South Attleboro, MA 02703. Stripers Unlimited is run by its founder, striped bass devotee Bob Pond. This agency is very active in research into striped bass problems.

Other conservation agencies include the *National Coalition for Marine Conservation, Jersey Coast Anglers,* and *United Gamefish Anglers.*

Bibliography

When you come to the coast, do it with an open mind, ready to read far and wide. There are not many books dedicated totally to our sport; without a doubt, a voracious reader could consume all of them quite quickly. Yet titles on other subjects such as marine fish, natural history, surf casting, and general saltwater fishing frequently contain valuable insights. Frankly, I would not be without them. I also feel that literary works, especially those that contain personal reflections on the natural world, play a significant role in an angler's education. True, these titles do not directly sharpen one's skills, but never forget that what is valid in our sport springs first and foremost from an allegiance to nature.

Books on Saltwater Fly Fishing

Abrames, J. Kenney. *Striper Moon*. Portland, Oreg.: Amato, 1994.

Brooks, Joe. *Salt Water Fly Fishing*. New York: Putnam's Sons, 1950.

Kreh, Lefty. *Fly Fishing in Salt Water*. rev. ed. New York: Lyons Books, 1986.

Nix, Sam. *Salt Water Fly-Fishing Handbook*. Garden City, N.Y.: Doubleday, 1973.

Samson, Jack. *Saltwater Fly Fishing*. Harrisburg, Pa.: Stackpole, 1991.

Sands, George. *Salt Water Fly Fishing.* New York: Knopf, 1970.

Tabory, Lou. *Inshore Fly Fishing.* New York: Lyons, 1992.

Books on Saltwater Fly Tying

Bay, Kenneth E. *Salt Water Flies.* Philadelphia: Lippincott, 1972.

Kreh, Lefty. *Salt Water Fly Patterns.* Fullerton, Calif.: Maral, Inc.

Roberts, George. *Saltwater Naturals and their Imitations.* Camden, Maine: Ragged Mountain Press, 1994.

Stewart, Dick, and Farrow Allen. *Flies for Saltwater.* North Conway, N.H.: Mountain Pond, 1992.

Wentink, Frank. *Saltwater Fly Tying.* New York: Lyons, 1991.

Books with a Section on Saltwater Fly Fishing or Tying

Bates, Joseph. *Streamers & Bucktails.* New York: Knopf, 1979.

Brooks, Joe. *Salt Water Game Fishing.* New York: Harper & Row, 1968.

————. *Streamer Fly Tying and Fishing.* Harrisburg, Pa.: Stackpole, 1950. Rev. ed. 1966.

Daignault, Frank. *Striper Surf.* Chester, Conn.: Globe Pequot, 1992.

Jorgensen, Poul. *Dressing Flies for Fresh and Salt Water.* Rockville Center, N.Y.: Freshet Press, 1973.

Karas, Nicholas. *The Striped Bass.* rev. ed. New York: Karmapco & Lyons, 1993.

Leiser, Eric. *The Books of Fly Patterns.* New York: Knopf, 1987.

Moss, Frank T. *Successful Striped Bass Fishing.* Camden, Maine: International Marine, 1974.

Post, Robert. *Reading the Water.* Chester, Conn.: Globe Pequot, 1988.

Rosko, Milt. *Secrets of Striped Bass Fishing.* London: Macmillan, 1966.

Sosin, Mark. *Practical Light-Tackle Fishing.* New York: Lyons/Doubleday, 1979.

Sosin, Mark, and Lefty Kreh. *Fishing the Flats.* New York: Lyons, 1983.

Waterman, Charles F. *Modern Fresh and Salt Water Fly Fishing.* New York: Winchester Press, 1972.

Woolner, Frank. *Modern Saltwater Sport Fishing.* New York: Crown, 1972.

Woolner, Frank, and Henry Lyman. *Striped Bass Fishing.* rev. ed. New York: Winchester Lyons, 1983.

Books on Saltwater Fishing with Little or No Fly Rodding

Adams, Leon D. *Striped Bass Fishing in California and Oregon.* Palo Alto, Calif.: Pacific Books, 1953.

Bates, Joseph D. *Spinning for Salt Water Game Fish*. Boston: Little, Brown, 1957.

Boyd, Lester C. *Atlantic Surf Fishing*. Boston: Stone Wall Press, 1976.

Camp, Raymond. *Fishing the Surf*. rev. ed. Boston: Little, Brown, 1950.

Daignault, Frank: *Twenty Years on the Cape*. Mystic, Conn.: MT Publications, 1989.

————. *Striper Hot Spots*. Chester, Conn.: Globe Pequot, 1993.

Farrington, S. Kip, Jr. *Fishing the Atlantic*. New York: Coward-McCann, 1949.

Francis, Phil. *Salt Water Fishing from Maine to Texas*. New York: Macmillan, 1963.

Heilner, Van Campen. *The Call of the Surf*. Garden City, N.Y.: Doubleday, 1920.

————. *Salt Water Fishing*. New York: Knopf, 1937.

Jansen, Jerry. *Successful Surf-Casting*. New York: Dutton, 1959.

Lyman, Henry. *Bluefishing*. New York: Barnes, 1959.

Lyman, Henry, and Frank Woolner. *Weakfishing*. New York: Barnes, 1959.

Reiger, George. *Profiles in Salt Water Angling*. Englewood Cliffs, N.J.: Prentice Hall, 1973.

Reina, Richard, and William Muller. *Surf Fishing with the Experts*. Sag Harbor, N.Y.: L.I.F. Publishing.

Reinfelder, Al. *Bait Tail Fishing*. Cranbury, N.J.: Barnes, 1969.

Rodman, O. H. P. *The Saltwater Fisherman's Favorite Four*. New York: Morrow, 1948.

Sylvester, Jerry. *Salt Water Fishing Is Easy*. Harrisburg, Pa.: Stackpole, 1956.

Walters, Keith. *Chesapeake Stripers*. Bozman, Md.: Aerie House, 1990.

Fish Identification, Natural History, and Tides

Amos, William H., and Stephen H. Amos. *Atlantic & Gulf Coasts*. The Audubon Society Nature Guides. New York: Knopf, 1985.

Berrill, Michael, and Deborah Berrill. *The North Atlantic Coast*. San Francisco: Sierra Club Books, 1981.

Bigelow, Henry B., and William Schroeder. "Fishes of the Gulf of Maine." *Fishery Bulletin of the Fish and Wildlife Service,* vol. 53. Washington D.C.: Government Printing Office, 1953.

Brindze, Ruth. *The Rise and Fall of the Seas*. New York: Harcourt Brace, 1964.

Bulloch, David K. *The Underwater Naturalist.* New York: Lyons, 1991.

Carson, Rachel. *The Edge of the Sea.* Boston: Houghton Mifflin, 1955.

————. *The Sea around Us.* New York: Oxford University Press, 1951.

————. *Under the Sea-Wind.* rev. ed. New York: Oxford University Press, 1952.

Carter, Samuel III. *Kingdom of the Tides.* New York: Hawthorn Books, 1966.

Defant, Albert. *Ebb and Flow.* Ann Arbor, Mich.: University of Michigan, 1958.

Eldridge, Capt. *George W. Elridge Tide and Pilot Book.* Boston: Marion Jewett White, printed annually since 1875.

Gordon, Bernard L. *The Marine Fishes of Rhode Island.* 2d ed. Watch Hill, R.I.: The Book & Tackle Shop, 1974.

Hay, John, and Peter Farb. *The Atlantic Shore.* New York: Harper & Row, 1966.

Robins, C. Richards, G. Carlton Ray, and John Douglass. *Atlantic Coast Fishes.* Peterson's Field Guide Series. Boston: Houghton Mifflin, 1986.

Ross, Michael R. *Recreational Fisheries of Coastal New England.* Amherst, Mass.: University of Massachusetts Press, 1991.

Scott, William Beverly, and Mildred Grace Scott. "Atlantic Fishes of Canada." *Canadian Bulletin of Fisheries and Aquatic Sciences No. 219.* Toronto: University of Toronto Press, 1988.

Teal, John, and Mildred Teal. *Life and Death of the Salt Marsh.* Boston, Mass.: Little, Brown, 1969.

Related Reading

Beston, Henry. *The Outermost House.* Garden City, N.Y.: Doubleday Doran, 1933.

Brooks, Win. *The Shining Tides.* New York: Morrow, 1952.

Cole, John H. *Striper.* Boston: Little, Brown, 1978.

Hay, John. *The Great Beach.* Garden City, N.Y.: Doubleday, 1963.

Hersey, John. *Blues.* New York: Knopf, 1987.

Ogburn, Charlton, Jr. *The Winter Beach.* New York: Morrow, 1966.

Reiger, George. *Wander on My Native Shore.* New York: Simon & Schuster, 1983.

Thoreau, Henry David. *Cape Cod.* Orleans, Mass.: Parnassus Imprints, 1984.

Index

Alewife, alewives, 88, 90, 95, 132, 141,
    142, 143, 218
American eels, 102, 146, 147
American Littoral Society, 308
American shad, 91, 141
Amphipods, 29, 151, 152
Anchovies. *See* bay anchovies
Angling etiquette, 293
Annelids (marine worms), 5, 31, 262. *See*
    also worm hatch
    Nereis, 99, 100, 101
Apogee tide, 12
Arbor knot, 192, 193
Atlantic bonito, 44, 73, 92, 107, 108, 111,
    115, 117, 124, 135, 139, 149, 150,
    151, 230–242
    best time of day for, 237
    description of, 231, 232
    diet of, 233
    eyesight, 234
    fighting, 230, 241, 242, 251, 253
    flies for, 237, 238
    habitat preferences, 233

    handling, 255, 258
    near inlets and jetties, 107, 108, 111,
        115
    retrieve for, 236–239
    run of, 240, 251
    running at you, 241
    season for, 239–242
    tactics near the beach, 233, 234
    teeth, 233, 237, 259
    unhooking, 258
    "up and down" style, 235, 237
    water temperature, 414, 416, 417
Atlantic herring, 90, 132, 143
Atlantic mackerel, 132, 138, 233
Atlantic menhaden (bunker), 124, 132,
    144, 150, 219, 222, 229
    as chum, 144
    immature (baby bunker), 145, 146

Backcast, 280–282
Backing, 175
    amount needed, 171
    getting burned by, 175, 247

Backing, *continued*
  maintenance of, 185
Backshore, 47
Backwash, 29, 43
  landing a fish in, 255, 256
Back eddy, 83, 112, 113
Bait. *See* baitfish
Baitfish, 5, 6, 19, 22, 26, 31, 32, 43, 44,
    52, 58, 81, 87, 88, 89, 90, 93, 94, 97,
    98, 132, 133, 136, 141, 146, 151,
    212, 219, 222, 224, 233, 235, 236.
    See also alewives, Atlantic
    menhaden, bay anchovies, blueback
    herring, butterfish, mummichogs,
    sand eels, silversides
  at night, 262, 264, 265
  importance of, 19
  in cordgrass, 94, 95, 97
  signs of, 32
  matching with a fly, 156, 157, 158, 162
  near bridges, 115, 119
  near inlets and jetties, 111, 113, 114
Barbless hooks. *See* hook and release
Barnstable (Massachusetts), 299
Barometric pressure, 121–123, 125
Bars. *See* sandbars
Barrier beach, 84–86, 95
Bass, striped. *See* striped bass
Bay anchovies, 87, 98, 111, 132, 148, 149
  importance of, 149
  matching with a fly, 150
Beach slope, 22, 23
Beaches, 15–59. *See also* shallow beaches,
    deep beaches
  composition of, 22, 39, 52, 55
  cusps and bowls, 24–26, 40, 42
  deep beaches, 38–59
  finding the fish on, 17–20
  fishing on, 34–38, 48
  inland elevation, 26, 27
  irregular shape of, 22
  runouts, 45, 46
  sandbars, 28, 29, 43, 51, 52, 53, 54
  seasonal changes in, 33, 54, 57, 82
  shallow beaches, 15–38
  shape of, 57, 58, 67

  slope of, 22, 23
  tides for, 33, 34, 57, 58
Berm, 47, 256
Big flies, 216, 229
Bioluminescence. *See* fire in the water
Birds, 17, 35, 48
Black zone, 56, 59
Blitzes, 17, 19, 35, 73, 221, 228
Blood knot, 201
Blueback herring, 90, 132, 141, 142, 143,
    218
Bluefish, 16, 34, 44, 52, 73, 92, 94, 97,
    101, 117, 124, 134–136, 139, 140,
    149, 150, 151, 221–230
  at dawn, 228
  at night, 227, 228, 262, 264, 266
  big flies for, 229
  bowing to, 254
  blitzes, 221, 228
  cycle, 221
  daisy-chaining, 227
  diet, 222
  fighting, 225, 251–253
  flies for, 223, 230
  habitat, 223
  handling, 255
  jump of, 225
  poppers for, 161, 223, 224, 225, 229
  preference for menhaden, 144, 229
  retrieve for, 224–226
  season for, 226–230
  shock tippets, 227
  teeth of, 221, 222
  unhooking, 258
  water temperature, 226, 229
Bonito. *See* Atlantic bonito
Boots. *See* waders
Bowls. *See* shallow beaches, deep
    beaches, points of land
Braided loop connectors, 197
Breachways, 95. *See also* jetties
Bridges, 115–120
  fishing, 116–119
  fishing at night, 119, 120
Bunker. *See* Atlantic menhaden
Butt extensions, 170

Butterfish *(Peprilus triancanthus)*, 132, 150, 151

Cape Cod (Massachusetts), 40, 41, 84, 85, 299
Casting, 275–292
    at night, 268, 269
    back-handed, 286, 287
    basic saltwater cast, 277–283
    correct grip, 279
    difference from freshwater, 275–277, 280, 281
    in the wind, 285–292
    physical conditioning for, 292
    rearward arm extension, 280, 281
    seating ferrules before, 278
    shooting line on backcast, 227, 280–282
    stretching line before, 278
    tennis elbow, 292
    with shooting heads, 284, 285
    with sinking lines, 283, 284
    with stripping basket, 277, 279
    working with the waves, 36–38
Channels, 88, 97
Chappaquiddick Island (Massachusetts), 300
Charlestown Breachway (Rhode Island), 298
Charts. *See* nautical or navigational charts, tide charts
Chest waders. *See* waders
Clamworms. *See* annelids
Cleats. *See* metal cleats
Clouds, 126, 271. *See also* overcast conditions
Clouser Deep Minnow, 58, 216, 218
    for bonito and little tunny, 237
    matching sand eels, 139
Coastal Conservation Association, 308
Coastal rivers, 88–93. *See also* Connecticut River, Housatonic River, Kennebec River, Merrimack River, Thames River, York River
    channels in, 88
    coves in, 89

salt wedge in, 92, 93
    time of current in, 91, 92
    tributaries in, 89
Cold fronts, 123–125
Connecticut fishing, 294–296
Connecticut River (Connecticut), 294
Conservation, 305–308
    hook and release, 306–308
    organizations, 308
Cordgrass *(Spartina)*, 95, 97
Countdown, 58
Crabs, 29, 52, 152, 153, 262
Creeks. *See* tidal creeks
Current, 5, 6, 11, 13, 19, 20, 25, 29, 30, 31, 34, 35, 41, 45, 50, 51, 53, 61, 62, 66, 69, 72, 73, 76, 78, 81, 82, 83, 89, 97, 101, 102, 108, 111, 113, 114, 269. *See also* rips
    attraction of, 19
    importance of speed, 13
    time of current versus time of tide, 12, 13, 91, 92
Cusps, 25–26, 40, 42, 49
Cuts. *See* sandbars

Daisy-chaining bluefish, 227
Dawn, 34, 44, 139
    bluefish at, 228
    bonito and little tunny at, 237
    high dawn, 126
    sand eels at, 138, 139, 140
    silversides at, 134
    striped bass at, 218, 219
Dead tide, 9
Deceiver. *See* Lefty's Deceiver
Deep beaches, 38–59
    best tide for, 48, 58
    cusps and bowls on, 40, 42
    fishing, 48–55, 58–59
    of sand, 39–55
    of rock, 55–59
    sandbars on, 43, 49, 51, 52–54
    seasonal changes, 127, 128
    shelf on, 44, 45
Depressions and holes, 20, 21, 31, 33, 34, 40, 43, 48, 53, 86, 95

Double surgeon's loop, 201
Drag, 172
  how to set, 245–248
  using finger to increase, 174
Dropoffs, 20, 24, 27, 29, 44, 45, 53, 54,
    88, 94, 104

Ebb tide. *See* low tide
Edges, 20, 54, 59, 94, 96, 113
  of channel, 88
  of first bar, 29
  of reef, 78, 81, 82
  of sandbar, 29
Eel grass *(Zostera marina),* 32
Eels. *See* American eels
Eldridge Tide and Pilot Book, 9, 92, 273
Elvers, 147
Epoxy flies, 158, 238
Equipment. *See* tackle
Estuaries, 87–104
  coastal rivers, 88–93
  hidden, 98
  importance of, 87
  salt ponds, 95–98
  salt wedges in, 92, 93
  tidal creek, 93, 94
  time of tide and current in, 91, 92
  worm hatches in, 99–102

Fall migration, 124, 125, 220, 221, 241,
    242
  bluefish, 229
  bonito and little tunny, 241, 242
Northeasters, 124
  striped bass, 220, 221
  weather and, 124, 125
Falling tide. *See* low tide
False albacore. *See* little tunny
False points, 77
Feeling the strike, 248, 249, 264, 266,
    269
Felt soles, 55, 56, 108
Ferrules, 278
  joining properly, 278
Fighting a fish, 243–260
  at night, 271

bluefish, 225, 251–253
bonito and little tunny, 230, 241, 251
from a boat, 259
from the beach, 251–257
in a rip, 260
landing, 108, 110, 112, 255–257
pumping, 253, 254, 259
setting the hook, 249
side pressure, 251
striped bass, 251, 252
unhooking, 258–259
Fighting butt. *See* butt extensions
Finding fish, 5, 6, 19, 20, 22, 23, 24, 25,
    26, 29, 31, 33, 34, 35, 40, 42, 43, 44,
    49, 50, 51, 52, 55, 99. *See also*
    Atlantic bonito, bluefish, little
    tunny, striped bass
  along deep beaches, 40, 42, 43, 44, 49,
    52
  along edges, 20, 27, 43, 53, 59, 78, 94,
    97
  along man-made structure, 59, 108,
    109, 112, 113, 115, 117, 119
  along points of land, 78, 80
  along shallow beaches, 17–20
  at dead low tide, 34
  at night, 119, 120, 264, 265, 266, 277
  baitfish and, 20
  birds and, 17, 35, 48
  "good-looking" water, 19
  in back eddy, 83, 84, 112
  in backwash, 29, 43
  in cuts, 51, 53
  in coastal rivers, 88, 89, 94
  in depressions and holes, 20, 21, 31,
    33, 34, 40, 48, 53, 95
  in salt ponds, 95, 97
  in sloughs, 29, 43
  in rips, 66, 68, 69, 70
  in runouts, 45
  in troughs, 30, 31, 43, 49
  near a reef, 78, 81
  near mussel bars, 52, 53
  near rocks, 56
  slicks, 18, 19, 35
  smelling the fish, 18, 222

swirls, 17, 18, 19, 35, 80, 264
water depth and, 22, 23, 24, 43, 58, 69, 79
Fire in the water, 272
Flashlights, 182, 257, 265, 268
signaling with, 268
Flats. *See* tidal flats
Flies, 155–166. *See also* epoxy flies, sliders, streamer flies, poppers
epoxy flies, 158
eyes on, 159
for bluefish, 223, 229–230
for bonito and little tunny, 237, 238
for striped bass, 216, 217
matching forage with, 131–154, 156–162
poppers, 150, 160, 161, 216
realism versus impressionism, 156
size and shape of, 155–162
sliders, 161, 162
staying in touch with, 36–38, 50, 71, 72, 248, 269, 270
streamers, 157–160
weighted, 39, 48, 50, 72, 111
Flood tide. *See* high tide
Fly lines, 173, 174
importance of stretching, 278, 279
maintenance of, 184
shooting heads, 174, 175
Fly reels, 171–172
amount of backing on, 171
drag characteristics, 171, 172
Fly rods, 168–170
Fog, 35, 128
Forage fish. *See* baitfish
Foreshore, 47
Free lining a fly, 82, 83, 111
Fronts, 123
cold fronts, 123–125
warm fronts, 125, 126
Full moon. *See* moon phases
Full Wells grip, 169

Game fish, 9. *See also* Atlantic bonito, bluefish, little tunny, striped bass
sensitivity to water depth, 22, 23

Gannets, 220
Grass shrimp, 153

Hampton Beach (New Hampshire), 302
Hand over hand retrieve, 215, 223, 250
Handling fish, 255, 257, 258
bluefish, 255
bonito and little tunny, 255, 258
striped bass, 257
Harkness Memorial State Park (Connecticut), 296
Hats, 179, 180
Haywire twist, 204, 205
Herring, 141–146, 90, 93, 95, 98, 143, 156, 233. *See also* alewives, Atlantic herring, Atlantic menhaden, blueback herring
Hickory shad, 141
Higgins Beach (Maine), 303
High dawn, 128
High tide, 9, 10, 11, 12
High-tide line, 30, 31
Holes. *See* depressions and holes
Hook and release, 306–308
Hook sharpeners, 182, 183
Hooks, 162–166
cadmium, 163
conical point versus cut point, 162
hook removers, 180
hook sharpeners, 182, 183
long shank, 165, 166
poppers, 166
sharpening, 244–246
stainless steel, 163
Housatonic River (Connecticut), 294

Inland elevation, 26, 54, 55
Inlets, 107, 110, 112, 113, 114, 236
Intermediate fly lines, 173
Isle of Shoals (New Hampshire), 302

Jellyfish, 35
Jersey Coast Anglers Association, 308
Jetties, 60, 108–115
fishing from middle of, 112, 113
fishing from shore end of, 113–115

Jetties, *continued*
    fishing from tip of, 108–112
    landing fish on, 108, 110, 111, 112
    tides for, 111, 115

Kennebec River (Maine), 303
Killifish. *See* mummichogs
Knots, 191–209
    arbor, 192
    backing to fly line, 194–200
    backing to spool, 192, 193
    blood, 201
    clinch, 206
    double surgeon's loop, 201
    fly line to leader, 200
    for leaders, 201
    haywire twist, 204, 205
    jamming in guides, 250, 251
    mono loop knot, 207, 208
    nail knot, 194–196
    surgeon's knot, 201–203
    surgeon's loop, 196, 202
Knots jamming in guides, 251

Landing a fish. *See* fighting a fish
Lead core lines, 285
Leaders, 201
    for sinking lines, 201
    shock tippets for, 118, 204–206, 227
Lefty's Deceiver, 216, 230
Lightning, 127, 128
Lines. *See* fly lines
Little Narragansett Bay (Rhode Island),
    297
Little tunny, 44, 107, 108, 115, 124, 139,
    150, 151, 230–242
    best time of day for, 237
    description of, 231, 232
    diet of, 233
    eyesight of, 234
    fighting, 230, 241, 242, 251, 253
    flies for, 237, 238
    habitat preferences, 233
    handling, 255, 258
    inlets and jetties, 107, 108, 111, 115
    mouth of, 232

    retrieve for, 236–239
    run of, 240
    running at you, 241
    season for, 239–242
    separating from bonito, 417–420
    size of, 232, 233
    tactics on a beach, 234
    teeth, 258
    unhooking, 258
    "up and down" style, 235, 237
    water temperature, 239, 242
Log keeping, 362
Longshore currents, 41, 50
Low light, 31, 33, 48. *See also* dawn, night
    fishing
Low tide, 9, 11
Lyme disease, 95

Maine fishing, 302–303
Man-made structure, 105–120
    bridges, 115–120
    jetties, 60, 108–115
Martha's Vineyard (Massachusettts), 299,
    300
Massachusetts fishing, 299–301
Matching the marine, 131–154
Menemsha Inlet (Massachusetts), 300
Menhaden. *See* Atlantic menhaden
Merrimack River (Massachusetts), 301
Metal cleats, 55, 56, 108, 177
Minnow net, 81
Monomoy Island (Massachusetts), 300
Moon phases, 11, 12, 34
Moon tides, 34. *See also* spring tides
Moonrise and moonset, 273
Mousam River (Maine), 303
Mullet, 98, 124, 132
Mummichogs, 87, 94, 132, 147, 148, 218
Mung weed, 130
Mussel bars, 52, 53

Nail knot, 194–196, 197
Nantucket Island (Massachusetts), 299,
    301
Napatree Point (Rhode Island), 297

National Coalition for Marine
  Conservation, 308
Nautical or navigation charts, 102, 103
Neap tides, 12
New England Coast, 293–303
New Hampshire fishing, 301–302
Night fishing, 34, 261–273
  bait on the beach, 265
  best retrieve for, 264
  casting, 268, 269
  effect of moonlight on, 506, 507, 508
  effectiveness of, 262
  fighting a fish at, 270, 271
  fire in the water, 272
  fish close during, 266, 267
  flashlight, 267, 268
  moonrise and moonset, 272, 273
  sand eels, 140
  staying in touch with the fly, 269, 270
  tides for, 271, 272
  tricks of the trade, 263–268
  unhooking a fish, 257
Northeasters, 124, 125
Norwalk Islands (Connecticut), 295

Odiorne Point (New Hampshire), 302
Old Orchard Beach (Maine), 303
Overcast conditions, 97

Parsons Beach (Maine), 303
Penfield Reef (Connecticut), 295
Perigee tides, 12, 30
  effects on tidal range, 12
Phosphorescence. See fire in the water
Piscataqua River (New Hampshire), 301
Playing a fish. See fighting a fish
Pliers, 179, 180
Plum Island (Massachusetts), 301
Pogy. See Atlantic menhaden
Points of land, 75–86
  back eddy, 83
  beaches leading to, 79, 84
  bowls near, 79
  false point, 77
  fishing, 80, 81
  reefs at tip, 77, 78

rips at tip, 77–79
  tides for, 80
  tip, 97
Polarized sunglasses, 180
Popham Beach (Maine), 303
Poppers, 49, 71, 157, 160, 161
  for bluefish, 223, 226, 230
  for striped bass, 218, 219
Portuguese man-o-war, 87
Power plants, 226
Provincetown (Massachusetts), 300
Pumping a fish, 253, 254, 259

Quonochontaug Breachway (Rhode
  Island), 298

Reefs, 77, 78, 81
Releasing fish. See hook and release
Retrieve, 215, 216, 224, 249, 264
  at night, 264
  hand over hand, 215, 223, 250
  for poppers, 215, 216, 223, 224, 225
  strip, 216, 249
Rhode Island fishing, 296–299
Rip line, 66, 67, 68
Rips, 30, 41, 61–74, 77, 78, 79, 89. See
  also tidal rips
  fighting a fish in, 260
  fishing in, 65–74
  fly speed in, 71, 72
  near a jetty, 111, 114
  presenting a fly in, 70–73
  rip line, 66, 67, 68
  safety in, 74
  sources of, 62
  spotting, 64
  structure in, 61, 68
  tidal, 62, 69, 70
  working a fly in, 72, 73
Rising tide, 56. See also high tide
Ritz grip, 169
Rocky beaches, 55–60
  black zone, 56
  fishing on, 58–60
  tides for, 57, 58

Rocky Neck State Park (Connecticut),
    296
Rods. *See* fly rods
Running lines, 174
Runouts, 45, 46
    rip formed by, 45

Saco River (Maine), 303
Salt ponds, 95–98
    baitfish, 97, 98, 154, 272
    channels in, 95, 96, 97
    cordgrass, 94, 95, 97
    flats in, 97
    inlet to, 95
    worm hatch, 99
Salt wedge, 92, 93
Sand eels, 21, 32, 87, 98, 111, 132,
    136–140, 233
    at dawn, 218, 219
    at dusk, 138, 139, 140
    at night, 140
    bass rooting for, 21, 139
    burying in sand, 138
    description of, 136, 137
    season, 304
    size, 137
    when and where to find, 138, 139
Sand hopper, 152
Sand launces. *See* sand eels
Sand shrimp, 153
Sand spit, 84
Sandbars, 28, 43, 51, 52, 53, 54, 92
    currents across, 53
    cuts through, 43, 51, 53, 54
    deep beaches, 43, 49, 51, 52, 53, 54
    dropoffs near, 44, 45, 54
    shallow beaches, 28, 29
Scarboro Beach (Maine), 303
Sea breezes, 128, 129
Sea herring. *See* Atlantic herring
Sea lice, 217
Season. *See* Atlantic bonito, bluefish, little
    tunny, striped bass
Seaweed, 30, 47, 49, 58, 130, 264
Setting the drag. *See* drag
Setting the hook, 74, 249, 266, 269, 270
Shad. *See* American shad, hickory shad

Shallow beaches, 15–38
    baitfish on, 22, 26, 31, 32
    best fly line for, 173
    composition of, 16, 22
    cusps and bowls, 25–26
    eel grass, 32
    finding fish, 17–20
    fishing on, 34–38
    sandbars on, 28, 29
    seasonal changes, 82
    shoreline shape, 22, 24
    shoreline slope, 22, 23
    slough, 29
    tides on, 33, 34
    trough, 43
    wading tour of, 30, 31
    working with waves, 36, 37
Sharpening hooks, 244–245
Shelves, 44, 45
Sherwood Island State Park
    (Connecticut), 295
Shilted water, 35
    effect on fishing, 35
Shock tippets, 204–206
    around sharp objects, 118
    for bluefish, 227
Shooting heads, 173, 174
    casting, 284, 285
    use around bridges, 116
Shrimp. *See* grass shrimp, sand shrimp
Side pressure, 251. *See also* fighting a fish
Silversides, 4, 32, 87, 94, 98, 111, 132,
    133–136, 148, 233
    at night, 135
    description of, 133, 134
    range, 133
    size, 133
    in cordgrass, 94, 97
Sinking fly lines, 173
    casting, 283, 284
    in a rip, 72
    in an inlet, 111, 112
    use for bonito and little tunny, 236
    use in the surf, 39, 48, 50
Slack line. *See* staying in touch with the
    fly
Slack tide, 9. *See also* dead tide, low tide

Slicks, 18, 19, 35
Sliders, 157, 161, 162
  at night, 136
Slope of the beach, 22, 23
Sloughs, 29, 43
Smelling fish, 18, 222
Solid wire. *See* shock tippets
Spartina. See cordgrass
Spearing. *See* silversides
Spring tides, 11, 12, 30
Squid, 102, 154, 272
Staying in touch with the fly, 36, 37,
  269–270
Steep beach. *See* deep beach
Streamer flies, 157–160
  color of, 159
  epoxy, 158
  eyes on, 159
  shape and size of, 158
Stretching a fly line, 278, 279
Striped bass, 16, 21, 34, 44, 52, 63, 73, 84,
  88, 90, 92, 94, 97, 99, 100, 101, 102,
  124, 134, 135, 136, 139, 140, 142,
  150, 151, 153, 210–221, 235
  amphipods and, 151, 152
  at dawn and dusk, 218, 219
  at night, 219, 220, 261, 262, 264, 266
  bay anchovies and, 148, 149
  big flies and, 216
  crabs and, 152
  cycle of, 211
  description of, 211
  diet, 214
  fighting, 251, 252, 256
  flies for, 216, 217, 218, 219
  habitat preferences, 212
  handling, 257
  in back eddy, 83, 84, 112
  menhaden and, 144
  mouth of, 211
  poppers for, 161, 218
  popping noise of, 264
  retrieve for, 214, 215, 217
  rooting sand eels, 21, 139
  sea lice on, 217
  season for, 217–221
  sense of smell, 213
  size of, 212
  unhooking, 259
  water temperature, 212, 219
  weather for, 214
  wintering over, 63, 212
Stripers Unlimited, 308
Stripping baskets, 175–177, 277, 279
  proper use of, 277, 279, 290–292
Structure, 20. *See also* bowls, cusps,
  dropoffs, edges, jetties, man-made
  structure, reefs, sandbars, shoreline
  shape, sloughs, troughs
Sunglasses. *See* polarized sunglasses
Surgeon's knot, 201–203
Surgeon's loop, 196, 202

Tackle, 167–189
  basic list of, 188
  care of, 182, 184–188
  chest packs, 178–179
  felt soles, 177
  flashlights, 182
  fly lines, 173
  fly reels, 171
  fly rods, 168, 169, 170
  hats, 179, 180
  hook removers, 181, 182
  hook sharpeners, 182, 183
  metal cleats, 177
  optional items, 188–189
  pliers, 180
  polarized sunglasses, 180
  shooting heads, 174, 175
  stripping basket, 175–177
  waders, 176, 178
  wading jacket, 178
Tennis elbow, 292
Thames River (Connecticut), 294
Tidal creeks, 93–95
Tidal flats, 16, 140
  waves on, 28
Tidal range, 7
  effect of moon on, 8
Tidal rips, 62, 69, 70. *See also* rips
Tidal sweep, 51
Tide charts, 9

Tides, 3–13
　　apogee tide, 12
　　bottom of, 9
　　charts, 9
　　crest of, 9
　　daily and weekly patterns of, 10, 11
　　dead high or low, 9
　　falling tide, 6, 7
　　fishing relationship to, 5
　　high tide, 8
　　how to pick, 6, 33–34, 48, 80, 114,
　　　　115, 271, 272
　　importance of, 4, 5
　　low tide, 9, 11
　　moon tide, 11, 34
　　moon's effect on, 7, 8, 9
　　neap tide, 12
　　perigee, 12
　　rising tide, 6
　　slack tide, 9
　　spring tide, 11
　　tidal range, 7
　　time of tide, 8, 9
　　wind's effect on, 129
Time of current, 12, 13
Tippet, 201, 204
　　effect on drag setting, 246, 247
Trough of a wave, 37
Troughs, 31, 43, 45, 49
　　on a deep beach, 43, 44, 49
　　on a shallow beach, 31, 43

Unhooking fish, 258–259
　　at night, 257
　　tool for, 180
United Gamefish Anglers, 308

Waders, 177
　　felt soles on, 55, 56, 177
　　metal cleats with, 55, 56, 177
　　　g jacket, 177
　　　　nts, 125, 126
　　　　　nt (Massachusetts), 300
　　　　　hode Island), 296, 297
　　　　　(Rhode Island), 297

Water color, 26, 27, 43
　　as indicator of depth, 27
Water temperature preferences. See
　　　Atlantic bonito, bluefish, little
　　　tunny, striped bass
Waves, 25, 27, 28, 43, 45, 62
　　as indicators of depth, 27, 28
　　breaking over sandbar, 28, 43
　　troughs of, 36
　　working with, 36, 37
Weakfish, 210
Weather, 121–130
　　barometer, 121, 122, 123, 125
　　clouds and fog, 126, 127
　　cold fronts, 123–125, 271
　　effect on fishing, 35
　　fronts, 123
　　lightning, 127, 128
　　Northeasters, 124, 125
　　radios, 122
　　sea breezes, 128, 129
　　warm fronts, 125, 126
　　wind, 128
　　wind and tide, 129
　　wind and weed, 130
Weather radios, 122
Weed. See seaweed
Weekapaug Breachway (Rhode Island),
　　298
Weighted flies, 39, 48, 50, 72, 111
Wellfleet (Massachusetts), 299
Wewewantic River (Massachusetts), 300
Wind, 34, 35. See also weather
　　effect on a rip, 63
　　effect on casting, 285–292
　　effect on time of tide, 129
　　sea breezes, 128, 129
　　seasonal changes, 128
　　shilted water and, 35
Wind lines, 64
Worm hatch, 99–102
　　Nereis limbata, 101
Wrack, 55
Wrack line, 30, 31

York River (Maine), 303